A Passionate Journey

A Passionate Journey

A MEMOIR

ROBERT MANN

EAST END PRESS

A PASSIONATE JOURNEY

Copyright © 2018 by Robert Mann

Published by

EAST END PRESS

Bridgehampton, NY

ISBN: 978-0-9975304-4-5

Ebook ISBN: 978-0-9975304-5-2

FIRST EDITION

BOOK DESIGN BY PAULINE NEUWIRTH, NEUWIRTH & ASSOCIATES
COVER DESIGN BY STEPHEN VIKSJO

Manufactured in the United States of America

10 9 8 7 6 5 4 3 2 1

DEDICATION

I dedicate this memoir to the most influential and meaningful individual in the composition of my life, Lucy Rowan Mann. Strange that
she does not appear until my twenty-seventh year, but there cannot be
one doubt that from then on she shapes my development and the re-
capitulation of a long and fulfilling existence. Even now in the coda
as I write, she is still the composer. Thank you, Lucia.

TEACHER
PERFORMER
MUSICIAN
COMPOSER
ROBERT
MANN
HUSBAND
FATHER
FRIEND

PREFACE

While our father, at ninety-seven years old, no longer plays his violin, he was an active musician through his ninety-first year, concertizing, teaching, and coaching. This book is a collection of both spoken and written words in the form of essays, letters, lectures, and transcribed interviews from various times in his life. Together they record a remarkable life in music; his experience and philosophy. They offer a glimpse into a life filled with musical milestones and the fascinating mind of a musical giant. When he was in his early twenties he wrote, "(I have) a will to study and a will to seek the truth of things, in myself, in music, and in the world that surrounds me." These writings reflect his passionate journey.

Lisa Mann Marotta
Nicholas Mann

CONTENTS

PART III · Relationships

PART IV · Looking Back

[INTRODUCTION]

IT WAS 1961. I LOOKED OUT MY NEW YORK APARTMENT WINDOW. The world outside was gray and wet. I felt lousy, depressed, coming home from a bad rehearsal. To all of you who have never been a member of a serious string quartet, I must confess that at this moment I was damn tired of the constant struggles. Struggles that four human beings playing two violins, a viola, and a violoncello must survive to keep such an ensemble alive. Always, you ask? Well, almost always.

There are exceptions, as in a rare, harmonious marriage. The inescapable reality of a string quartet life encompasses the unrelenting pressure of earning four separate livelihoods; the incessant clash between four personalities, each possessing a well-fortified, inflexible ego; the compelling desire to perform new music that demands a difficult learning process and, when played, will not be easily digestible to the listeners. The frustrating efforts to build a sound career, capture a loyal following, win critical acclaim while keeping abreast of the burgeoning competition in the string quartet field, accepting the sonorous audiences, of course over groups that will have nothing to do with a string quartet at all. Did I possess a tough enough spirit? Could I gather the inhuman patience required to survive?

On this gray, wet day in the sixteenth year of the Juilliard String Quartet's existence, I was unsuccessfully trying to recover from the previous day's explosive rehearsal. To be honest, this talented but flawed group of young musicians didn't like each other, yet had to rehearse and perform in public as if we did. My wife Lucy's words, "What the hell do you need this kind of life for?" raged like a brushfire through my brain. Perhaps she was right!

Then the telephone rang. Should I let it ring or answer it?

"Hello."

"Robert, this is Harold Spivacke."

I perked up. Dr. Spivacke was head of the music division in the Library of Congress in Washington, D. C. On a few special occasions he had invited our quartet to play in his hall, the Elizabeth Sprague Coolidge Auditorium. We would play difficult modern pieces that the Budapest Quartet would not even touch.

"Hi, Dr. Spivacke, what's on your mind?"

"Robert, please answer me, are you standing up or sitting down right now?" *What a peculiar question*, I thought.

"I'm standing."

"Well, young man, sit down, because I want to tell you something that requires sitting down to be heard and responded to."

Completely baffled and uneasy, I said, "Yes?"

"The Library of Congress has a strong commissioning program of young composers or outstanding composers of new works. The Budapest never plays these works. Can you guess what I have decided?"

"Come on, Dr. Spivacke, I haven't the slightest idea."

"Well, after a long, difficult, internal debate and a most guilty conscience, I am letting my dear friends, the Budapest String Quartet, go. I have to have a quartet in residence that will play these new works. I know that you guys will play them. I am asking you, the Juilliards, to replace them as the quartet in residence at the Library of Congress. What's your answer?"

I was speechless. I was struck dumb. Any response at that precise moment to Dr. Spivacke's words would have been inadequate to describe the raging storm of emotions battering my mental and physical consciousness.

Robert warming up backstage, Coolidge Auditorium, Library of Congress

Yes, there was an enormous wave of exhilaration that instantly swept away the pain of yesterday's crises and all previous pains, but an equal backlash of trepidation numbed my senses. How could the young, much less experienced Juilliard Quartet replace one of the greatest quartets of all time, the Budapest, functioning in the most prestigious chamber music residency in the musical world? Even as these storm waves crashed and subsided, there still remained deep questionable currents flowing below the surface.

How could Robert Mann, at best an adequate violin player, lead his quartet as Mr. Roisman of the Budapest led his? Even now, so many years later, I still ask this question.

Holding the telephone in shock, I traveled instantly back in time to another dreary afternoon long ago in Portland, Oregon, listening to a static-impaired radio broadcast of a Library of Congress concert from the Coolidge Auditorium played by the Budapest String Quartet. Was it possible? Could my lifelong dream become a reality? The Juilliard String Quartet playing twenty-four concerts a season in one of the most perfect acoustical chamber music halls on the Library of Congress-owned Stradivarius instruments? Heaven on Earth.

Dr. Spivacke was not a patient man.

"Robert, are you still on the line?" Would my vocal chords fail me now? "What's your answer?"

"Why, Dr. Spivacke, yes, yes, yes, yes."

My life in chamber music, no matter how difficult, challenging, or successful, has been the life for me.

PART I

The Early Years

[EARLY LIFE]

MY PARENTS, CHARLES AND ANNA MANN, MET IN PORTLAND, Oregon. My father was born in England where his family worked in the garment industry, and following his time in the British army in World War I, he moved to Oregon. At five years of age, my mother and her family arrived there from Poland. I was their first child and we stayed in Portland until I was close to eleven. My brother, Alfred, was born five years after my birth and my sister, Rosalind, eight years later. During this time my father had a tailor shop in Portland. He was a good tailor.

My parents were not trained as musicians. Following high school, my mother got a job with a man who sold pianos. An upright piano was included in her pay. She learned to play and she loved to sing. She had a beautiful singing voice and sang in the Portland Symphony Chorus. When she came to New York, she sang in the Brooklyn Philharmonic Chorus and later in the YMHA Chorus. My father didn't play any instrument but he loved classical music.

It was important to my parents that their children play musical instruments. As the oldest (at 9 years of age) I was told that I must choose a musical instrument to study. They didn't specify which instrument. We had an upright piano in my house, but I selected the violin. I don't know why. I believe because it was smaller than the piano and I could carry it. Alfred tried the piano, oboe, and cello, and ended up not playing an instrument—he became a scientist instead. Rosalind started piano, and played successfully.

I started my music lessons at the Portland College of Music, after my parents saw an advertisement in the Portland daily paper: "Portland College of Music, Instrument provided, inexpensive weekly lessons." Every Saturday, for $2, I was sent across the Willamette River to the Holiday School where they had a class of six girls and me, Robert Mann. I was loaned a cheaply made violin for free. I attended all of these classes for my parents. The teacher was more interested in the young girls' playing so I was never called on to demonstrate my ability, which was good because I never practiced. My mother would ask, "Why aren't you practicing violin?" I would say, "Mom, I'm learning to read music." I would show her the music, and had tucked my favorite science fiction story inside the music book, which I would read instead. I don't know if I even learned to draw a bow at that time. After six months, I was informed of my "graduation" and handed the violin, bow, and violin case.

WHEN I WAS TEN and a half, my friends and I had a gang headquarters that was a construction ditch. It was very deep with planks overhead and we could get down below. The day I got my violin, I went directly to my underground club where my friends were. I showed my gang my bow and violin. We decided that we all should have instruments. We collected broom handles, three cigar boxes, a few pieces of wood, and nails. I stripped my violin of three of its strings. I attached one string to each of the cigar boxes. We even stripped the hair on the bow to put on three other hickory sticks so they could make a sound. Without any knowledge or understanding, I created my first string quartet and had a great time. I just wanted to play music in a group. I brought all the cigar boxes home, along with my violin. When my parents discovered what I had done, I learned that chamber music is very pleasant up front and very painful behind.

My father decided to start a new tailor business in Tillamook, a town of around 900 people near the coast of Oregon, where we lived for two and a half years. Tillamook, named after an Indian tribe, is where I have my most vivid, early memories and where I discovered earthly paradise.

I remember my father met an elderly Norwegian furniture maker who lived in Tillamook. This man's hobby was his passion for building crude violins out of fresh maple wood. He didn't know how to make a good violin, but what he made looked like a violin and sounded a little bit like a violin. My father made a suit of clothes for this old man and in exchange, my father received a violin. And that is how I got the first violin that was really mine.

In Tillamook I began to learn what it was like to play for other people. We were the only Jewish family in the town and there were about nine churches. There was one congregation on Saturday, the Seventh Day Adventists, and there were Methodists, Presbyterians, Catholics, and all kinds of denominations on Sunday. I became very popular in Tillamook, going to all of these churches. When it was time to pass the hat for the offertory, I'd play some piece of music on my violin. They loved to have me play rather than a little old organ or piano.

AFTER ABOUT A YEAR of living in Tillamook, someone new arrived in the town. His name was Mr. Bergeron, from Belgium. He came to town to grow tulips. Bergeron also played the violin and claimed that he had studied with the great Norwegian violinist Ole Bull. My father decided that I should take violin lessons from Mr. Bergeron. He was a disaster and didn't teach me anything. However, he did do one thing that I loved. He would take me fishing, to my delight.

He loved to fish as much as I did. He had a small, leaky boat, and he rented a dock space close to Tillamook Bay.

One night, after a night of cards and carousing, the dock owner and Mr. Bergeron drunkenly argued over the amount of dock rental. My teacher was short, stocky, and strong. He threatened to beat up his friend, who actually asked his wife to retrieve his shotgun. She did. He fired. Mr. Bergeron and his wooden box of a boat seemed surprisingly lifelike to a young boy who had never seen a dead man before.

The Tillamook Press printed, "No Violin Teacher in Our Town." Without hesitation and surprisingly little resistance from my parents, I immediately reenlisted in nature's conservatory. Paradise, for me, restored. My passion was fishing. I loved to go through the wetlands of Oregon because there was a lot of rain. Tillamook was bounded on each side by two very good fishing streams, the Trask River and the Tillamook River. I would take a pail of dirt and worms and very minor fishing equipment. I would fish during the day while my parents were working in their tailor shop and make sure that I was home before they got home. They would ask if I had practiced, and of course I was a good liar. As a child I didn't have a fiery feeling for music, not at all.

Tillamook is where I discovered my love of nature. I caged a pet porcupine, slept on the ground in the wild, and listened to the whimpering night cries of mountain lions in the distance. I also loved hiking. The mountains on the coast of Oregon are not precipitous, but they are pretty high and remarkable. No coast could be more beautiful. I loved climbing cliffs. I took chances all the time. On the Pacific coast a few miles west of town, there was a dramatic confluence of jagged, granite cliffs, hundreds of feet in the air, precipitously dropping down into small, deep indenting sea bays overflowing with gritty sands beneath carpets of sea-smelling seaweeds, barnacle-encrusted rocks, shells of living and dying miniature sea animals, all depending on the back and forth path of monthly charted tides. This scene in daylight was crowded with large orchestras of seabird harmonies clamoring a cappella. At night it became rushed crescendos and decrescendos of an ageless repetition of waves. In this dramatic geographical mix was a reminder of sadness called the Lost Boys Cave. Two young boys had entered at low tide and were trapped by the incoming tidal waters, deep under the mountainous cliff. By accident I discovered this place of magical power.

One misty, wet afternoon, I clambered over a rocky cliff unsuspecting of the cave beneath. The view from the summit was obscured by the drizzling rain, but the percussive roar of mighty waves drew me down a most slippery descent. I succeeded because I was young and agile. I found a thin ledge thirty feet above a violent, unending attack of powerful cascading waves. What a discovery! The waves that would hit this cliff were fantastic. They were mountains of waves. While the waves sprayed over me, they never threatened to dislodge me into the roaring water. There is something ego fulfilling about being able to get along in the wilderness by yourself. I would perch on the ledge above and listen to the waves and their rhythm. I believe one of the reasons why I have such fantastic rhythm is because I was so fascinated by watching these waves. I would spend an entire day there when I wasn't in school, sitting on the ledge by myself, just watching the waves.

Once I had discovered the cliffs, I would spend hours silently responding to the rhythmic cycle of lesser to greater waves building into an orgiastic climax as they hit and surged over the rocky crest into the pond. The musical elements of this early experience have provided unending resources throughout my musical journey. Another fascination of mine was watching meteor showers. I would sleep outdoors and watch the meteors cross the sky. It was fascinating to see the variance of the large ones that didn't go that far, and the little ones that went farther.

Pardon Ludwig (van Beethoven), for my daring to mention that my first concerts were composed of Pastoral Symphonies consisting of the subtle melodies of pastured cows modulating inharmonically into milk cans, tonally resolving into long, slanted vats of Tillamook cheese. What better environment to develop a keen ear, a sharp eye for alert response in future existing chamber music teamwork. Every round trip of the sun, every change of season added a new dimension to my unborn musical vocabulary. New variations constantly stirred my imagination with every furious storm. With all the senses brought to life in a very young body, I think Tillamook's conservatory that I attended before the age of thirteen was the best.

Robert, middle school years

Mr. Hurlimann

My days in verdantly wet Tillamook were numbered as my father decided to return to Portland to try another trade, grocery merchant. I was twelve years old when he brought me to play for Eduard Hurlimann, the concertmaster of the Portland Symphony Orchestra. He was Swiss, and was not only a fine violinist but also a wonderful, tasteful musician. It is not an exaggeration to declare that before World War I, the most active musicians in America came from Europe—teachers, important members of orchestras, concert performers, conductors, and composers. Mr. Hurlimann was no exception, but he was a rare bird. He studied in Prague with Adolph Pick who later moved to Chicago, where he became an important teacher. Hurlimann was not a Jew, but he understood and hated Adolf Hitler with a passion before most in America knew who Hitler was. He was equally at home playing chamber music, leading the symphony violin section, or performing a concerto. Mr. Hurlimann had one of the most beautiful bow arms of any violinist that I've ever seen. When he played, it was as masterful as his handling of a fly fishing rod. He knew all about wild mushrooms, and was a good fisherman who loved fishing as much as I did. That caught me and I was lucky that he accepted me as his pupil.

Mr. Hurlimann said to my father, "You know, Mr. Mann, your kid is no wunderkind. He will not be a great soloist, but if he works hard and practices, I'm almost certain that he can make his living with music. I will take him as a student but you must promise that only Robert will come to his lessons from now on."

He agreed to teach me on scholarship, and, when I was fifteen, introduced me to Bach's solo works, including the partitas and sonatas. You might say that these are the Bible for violinists. Everyone from the great violinist Joseph Joachim on up through the years has studied them. I would come to my lesson not having practiced more than about fifteen minutes a day. I couldn't fake anything with him. If I hadn't practiced, he'd get very severe and would listen for about five minutes. Then he would say, "Okay, Bobby, I don't want you to waste my time. Go home and when you've practiced enough, call me and I will give you a lesson."

I was learning the Bach C Major sonata, which is a difficult one. The slow movement, the Largo, has a very beautiful and simple melody. This three minutes of music has remained a musical touchstone throughout my life. One day, I arrived around 1pm for my lesson. Hurlimann was intrigued with how I was translating the sounds into phrasing and nuances so that listeners could enjoy them, without knowing what the variation and differences were. He cancelled all of his lessons that came after mine. We spent the whole afternoon working on the third movement. He played it. He had me play it. We broke it down and studied every note, harmony, and phrase. From the opening double-stop sound (of melody and bass line) continuing the music's course until it cadentially came to rest with its three-note broken chord, there wasn't a nuance of phrase, any evolvement of harmony, any structural arc that he didn't gift to me with profound love for Bach, the violin, and me. I honestly felt that I was born musically on this day. I began to think music was very interesting and started to practice more. This was the day I gave up my dream to be a forest ranger in a national park and became a true acolyte musician.

I studied with Mr. Hurlimann from age twelve until I moved to New York at eighteen. He later became the conductor of the Bakersfield (California) Symphony Orchestra, and when I was in New York, he invited me to Bakersfield to play the Prokofiev G Minor Concerto with him. It was wonderful. We continued a close relationship until his passing. If he and a few other European musicians had not worked their musical magic on me, I would have become a forest ranger (hopefully, in some western national park) or at least a potato farmer in one of my favorite places on earth, Idaho's Salmon River country beneath the rugged Sawtooth Mountains.

I wasn't aware that when I played, people liked the emotional message. They would tell me, "That was wonderful." They seemed to recognize something I was totally unaware of. I wouldn't know why. I really didn't. I was always struggling to play better. But I was aware that music not only intrigued me, it meant something deep to me. In Portland, we had a wonderful music librarian, Miss Knox. She was elderly and very severe. Yet she liked me and she allowed me to go into the reference room. I looked at copies of manuscripts from not only Beethoven and Mozart, but also Schoenberg and Bartók. I took home six little pieces of Schoenberg and tried to play them on the piano. I would arrange the Bartók folk songs for little groups of the orchestra. Bartók and Schoenberg were both influences on my life. Later, I even took home scores by Berg, though I didn't understand anything. At that time Berg had just finished writing *Wozzeck*. Ms. Knox even invited Béla Bartók to visit Portland, and he played, gave a lecture, and a demonstration on an upright piano. It is one of the regrets of my life that I didn't get to see that.

Portland had one other important personality—a crazy Russian guy named Jacques Gershkovitch, who had fled the Russian revolution. He had not gone west like most of the Russians who were fleeing, but east to Siberia. He got to Portland and took over a little junior symphony made up mostly of students from Portland's six high schools and from Reed College. That Portland Junior Symphony actually became quite famous throughout the United States.

I joined the Portland Junior Symphony when I was thirteen and became the concertmaster when I was sixteen. This is where I got my first experience playing in an orchestra as well as an introduction to weird repertoire. We played a stage version of Mussorgsky's *Khovanshchina*, entire operas, and Russian tone poems by Liadov, Glinka, and other Russian composers. I met many friends playing in the junior symphony; we loved to play music together and developed lifelong relationships. We also used to sing madrigals and a cappella music and even hiked together.

In my teenage years, there were four people from the Portland Junior Symphony who were of great meaning to me. One was Isadore Tinkleman (crippled by polio) who became a great violin teacher. He studied in New York at the Manhattan School of Music with Rachmael Weinstock and came back to Portland where he started a community music school. When I was in the Army and traveled to New York I would stay in his apartment. Another friend, James Niblock (Jimmy) became a composer and later the head of the music department at Michigan State University in East Lansing.

Isadore Tinkleman

Max Felde

Also, there was Max Felde, my dearest friend who also went to New York to study viola. He was a Norseman and an extraordinary guy. He became the original violist of the La Salle Quartet, and later moved to Vancouver.

The fourth person in that group, besides myself, was a talented young violinist, violist and conductor, Warren Signer. He went to the Curtis School of Music in Philadelphia to study. When we were teenagers, Max, Jimmy, Warren, and I went on a camping trip to Tillamook, located on the most western part of Oregon that goes out to the ocean. In Portland we bought cheap ferry tickets that went down the Columbia River to Astoria. After that, we hitchhiked. That first night it rained hard, like it can only rain on the coast of Oregon. We had our supplies, but we didn't have a tent so we put our belongings under large logs and built a fire. The heat warmed our stuff so at least it was not dripping wet and Max and I were able to sleep. However, Jimmy and Warren didn't join us. I don't know what they did—maybe they walked the beach all night. They came back to our campsite in the early morning while we were still half asleep and said, "We're leaving." They left and they took all of our food, except for the chocolate syrup. Max and I were determined to stay. We ended up living on clams and nuts and berries that we found in the forest. We stayed the week and we finally hitchhiked back up to Astoria arriving late at night. We weren't able to take the ferry back to Portland until the morning so we needed to find a place to sleep. The hills in Astoria are very steep, much steeper than many of the hills in San Francisco. We climbed up and finally found a place to lie down. When we woke up in the morning we discovered that we had actually climbed into the Astoria Zoo. There was an animal, I think it was a moose, looking at us when we opened our eyes. We finally made it back to Portland and I hiked with Max to his house, which was about four or five miles from the ferry. Then I hitch hiked to my own home a couple of miles further, and I walked into my father's grocery store. He thought I was a beggar and told me that he didn't have any food. I said, "Don't you recognize your own son?"

• • •

ANOTHER SEMINAL EVENT OCCURRED while I was in the Portland Junior Symphony. For one concert held in the school's gymnasium, that was going to feature solo and chamber music, I decided to compose a piece for the occasion. It was my first composition and was kind of a gypsy piece. After that, I kept composing. I didn't study any formal theory. But I knew there were fugues, so I would compose a fugue without knowing any of the rules. I also wrote a long sonata, following a Bach solo sonata, for a girlfriend who was a cellist in the Junior Symphony.

Robert at the beginning of his musical career

Wanting to be a chamber musician

There were two realities for my wanting to be a chamber musician. Musicians such as Yehudi Menuhin, Isaac Stern, and Ruggiero Ricci would come and play concerts in Portland. I knew, and Mr. Hurlimann knew, that I was never going to be a great solo violinist. I didn't have the chops to play, to control the instrument in that way. I also didn't have the desire.

In my early days in Portland there was a hall in a labor building called The Neighbors of Woodcraft. It was a beautiful hall and had beautiful acoustics. As an adolescent I used to sneak in to hear the Budapest Quartet, the Pro Arte Quartet, and other groups. They all came to Portland on concert tours. I was inspired.

In Portland, Howard Trugman, the manager of the symphony, loved to have kids come to his apartment and play. I had a group and we read at least once a week all of the chamber music that we could get our hands on (and Ms. Knox, at the Portland Public Library, got all of the music for us). Haydn wrote oodles and oodles of quartets, and so did Mozart. Beethoven wrote sixteen quartets and so on. It seemed to me, since I was quite good at reading classical chamber music, that I could be a chamber musician.

New York and the Institute of Musical Art

When it became time for me to study elsewhere, Mr. Hurlimann, who was a very bright man, said that I had to go and study in a very sophisticated city where music was more meaningful than in Portland.

At this time, for serious young string players, there were two outstanding schools to go to for study, the Curtis Institute in Philadelphia and the Juilliard Graduate School in New York. Both were free at the time. At age eighteen, I sent my application to the Juilliard Graduate School and was accepted into the Institute of Musical Art (which later merged with the Juilliard Graduate School to become the Juilliard School of Music.) I can't tell you why I chose New York over Curtis.

I think I thought I wasn't that good, and that it would be easier to get into Juilliard than Curtis.

We were a poor family, so I played a concert in my high school, Lincoln High School, to raise money for my studies in New York. I was playing a violin that was given to me by my English teacher, Miss Frances Gill, whose family owned the big paper, stationary and furniture store in Portland. She gave me a violin to take to New York. It was old and she thought it was a Guadagnini, but it wasn't—it was an old Tyrolean violin and I still have it. A very wealthy lady, Edna Holmes, came to the concert with a Ms. Rothschild, who was supporting young musicians. They felt that they had to support me and were able to raise enough money on my behalf. Ms. Holmes was a marvelous lady. Not only did she provide most of the money for my going to New York, but she also sent me $80 a month throughout my

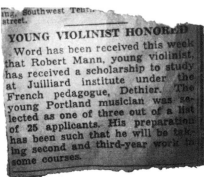

High school concert publicity

student days in New York. Even later, when I was married, she would send presents to the children. Later in life I wrote a letter to her saying, "Edna, you've been one of the most meaningful people in my life and I want to repay you now." She replied, "Don't repay me, you continue to help young people and I will be repaid."

I always loved peanut butter and everybody knew it. So when I got to the train for my send-off to New York, about five mothers were there who all produced boxes of peanut butter cookies for me to take across the country. I traveled via Washington state to Vancouver and took the Canadian train across the country, down to Minneapolis and east to New York.

I was met at the train by the husband of my mother's cousin, who was a rabbi in Mount Vernon. Then I had to find a place to stay. Mrs. Howard Brockaway, who was the placement person at Juilliard said, "There is this absolutely marvelous family and they have a daughter who is a wonderful young violinist, Carol Glenn. The mother runs a couple of apartments where she rents out rooms that are affordable for students. You should go there because it's very homey and it's your first year away in New York." So I went there.

When I arrived at the Institute I had to take exams, and the first thing that happened to me was that I failed them. They wanted to know if I knew what a Neapolitan six was, if I knew all of the modes, or whether a given chord was major or minor, this or that chord form. While I knew all the chords and their functions, I didn't know any of their technical names. I was placed in the first year. Within two weeks I learned all of the names and the teachers stuck me in the second year and by the third month I was in the graduating class.

My teacher, Edouard Dethier, was from Belgium. I wanted to study with Louis Persinger. All young kids wanted to study with him because he had taught Menuhin and Ricci. But I couldn't because I hadn't been assigned to him. Dethier had studied at the French conservatoire and with the great Belgian violinist, composer and conductor Eugène Ysaÿe. At that moment, being assigned to Dethier was the luckiest thing that ever happened to me because Dethier was a continuation of the path that Hurlimann had sent me on. Not only did

Dethier have a perfect technique but he loved chamber music. He was a passionate, wonderful, warm, and rather shy man.

I loved my studies with Mr. Dethier, although he had a certain idiosyncratic way of teaching which I often rebelled against. He would say, "You're going to study such and such composition. Go to Carol, or go to another student, and copy the bowings and fingerings." I wouldn't do that. I would struggle through the piece and make my own bowings and fingerings. When I went to my lesson he would say, "Well, didn't you copy the bowings and fingerings?" and I would reply, "Mr. Dethier, I didn't really want to do that. I wanted to find out for myself." He would say, "I'm trying to save you time. I mean I've gone through all of these struggles." And I would say, "Yes, but I need to go through those struggles, too." His reply in his fantastic French accent, "You know, I get so mad at you. I could take my fingers and pluck out your eyeball, spit in the socket and let it splash back."

Every Friday, Mr. Dethier would play string quartets for his own musical health. He played in a quartet with a female student on second violin and a cellist by the name of Bedrich Vashna, who was much older and had played the Dvořák concerto in Prague, with Dvořák conducting. Another requirement in Juilliard in those days was for violinists to also learn viola. Juilliard didn't have a viola department. Dethier's quartet needed a violist and since I could also play viola, I was elected.

So, every Friday we would play for three hours, have refreshments, and play for a couple hours more. I learned all of the chamber music repertoire from pre-Haydn into the twentieth century during these sessions. Dethier didn't get past Dohnányi, he didn't understand Bartók or anything modern, but he did love Debussy.

Dethier had a house in Blue Hill, near the Blue Hill Music Festival, which was a gathering place for many important musicians. In the summer, I would go there to study with him. Franz Kneisel also had a home there. Kneisel was a friend of Dethier's who had also been a friend of Brahms, as well as the concertmaster of the Boston Symphony in the nineteenth century. He was America's first serious quartet player; his quartet was the first to play the complete cycle of Beethoven quartets in the United States. It was at Blue Hill that I also met the legendary violinist and composer Fritz Kreisler for the first time. Kreisler was a very strange and funny man. He never touched the violin all summer. He would study a piece without practicing it and then play it in a concert.

That summer I also met a man who was very important in my life, Stefan Wolpe. He was at Blue Hill composing and he had a whole group of students with him. I would join his group and read music. Wolpe had a theory that you could read contemporary music and develop skills for playing it. I really became enamored of this man. I didn't officially study composition with him, but I would compose a piece, bring it to him, and he would criticize it. He was an important influence on my compositional development.

My first theory and composition teacher was Bernard Wagenaar, who was a Dutchman. He could play any score on the piano. But I also

Stefan Wolpe

remember studying the Bach chorales with Judson Ehrbar, who later became the Registrar at Juilliard. Ehrbar gave us the melody, an old Lutheran melody, and our job was to harmonize it. He was young and didn't really know that much. He would put out the Bach score to show us what Bach had done with this melody, and then he would take our harmonization and put it up next to Bach's work. The red pencil was going all through our work all of the time, and after three or four lessons I got tired of that. I made friends with the librarian at the New York Public Library's music division, located at 58th Street on the East Side. I knew that Bach had harmonized many chorales more than once, and I asked her if there were any other editions than the one that Ehrbar was using for his teaching. She took me to the reference area and found them, and I begged her to let me check them out. She agreed that I could have them for a week, on the condition that I didn't tell anyone. I found the assigned melody and copied in my handwriting Bach's other version out of the book. I went to class, and Ehrbar did his usual teaching and crossed out everything in red that I had copied from Bach's other score. Finally, when he finished his red markings, I took my borrowed book with Bach's alternate harmonization and said, "Would you put the red pencil through this book, too?"

Of course this was a terrible thing for me to do. Ehrbar got up after a minute, left the room and was gone for about twenty minutes. When he came back he said that Mr. George Wedge, who was the head of the school and had written a famous harmony book, would like to see me. I was sure that I was going to be thrown out of the school. Mr. Wedge was behind his desk busily writing and didn't say anything to me for at least three minutes. Finally he said, "Sit down, young man." He was smiling, and said, "Now look, all of us are learning, even our teachers. You shouldn't put a person in that kind of position. That was rough, but since you seem to know what you are doing, I'll excuse you from the class. You will just take the exam at the end of the year."

I studied quartets with Hans Letz who came to the United States with Franz Kneisel, and played in Kneisel's quartet. I remember an instance when my quartet was in Hans Letz's studio having a quartet lesson. He had picked up four pieces by a Dutch composer, Julius

Hijman, who had fled the Nazis. Hijman was going to have a concert of his music played at Carnegie Recital Hall, and he hoped that a student quartet would be willing to play on this recital. The work was very complicated, there wasn't a harmonic scheme that we could conceive of, but we were playing it. In walked Felix Salmond, the great cellist and chamber music musician, who listened for a while and said, "Enough of this. How can you let your kids play this, Hans?"

Hans began to retreat and said, "Well, perhaps we will tell the gentleman that we won't play the work." I was upset and found out where Mr. Hijman was staying so I could call him. I said that Juilliard wouldn't help him with his performance, but if he wanted, I would ask three of my friends and we would perform the work, and we did. The reason that I tell you this story is that Mr. Hijman got a job so very quickly afterwards at the Houston Conservatory of Music, teaching theory and composition. When he left New York, he had to leave his upright piano and he offered it to me. I'd gotten my first reward for playing a contemporary piece.

The discipline of chamber music

The discipline of chamber music emerged in America when I was a student*. Before World War I, many people played chamber music in

---

* Chamber music started in the 1700s or even before. In the 1700s, 1800s and into the 20th century, playing chamber music was not considered a profession. Playing chamber music was a way that musicians enjoyed each other. They got together, even the greatest violinists, to play an evening of quartets. That was the way everyone experienced chamber music.

One of the first great performers was Josef Joachim, a friend of Brahms. He had a quartet in London and one in Berlin; the other members were colleagues or minor colleagues. He was not a dictator so much as a mentor and a leader. The music's interpretation was how he felt about the phrasing and the way the piece was revealed through the performance was his doing. Everyone wanted to please Joachim.

In the early 1900s, concert venues were becoming more important and a few quartets began to appear and have big careers. The first one in the 1900s was the Flonzaley Quartet. The quartet's first violinist, Adolfo Betti, came to the Mannes School in the 1940s and taught chamber music. In one of his groups he needed a violist and I killed myself to get into it. I took lessons with this great musician. The Flonzaley Quartet you could say was the first quartet that traveled the world playing concerts and earning a living as a chamber music group.

Europe, but mainly amateurs who held evenings where they sight read quartets, trios, and quintets, and maybe even sextets. When I came to New York and I needed money desperately to study, I learned the underground way of making a kind of student living was to play in amateur chamber groups. There was a strong amateur society in New York and I knew the lady who ran it, Helen Rice. She was marvelous and I would join her group as a violist or second violinist when she would play with her friends. We would spend the evening, at least three or four hours playing chamber music. The groups usually needed violists, and I could play viola quite well, so I got a lot of jobs and would earn $50 for spending an evening playing chamber music with these amateurs.

But I was a lousy student. I was discovering New York and didn't practice much that first year. At Carol Glenn's house, where I was living, there was a jazz fellow who was learning classical harmonization, and we used to go to his room and sit around. We would listen to a radio show called *Lights Out*. At around three o'clock in the morning we would go down to Blenheim's cafeteria and have what we called the one-eyed Egyptian sandwich, which was an egg fried in the middle of a white piece of bread.

It was a terrible year for developing my violin playing but a wonderful year of growing up and, unfortunately, getting an ulcer. One man, Conrad Held, who was on the Institute faculty and taught violin and viola, wrote in his notes on my end-of-the-year jury, "Never in my whole life experience have I ever seen such a talented well-prepared young man deteriorate so much in the space of one year." I never forgot that. And, I did manage to pull it together, practice a bit, and graduate from the Institute of Musical Art that year.

After graduating, I didn't want to go home to Portland. I learned about an interesting spot near Tanglewood named South Mountain, which was the estate owned by Elizabeth Sprague Coolidge. There she had sponsored and commissioned the Webern string trio, the Third String Quartet by Schoenberg, and other pieces. Maestro Willeke, the conductor of the Institute of Musical Art's orchestra, was there; he invited faculty and students for a festival of studying and playing chamber music at South Mountain. Since they needed a violist and I was willing, I was in demand again. I ended up spending that summer at South Mountain, practicing and trying to improve my technique before taking the exam to enter the Juilliard Graduate School.

After that, it was time for me to play for Mr. Dethier before taking my exams. He was very upset because he thought my Bach was terrible. I had also prepared the Beethoven concerto with the Kreisler cadenza. At the exam, they would ask you what you wanted to begin with so I chose the Beethoven concerto. I played a good part of the first movement and then I was asked to play Bach. My heart sunk because I knew that my teacher thought it was terrible. Someone else said, "No, I'd like to hear the cadenza." I was in luck. Afterwards, Mr. Dethier said, "God is kind to fools and drunkards. I wonder which you are." I got into the Juilliard Graduate School, but I was still more interested in chamber music than I was in solo violin. I must have been involved in at least four chamber music groups at that time.

At Juilliard I loved to play in the pit ensemble for the operas. That was a marvelous way of getting to know Mozart's operas. I also loved playing in the orchestra. Most of the students tried to avoid playing in the orchestra. Lynn Harrell was one of the only successful soloists who talked about going back at the end of his life to play in an orchestra again, because he loved it so much.

I remember an orchestra concert conducted by Alexander Siloti, a crazy Russian. We were on stage waiting for him to come out. We waited for five, ten, then fifteen minutes. Everyone was wondering what was going on and finally somebody went backstage to find him. He said, "I won't come out until Liszt tells me it's okay to come out." Some of his pupils would come to a lesson and recalled that he would say he talked to Liszt down at Columbus Circle.

Albert Spalding also taught violin at Juilliard. He was maybe the first famous American violinist. He was a member of the family that sold all of the sports equipment including the Spalding tennis balls.

I played sonatas with Billy Masselos who was a student of Carl Friedberg. Other friends included Willy Kapell, who studied with Olga Samaroff Stokowski. Willy Kapell was different than the typical student. His language in those early days was tempered with a lot of epithets and he had a short fuse. I remember we studied sonatas with Louis Persinger. Since we were both busy doing so many other things, we would get together about two hours before our lesson and run through the sonatas. Then we would arrive to play for Persinger and pretend that we had worked all week on the sonatas. Of course we hadn't. It didn't take Persinger long to catch the drift. After three or four lessons we came in with the Brahms G Major Sonata. The sonata starts out with a G Major chord on the piano, two of them, and then the violin comes in. Kapell played the two chords and I came in. Persinger says, "Wait a minute, wait a minute," and he spends the whole hour on me and the upbeat. Willy sat fuming, waiting and not being able to play.

In those days at Juilliard, students had a curfew. You had to be out of the building by ten o'clock at night. Willy and I would hide in the cleaning closets until the guards had gone through the school to make sure that everyone had left and we would stay all night and practice. I remember Willy used to practice Scarlatti so furiously that his fingers would bleed.

[NAUMBURG COMPETITION]

When I was a student in New York, there were the Naumburg and Leventritt Competitions in New York and the Schubert Memorial that took place in Philadelphia. In Belgium there was also another great competition, the Queen Elizabeth.

The Naumburg Competition, named after Walter Naumburg, an amateur cellist and avid chamber music player, was a competition for soloists. It gave the winner a concert debut in Town Hall in New York City, completely free. Mr. Dethier said, "You know you're not good enough to win the Naumburg but it would be a good experience for you to try out." Virtuosos from all over the country entered the competition. Most of the players were so much better than I was. In those days, the Naumburg included several different instruments and voice in the competition. In other words, Walter Naumburg started his competition for any talented young solo musician. Later, Lucy and I, in our roles as Naumburg President and Executive Administrator, would add chamber music to the array of competitions.

I practiced all the requirements but didn't take it seriously. If I would have, I would have dropped out. You were required to have two complete solo programs and a concerto. My program included a Nardini sonata, the Bach partita in D minor and the Chausson *Poeme*. My concerto was Prokofiev's second concerto, the G minor, and when it came time for the competition, I only knew the first movement by memory. The judges wanted to hear everything you played. If they were nice in the beginning, they would ask, 'What would you like to start with?" Luckily this happened and I said very politely, the first movement of the Prokofiev concerto and I played it. I was hoping that the judges would immediately go to another piece because they wanted to hear me play Bach and so on. It worked, and I didn't have to play the last movement. I got into the semi-finals, which were held a week later. I killed myself and memorized the Prokofiev concerto so I could get through the slow movement. It was the last movement that was a problem for me. It's a rondo and very brutal and I wasn't confident playing it.

Also making the semi-final round were six other violinists—all girls. The semi-final round also had a different jury. So when they asked me, "What would I like to start with?" I said, "The first movement of the Prokofiev concerto," and that was fine. All of a sudden a member of the jury said, "You know, I'd like to hear the last movement of the Prokofiev." I turned to my pianist, who had gone on tours with Paul Robeson and William Primrose and had a funny sense of humor. I turned to him and asked, "What do I do now?" He said, "You have two options. You can say you don't know it and they kick you out. Or, you can start playing and stop when you have to." God's truth, I went through and as I reached the end of the part I knew, the judges said, "thank you." I just couldn't believe it. Next the jury wanted to hear the Chaussone *Poeme*. I made it to the final round.

The final round took place at Town Hall, a performance hall in midtown Manhattan. In the finals were a number of violinists as well as other musicians in other disciplines. Willy Kapell made it to the finals. There was also a young man from The Curtis Institute, a violinist named Rafael Druian who had a fantastic technique; we all thought he would win. He later became the concertmaster of the Cleveland Orchestra under George Szell.

At the finals, a lady juror who I learned later was one of the great *lieder* singers of the day who was famous for her singing of Debussy, asked, "You have this Nardini sonata on your program. What is that?"

I explained that Nardini was an Italian Baroque composer from the early eighteenth century. She asked me to play the *larghetto* movement, the slow movement of the sonata. The one thing that I could do well was to communicate warmth in my phrasing, the reason anyone listens to this kind of music. The lady juror later told me that they recognized that the other violinists had better technique and were much better, but no one communicated the slow movement the way I did with the Nardini *larghetto*. Two winners were chosen in the 1941 competition—Willy Kapell and me. Playing that movement was the reason I won the Naumburg competition.

My teacher's response to my winning was what he always said, "God is kind to fools and drunkards. I don't know which you are." He was amazed.

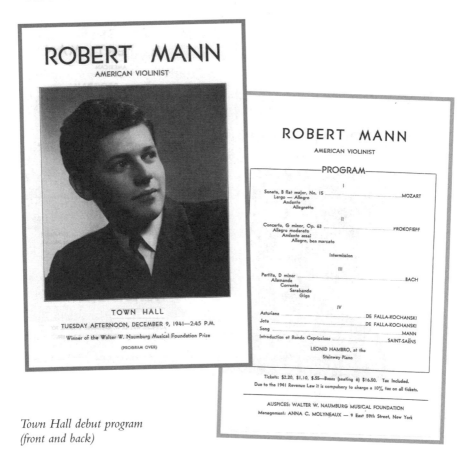

*Town Hall debut program
(front and back)*

I played my debut in New York City's Town Hall on December 9th, two days after Pearl Harbor. The program included the Prokofiev concerto (you had to play a concerto on your program in those days). I opened the concert with a Mozart B-Flat Sonata and an American contemporary piece that I wrote. That was a Naumburg requirement that you had to play an American work. My pianist was my very good friend, Leonid Hambro.

Since Pearl Harbor had taken place two days before, a third of my audience was scared that New York City was going to be bombed. People were directed to stay in the basement of buildings downtown. A third of my audience didn't even get to the concert, so I didn't have a full house. However, my mother came. After my concert, I got reviews from all of the New York papers, Brooklyn too. I mean every single one. And by the way, all of my reviews were wonderful*.

PHOTO CREDIT: G. D. HACKETT

Robert and Leonid Hambro

---

* "(Robert Mann) deserved the applause. His playing was technically secure. His into-nation and the quality of his tone were good no matter how fast the music. There was a wide variety of color in his playing, . . . His final group revealed another talent, for it included 'Song,' a work of his own." *New York Times*, Dec. 10, 1941

After winning the Naumburg, I played the Prokofiev concerto with Albert Stoessel conducting. That performance of the Prokofiev was played note perfect, the whole piece. I don't know why. I'd never done that before and I've never done it since.

Another story involving my friend Leonid Hambro took place after he won the Naumburg himself in 1946. Lee asked me to compose a piano work for him to play as his American piece. At the concert, I was sitting in Town Hall with his teacher, Rosina Lhevinne. Lee had decided that he was going to perform his entire concert from memory. He got to my piece, which starts with a two-minute slow section followed by a very fast section that lasts about six minutes and then a short coda. During the fast part, he became unbelievably lost and started to improvise. I thought *why don't you stop, go off the stage, get the music and play it with the music.* But no, he kept improvising, trying to figure out what to do, which had nothing to do with the piece that I had written. Finally, he jumped to the coda, which he remembered and finished the piece. Ms. Lhevinne turned to me and said, "Lovely piece dear." I was dying. It wasn't my piece at all.

[ARMY YEARS]
(1943-1946)

THE SUMMER BEFORE PEARL HARBOR, THE COOLIDGE QUARTET WAS looking for a new second violinist and they were also about to record the complete cycle of the Beethoven quartets for Columbia Records. Established by William Kroll, the Coolidge Quartet was an early American string quartet named after its patron, Elizabeth Sprague Coolidge. I auditioned for the job, and to my happiness, delirious happiness, I was asked to join them. They asked me, "Is there any danger of your being drafted?" My answer, "Well, I have two draft numbers, one in New York and one in Oregon. I think I'm free for this year, but I'm going to be drafted after that in Oregon. I don't think that I will be able to avoid the draft unless my stomach ulcers get me out." That said, they decided to keep looking for a second violinist, not because they didn't like me, but because they didn't want to interrupt the recording of the Beethoven cycle, which was a two-year project. So I lost my chance to have been in a quartet because of the war.

I was sure that I was going to be drafted at the end of the summer, so that June I went to a music festival in Albuquerque, New Mexico. I was lucky to meet an absolutely astonishing lady there by the name of Ruth Hanna McCormick Simms. She was the daughter of Mark Hanna, the famous Republican politician from Ohio in the early part of the twentieth century. She had married Bertie McCormick, who owned the *Chicago Tribune* and who also happened to be one of the most arch conservative reactionaries in the country. Following their divorce, she married a man by the name of Simms, who was the president of a bank and later became the governor of New Mexico. Mr. Simms couldn't have cared less about music but Mrs. Simms was the major patron of the festival and had a wonderful home outside of Albuquerque. It had a swimming pool and concerts would take place on her overhanging terrace. The audience, which generally included around three hundred people, would sit on the other side of the swimming pool. At this time, I was pretty much a political radical. I didn't belong to any party but I thought the poor people of the world should unite and be better off.

Of course, Mrs. Simms couldn't have been more reactionary. She hated Roosevelt. She had been Tom Dewey's western campaign manager. On top of that she had this enormous ranch in southern Colorado. It was thousands of acres. At one point before the end of the war, she rode down to Northern Mexico on horseback with cowboys from her ranch, bought some 25,000 head of cattle and came back with them across the border. Roosevelt had a beef subsidy and she was going to try and flood the market or break it or something political. I talked with her and I didn't hide my more liberal views. She would sort of look amused at me, but we liked each other. Following the festival, we

*Ruth Hanna
McCormick Simms*

kept up our relationship. I ended up going to the Albuquerque Music Festival for two summers. Mrs. Simms would write me letters saying, "Do you think the young men in the Army will vote for Mr. Dewey?" I would write back and tell her that they didn't really know who Tom Dewey was.

In the meantime, I had a quartet that I had put together and we were playing late Beethoven quartets. I played first violin, Herbert Sorkin played second, Tom Lanese was the violist and Joe Tekula was the cellist. There was a conductor and clarinetist named Rosenkranz who after the war became a major conductor on Broadway. He was forming a show called, "This is the Army," that would travel the world to entertain the troops. He would be conducting an orchestra and he told my quartet that if we enlisted that he would guarantee that we would all be brought in to be the principal players. That way, we wouldn't have to fight and we would just travel around. Well, I had my two draft numbers and the Portland number was high enough that I was sure that I wouldn't be called that year. I didn't want to lose a year of study. So I didn't take Rosenkranz up on his offer and didn't stay with the quartet. That was fateful, because when the opportunity for the Juilliard String Quartet came, Rosenkranz's group was off playing somewhere in the South Seas. If I had been with them, I wouldn't have been given the chance to start the Juilliard String Quartet.

Eventually I was drafted into Fort Lewis in Washington and sent to Camp Crowder in western Missouri, near Joplin. We were told to bring only a toothbrush and an extra pair of underpants. All else—*verboten!* "Dare I? Yes, damn it." Covering my Tillamook "Strad" and bow inside a canvas bag, I concealed it during the train ride and barracks assignment.

Avoiding prying master sergeant eyes, I covertly shoved the fiddle under my bunk. Standing in line at attention, reality interrupted. The loudspeakers in Fort Lewis spoke loudly: "Private Robert Mann; Private Robert Mann—report on the double to Barracks C 102." I dropped out of line and ran. Breathless I entered C 102. At the end of the room, three soldiers were lounging on a chair and a bed. A corporal held a guitar under his arm. A master sergeant barked, "You the creep with the fiddle under your bunk in A 105?" I thought that they were going to confiscate my fiddle. He threatened, "Go get it now on the double."

Miserably crushed, I ran, I got it, and I returned. The guys hadn't moved. The guitar corporal said, "You play?" I nodded. "All right," he continued, "You know that there 'bumblebee' piece?" *What the hell is going on?* Truth was, without knowing why, before induction, I had practiced the Bach "Ciaccona," "Smoke Gets In Your Eyes," the popular movie theme from *Intermezzo* and (jackpot!) "Flight of the Bumblebee," by Rimsky-Korsakov.

The corporal added some information for his buddies. "The world record for this piece is one minute and fifty-three seconds, held by an accordion player." He turned to me, "You think you can beat that?" I shrugged. "We're going to time you!" The master sergeant took out his watch. "Get set! Go!" I hadn't even tuned up and of course had no accompaniment. I scrambled down the opening chromatic runs as fast as cold fingers could move. The seconds ticked by and then I approached eight bars of music that must repeat. *Excuse me God,* I cheated as I didn't repeat. That helped save my skin. Having shaved off five seconds, I desperately headed into the final notes and ended on a pizzicato chord. The drab room sensed the tension (mine) and silence (theirs). "Waddayou know, fellas," the master sergeant chuckled. "This creep is only one second behind the world record. We can't put him on kitchen police." "Naw, you can't do that," echoed the corporal. "So we're not going to send you to the artillery in Missouri or whatever." "Let's send him over to the officer's mess. He can play for them while they eat." So you see, I got to keep my Tillamook "Strad" and continued to play "that there 'bumblebee' piece."

I had to go through basic training and I didn't touch the violin for six weeks. Camp Crowder was in the Ozarks and on the one day that we had off, most of the guys would rush to Joplin to try and find girls. Instead, I would go outside of the camp and find little streams that had these wonderful vines hanging from the trees. I would practice like Tarzan, trying to cross the stream on one vine.

Camp Crowder is where I met Arthur Winograd, a redheaded cellist, and Bernie Leighton, a rarity of a pianist. Leighton's chops in Brahms were as thrilling as the jazzy improvisations which he produced for six years in Benny Goodman's band. He had a trumpet playing buddy who pulled mysterious strings and Bernie, Arthur, and I were diverted to Fort Wright, an island on the Long Island Sound where our major job was watching the radar screens for U-boats that were trying to do damage. We jazzed it up every night for dancing soldiers and the WACs (girl soldiers). Arthur and I were squares but we could play "April in Paris" type tunes when called upon. The piano trio flourished. We played in the barracks, we played in churches of nearby towns, we played for the officers drinking and eating in their club.

The minute I finished my basic training, a group of us musicians were told to report to the band school inside the signal corps. In this camp, a man from Wisconsin named Skornika was starting a band-training school. I was in the first cadre and Winograd and Leighton came in the second cadre. We were told to choose an instrument. I chose the E-Flat horn. Winograd picked up a couple of drum sticks. The lieutenant's name was Tremaine and he was a jazz guy who took Skornika's place when he was called to go to Washington. In this band, we played Carl Maria von Weber's *Euryanthe* overture and the last movement of the Tchaikovsky Fourth Symphony. Winograd was playing the timpani and I couldn't handle the horn part and Termaine couldn't conduct. So he turned to Winograd and me and we did the conducting for him.

We also had to take people on training marches. You know where they shout, "Attenshun." Then they say, "Left, Right, Hup two, three, four," and we had a fantastic time. We would be leading a group and we would order them to make all kinds of turns and they would end up in a ditch with everyone laughing. In the meantime, we didn't know where we were going to be sent.

We played for the officers and at our first concert the colonel's wife was in attendance. The colonel ran the military post but his wife ran the colonel. She liked us and she cracked the whip telling the colonel not to send us to Guadalcanal or other points in Southeast Asia. She asked, "Do you boys know *Fingal's Cave* or *Afternoon of a Faun?*" This gave us an idea of what kind of music she liked, all the pot boilers like *Scheherazade, Polovstian Dances,* Strauss tone poems galore and other big pieces for orchestra. I arranged them for our jazz band or for our piano trio that gave concerts.

My friend Lee Hambro, the pianist, was then in the Navy; he came to visit on one of his leaves. I arranged for Bernie Leighton and Lee to play a two-piano accompaniment of the Brahms' Double Concerto; Winograd and I joined them on violin and cello. For another gig, I played the Tchaikovsky concerto with a jazz band accompaniment that I arranged. We made arrangements of everything for these instrumental combinations. At one point, at the colonel's wife's suggestion, we put on an act of Gounod's *Faust.* We had a girl soldier and a boy soldier who could sing the main roles, so I made an arrangement.

I didn't have to go overseas. Thanks to the colonel's wife, any time we were on the list to be transferred she was able to get our names removed. I stayed at Camp Crowder for about two to three years. In the morning we had to go to the motor pool and change tires. We would sit around chewing the rag and having fun, and then a sergeant would come along and curse us out. We also used to collect garbage. My main memory of the garbage was that there were a lot of grubs that used to get into the garbage cans and eat through the garbage bags. In the afternoon we were free to make arrangements and to prepare for the dances where the band played for all the soldiers stationed at the various forts.

There were a whole string of forts: New London (that's where they made our submarines), Montauk Point, Block Island and our own place, Fort Wright on Fisher's Island. We used to take boats, in all kinds of weather, to go and play for an evening's dance at these various forts. In Fort Wright I used to swim. It was dangerous and I really tempted fate a couple of times when I had difficulty getting back to land. I also remember that we had a terrible gale there one night during which I went to the library. I had a hard time standing up because the wind was of such a strong velocity. We didn't always work so hard at Fort Wright. In fact, one of the funniest moments was when

Army band with Robert, Arthur Winograd, and Bernie Leighton

the army taught us a lesson by sending a group of soldiers on a mock raid of the island. We thought we were captured until we were let in on the secret. That was a definite embarrassment!

In 1944, I passed through Chicago on an army furlough to go back to Portland to see my family. My scientist friend Hy Goldsmith was in Chicago, where they were working on the atomic bomb. A group of us were going to play chamber music at his house. Also invited to this chamber music evening was Leo Szilard, who was a physicist and inventor. He conceived the nuclear chain reaction and in 1939, wrote the letter for Einstein's signature that resulted in the Manhattan Project. That evening as I played for Goldsmith's guests, I witnessed Dr. Szilard reading a Sunday edition of *The New York Times* cover to cover in a somewhat noisy accompaniment to Haydn, Mozart, Beethoven, and Schubert. Aware of my reaction to his newsgathering during the proceedings, Dr. Szilard insisted that he heard and digested every note.

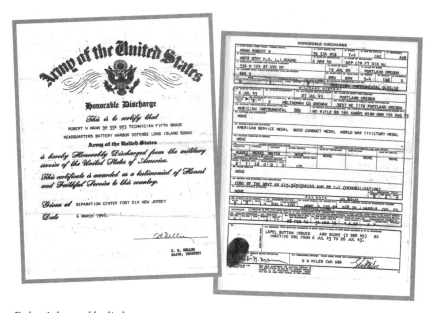

Robert's honorable discharge papers

PART II

Quartet Life

[THE JUILLIARD STRING QUARTET IS BORN]
(1946)

*I*N 1944, WHEN I WAS IN FORT WRIGHT, ON FISHER'S ISLAND, I WAS still corresponding with my friend from the Albuquerque Music Festival, Ruth Hanna McCormick Simms. She had promised me that if we both survived the war she would set up a string quartet at the University of New Mexico and I had been absolutely thrilled. That was my dream. In fact, when I was a high school student in Portland I used to listen to a very static-filled radio broadcast of the Budapest Quartet playing from the Library of Congress where they were the resident quartet. I would say, *that's what I want to do.* Mrs. Simms was riding the range in the West when her horse slipped into a gopher hole and fell. Mrs. Simms broke her hip and went into the hospital, and, sadly, despite all of her money she died two weeks later of an infection. That was the end of my dream of a string quartet in New Mexico.

In the army we were given two-day passes about once a month. We lived for our passes. It provided us time so we could take a ferry boat over to New London, Connecticut, get on a train, and have a day or two playing chamber music with friends in New York City. Of course, Winograd and I headed to New York City. I would stay with my friend from Portland days, Isadore Tinkleman, who became one of America's finest violin teachers. We also used to congregate at the Larchmont home of Edgar Schenkman, who was a violinist and a conductor. We became very close. Schenkman was also a friend of William Schuman, a composer who became the head of Juilliard. In fact, when William Schuman came to direct the Juilliard School, Schenkman became the main conductor at Juilliard.

Schenkman and his wife Marguerite played violin and viola, and I would get Arthur Winograd to come with me to read chamber music with my older friends. Bob Koff, a violinist who I knew a little bit, also would join us. Koff came from Oberlin, like Dorothy DeLay, the great violin teacher, to study at Juilliard. He was stationed at Camp Kilmer in New Jersey, and we would arrange our passes so we could meet at Edgar Schenkman's home for a long evening of playing chamber music.

One night after we played and were having fun eating and drinking, I mentioned to Edgar, "You know, there used to be a Curtis String Quartet, and there was even a resident quartet at Oberlin. Don't you think, now that Juilliard has William Schuman as a new president, that there should be a quartet at Juilliard?" Edgar, who was an absolutely wonderful and marvelous man, said with his severe but friendly wit, looking like he was the Cheshire cat from *Alice in Wonderland*, "I happen to know that is one of the things William Schuman is interested in." Hearing this news, Winograd, Bobby Koff and I started talking about this idea. Edgar told us, "I want you to write a letter to me. In this letter it has to say what role you think a resident quartet would play in the future of Juilliard. Send the letter to me and I'll see that Schuman sees the letter." So the three of us got together and wrote a letter.

After Edgar received our letter, he got back to me and said, "You know, Mr. Schuman is a composer. In your letter, you didn't stress enough about the importance of playing contemporary music. That is something you should think about." Now it was getting near the time that I was getting discharged and all of a sudden Edgar told me that William Schuman wanted to have an interview with me.

We were dying because, while we had Winograd, the cellist, and the violinist Robert Koff, and myself, we didn't have a violist. We were trying out every violist we knew to make a full quartet. I went to the interview with Schuman and confessed we were without a violist for the quartet, and I said that we would find one. Schuman was the most unusual combination of an absolutely marvelous free-wheeling imagination and a strict, formal, responsible mind that made him perfect to head Juilliard. He put me at ease because we immediately started to talk about Beethoven, chamber music, and contemporary music.

He asked, "Well, what kind of a quartet would you like to have? Why should I hire you? Why shouldn't I hire the Budapest Quartet? I've considered them for the job, but they would cost a lot of money. I'm interested in having a young quartet that really has potential." The Budapest was a great, great quartet; however, they never played contemporary music. They didn't like it. They only played the music of Haydn and Brahms and maybe Ravel. Schuman was a composer himself and he wanted a quartet that would play not only his music, but music written by composers such as Aaron Copland, Wallingford Riegger, some of Schoenberg's quartets and the music of other important contemporary European and American composers.

William Schuman, founder of the Juilliard String Quartet

I said to William Schuman, "Look, when we find our violist, all of us are interested. I'm a composer, and we want to play music just written. Our goal is to play new music as if it had been composed long ago, and to play a classical piece written hundreds of years ago as if it had just been written." At the time people listened to string quartets as if they were in church. We were not going to play that way and felt the music was alive and living in today's atmosphere. It wasn't that we were against traditional playing, or how the music sounded when it was written. We just wanted to make it as alive and meaningful in our time as it was back then.

I learned years later when Schuman and I became good friends that it was that thought that convinced him to hire us, a young quartet with a fresh point of view.

We did have a problem. The quartet still needed a violist. Schuman laid out our terms and said we could take our time to find a violist. He said that he had convinced the Juilliard board to invest $10,000 in the idea of a string quartet. Each of us would get $2,500. We would have to prove ourselves and it wouldn't be guaranteed that the quartet would be able to continue for a second year. He did say, "If everyone likes you, I will do my damnedest to make it work." William Schuman also wanted us to be introduced to New York audiences and set our first concert for the fall. We would have a summer to prepare as a quartet.

We found our violist, Raphael Hillyer, through the recommendation of our mentor, Eugene Lehner. We spent the better part of two days rehearsing with Hillyer and he was terrific. I remember we played the Beethoven late quartet in C sharp minor, Opus 131. We agreed that Hillyer should be invited to complete our new ensemble and asked him to join the quartet. He responded eagerly but explained that he had a lot to consider and needed to consult with his family. He faced the strain of many difficulties.

At this time in 1946, Hillyer lived in Boston and was still under contract with the Boston Symphony. He also had a family and two children. His present salary was ample while what William Schuman offered us was measly in comparison, with no guarantee that it would continue for a second year. The financial reality was just the tip of Hillyer's challenges.

His wife, Gerda, had barely escaped the worst of the Austrian Holocaust with her parents and sister. She was a wonderful woman who had been a medical doctor in Vienna. She worked hard and had gotten her Massachusetts medical license and was now practicing medicine in Massachusetts. If Hillyer were to join the Juilliard String Quartet, he would have to move to New York. This would mean that his wife would have to give up her license in Boston and go through the whole process again in New York.

He also consulted with his father, Dr. Louis Silverman, who was a mathematics professor at Dartmouth. (Rafael had changed his name from Silverman to Hillyer, mainly I think because he thought anti-Semitism would work against him.) Dr. Silverman wanted his son to be in the string quartet and agreed to help him financially. So Hillyer made the decision and we got our violist. I am still amazed how, with all of his problems, he assented to become the fourth member of our group.

We faced another impossible problem. Both the Winograd and Hillyer families had to find places to live in New York, which has always been hard. This was a much greater impediment than many of us realized. After the war, hordes of hopeful families descended on the greater New York area and vacant, rentable apartments no longer existed. Not one single space was available. Hovering over this situation was the challenge of the quartet's permanence.

I found a slum apartment at 103 LaSalle Street just off Broadway close to 125th Street. Robert Koff, our second violinist, and I each lived in an apartment with many roommates paying individual rents. Both the Winograd and Hillyer families searched and searched for places to live and couldn't find apartments to save their lives. A flawed solution finally emerged. The two families found one house in Long Branch, on the New Jersey coast, about a two-hour drive from New York City. It was a house large enough to allow both families to exist under one roof. That first year, for three days each week, Koff and I took a train to New Jersey to rehearse, while Hillyer and Winograd came two days into our crowded apartments to complete our weekly work. It was a monstrous, stressful situation, but it worked.

More troubling was the effect on the wives and children of the two families. There can be no doubt that Gerda Hillyer, who had already suffered so much in her life, was the most stressed. Eventually after a few years the Hillyer family found a house in New Jersey across the Hudson River from New York and the stress decreased.

In the beginning, the members of Juilliard String Quartet didn't really know each other that well. We knew each other as work colleagues but there was little intermingling friendship between the families outside of the musical experience. Ideally, a serious string quartet that commits to a successful survival must consist of four individuals who like and respect each other, not only as human beings, but also as instrumentalists and musical personalities. One might compare such a group to a formidable car with four passengers who are taking turns driving the vehicle, deciding where to go, how fast or how slow, etc.

After our initial rehearsing, I am sorry to confess, the Juilliard four discovered a disastrous number of weaknesses and differences. I knew Winograd and his very intelligent and contemptuous personality. I knew Koff and his acerbic wit a little because we had played together. But I had never really gotten to know Hillyer. After two days of rehearsal, Hillyer appeared on the third day without a greeting. Through the day his silence grew louder and more uncomfortable and lasted as we rehearsed into the night. The other three members conversed about musical ideas, details and suggestions. Somebody would make a suggestion and Hillyer would breathe harder but wouldn't say a word in response. His silence was sensational. He left looking very angry. We didn't know what to do. The three of us were upset and confused. We conferred and agreed that another day of this behavior would be the moment of crisis. We felt a great weight pressing us down into the ground and the new quartet facing failure. *What's wrong with this guy? He shouldn't be in the quartet. We had made the wrong choice.* We persisted because we were desperate. Sure enough, on the next day Hillyer took his place and played, as before, but without speaking.

Early the following day, we met, unpacked our instruments, sat down, and I prepared to make our agreed-upon message of ending our relationship. Before I spoke one word, Rafe, with no word of apology or explanation, began to speak to us calmly and objectively regarding our future plans and musical concerns. We somehow sensed relief and began to work together as if nothing bad had occurred. Mostly our violist seemed quite reasonable but I was painfully aware that while he addressed Koff and me, he continued to ignore Arthur Winograd. Somehow this state of affairs would continue even as the group began to establish our firm reputation and career. It turned out that Hillyer hated Winograd. Hillyer was dark and brooding. Winograd was arrogant and brilliant. They were both great wits and had brilliant minds, but their personalities clashed.

Now back to our first summer as a quartet. I was determined that the quartet should persevere. We were going to be presented as a quartet in the fall. Eugene Lehner, our mentor, and his family lived in Newton, Massachusetts, but in the summer they went with the Boston Symphony to Tanglewood. His Newton home was empty and available and we were able to stay in the Lehner home. This was convenient for rehearsing as Hillyer's own Massachusetts home was near Harvard across from the Charles River. He would come to Lehner's and we would rehearse morning, afternoon, and evening. We chose some repertoire and the rehearsals began, tentative and exploratory. Each of us brought his own past chamber music experience into the daily work schedule of two and half hours in the morning, two and half hours in the afternoon, and as long as we could tolerate after dinner. My memory of that time was that the rehearsal schedule worked but wasn't particularly joyful. All of us felt an abiding pressure to produce something over the next two months so that we could perform before our Juilliard School's audience convincingly as a fine string quartet.

We learned Beethoven's Opus 127, and the Third Bartók amongst other works. We asked the composer Irving Fine, Harold Shapiro and a few friends of ours in Boston and Newton if we could play for them. This was our first performance. That summer the quartet also played two try-out concerts at Dartmouth, arranged by Hillyer and his parents. We played Beethoven's Opus 59 No. 3 and Opus 127, and Ravel.

At the end of the summer I left Tanglewood with my friend Willy Kapell, a pianist who had played the Rachmaninoff C Minor Concerto with the Boston Symphony. Driving back to New York he said, "What's this shit I hear about you starting a string quartet?" And I said, "Yeah, I'm very excited." He replied, "Come on, I know that you could have a solo career if you want one. Why don't you come and start a solo career. I'm sure I can get you in with Arthur Judson, my manager." I wasn't interested and told Willy not to bother.

Willy later played Robert Schumann's quintet with the Juilliard String Quartet. And then of course, he began to get very busy with concerts. He was in Australia and was coming back to the States when his plane crashed outside of San Francisco. He was only forty and at the height of his career. He would have been one of the biggest stars of the piano.

Our debut New York concert, arranged by William Schuman, was on October 11, 1946, in the little hall at Juilliard (located at that time on 122nd Street and Claremont Avenue where Manhattan School of Music is today). We opened with the Third Bartók Quartet, followed by a Walter Piston quartet and after intermission, Opus 127. Menuhin and Zoltán Kodály were in the audience. It turned out to be a successful concert and so began our incredible sojourn in Juilliard.

Even though they might not have liked each other, the members of the Budapest Quartet were civilized gentlemen. They would not get angry with each other in public or have fights in rehearsals. They would compromise. The Budapest had a marvelous solution. They divided the repertoire into four parts; each person had a quarter of the repertoire on which they had two votes and so therefore could break a tie if the group was evenly divided in their opinions.

It took the Juilliard String Quartet a long time to learn how to live as a string quartet. The deep arguments and unhappiness were part of the quartet life. I would come home after rehearsals and my wife, Lucy, would say, "What do you need this for?" And my reply would be, "The music is too great to give up."

I always tell one story. We were at Juilliard studying Haydn's D Major Quartet, Opus 20 No. 4, which starts with an octave unison melody. The question was, where were the phrases, pulses? We had four different points of view. I was the one who got very angry first, because we were not agreeing, and picked up my stand and threw it behind me on the floor. The next thing I knew, there was a stand coming at me from Winograd. Throughout the early days, we had many arguments of a vociferous and horrible nature.

Another serious quartet argument had to do with repertoire. Through William Schuman's intercession with Koussevitsky, we were given our first concert at Tanglewood during the summer of 1947. We were told to play a program of American composers, including a work by William Schuman, who at that time had written three quartets. We wanted to play some Copland, who had only composed two different movements for a string quartet. We also programmed a Walter Piston quartet, and for our final work we had a huge disagreement. Hillyer and I loved Roger Sessions' quartet. Winograd and Koff hated it. A terrible fight ensued over whether or not to play it. There were strong personalities that clashed, but in the end what is important is that we worked it out (and we did play it!)

Our Town Hall debut was in December of 1947. During our first year as a quartet we played almost every American composer. During our second summer, we had convinced the people at Tanglewood, Koussevitsky mainly, to let us come teach and play a number of concerts. We would play the Viennese composers—Schoenberg, Berg and Webern, and we would also play Beethoven. We opened our first concert playing Opus 130 and the "Grosse Fugue." We got the most horrible review that anyone ever got from a guy who wrote for the *Berkshire Eagle* in Pittsfield. He said that we didn't understand the first movement and played it too fast. The "Cavatina" was beyond us. He paraphrased Winston Churchill and said, "The Grosse Fugue never had so much sweat and muscle expended for so little result."

At Tanglewood we learned the six Bartók Quartets. This was publicity-worthy for us because all of the magazines picked it up and talked about our young quartet. It shocked all of the elders because the

Juilliard String Quartet, original members, 1946. LEFT TO RIGHT: *Robert Mann,*
Robert Koff, Raphael Hillyer, Arthur Winograd
PHOTO CREDIT: G. D. HACKETT

articles said that we played old music with vivacity and verve as if it
had just been written! So despite the *Bershire Eagle* review, we had
success at Tanglewood. In 1949, we played all the Bartók quartets in
two concerts at Times Hall in New York City, something no one had
ever done in America, and only one other quartet had done in Europe.
According to the *New York Times* review by Olin Downes, so many

people wanted to attend that "the stage was crowded to the last seat and the listeners eddied about the quartet which had just enough elbow room, and no more, for its performance." There was not a seat in the house and there were mounted policemen to control the crowds! Shostakovich, who was visiting New York at the time, actually came to that concert and told us he liked it very much. Our reputation for playing contemporary music was firmly established. Playing this music wasn't a duty for us, we wanted to do it.

PHOTO CREDIT: G. D. HACKETT

Tempi and contemporary music

One of the hallmarks of the Juilliard String Quartet was its reputation for playing fast tempi. Especially in the Beethoven string quartets. If you know your musical history, however, we were just following Beethoven's wishes.

It was actually Rudolph Kolisch (1896-1978), the violinist, whose 1943 article "Tempo and Character in Beethoven's Music" was responsible for the promulgation of the Beethoven metronome markings. Now this is something that's quite historic because there have been many fights raging about these marks.

Before Beethoven wrote his late quartets he had a relationship with a man named Maelzel, the inventor of the metronome. It was a strange relationship because they were sometimes friendly, and sometimes they wouldn't talk to each other. Maelzel was going to London and he invented something called the Orchestriam, a mechanical orchestra. Beethoven composed his Wellington Symphony, the *Battle Symphony*, for this instrument. Beethoven wanted to go to London with him but unfortunately it didn't work out and they had a fight. Later, Beethoven began to write to friends saying, "How can we tell if we have simple Italian directions, how fast or how slow a piece goes?" An example that Beethoven wrote about is that if you have a piece marked *andantino*, how do we know whether it's faster or slower than *andante*? He also made reference a number of times to the fact that his music was played in such a way that it didn't possess his character. In one famous letter that he wrote to a friend, he heard that his Ninth Symphony had received enormous success in Berlin at its premiere. He said, "The metronome markings will be sent to you very soon. Do wait for them. In our century such indications are certainly necessary. Moreover I have received letters from Berlin informing me that the first performance of the [Ninth] symphony was received with enthusiastic applause, which I ascribe largely to the metronome markings."* What he

---

* Ludwig van Beethoven, Letter to Bernhard Schotts Söhne, in *The Letters of Beethoven*, Vol. III, trans. and ed. Emily Anderson (New York: Norton, 1961, 1325).

did was to add metronome marks to all his quartets up through Opus 95. He also metronomized all of the symphonies, the Ninth Symphony included, and some songs, and his metronome marks were printed. But nobody ever played them. I used to like the Budapest's playing because they played this music a little faster. We all loved it.

Once, when we were practicing the allegretto from Beethoven's string quartet Opus 59, No. 2, studying with Lehner, he asked, "Why do you play it so slow?" We answered, "What do you mean?" He said, "Well you know what the metronome mark is—a 69 to the whole measure (dotted half note)." We tried it and we couldn't believe our ears. That was crazy, nobody played it that fast. He said, "What does Beethoven ask you to do?" So we looked and in Italian, Beethoven had written, "Play the first part with repeats. Then, play the second, the trio through, and then play the first part again, *senza repetizioni* (without repeat) and then play the trio a second time. Then come back and play for a final third time, the first part." Nobody ever played it this way. Everybody only played the trio once. The one thing that convinced us that there was something to it was that in the faster tempo, you were propelled to play the trio a second time. In other words, the timing of the whole piece assumed a different time structure. So we became convinced that there was something to Beethoven's metronome marks. You have to understand, to play fast you have to develop a new kind of technique. Over the years we did this.

Lehner pointed out that Kolisch hadn't thought to follow Beethoven's metronome markings all by himself. Many musicians had considered it. Mahler had been interested in it, and Mahler interested Schoenberg, and Schoenberg interested Kolisch and so on. That's how it came down to us. Of course when we were practicing Opus 59, No. 2 in Felix Salmond's studio, he came in to listen to us play the last movement. This movement in the old days was played moderately fast. It was marked *Allegro molto* and 88 to the whole note. When he heard us playing it faster, Salmond, who was cross-eyed and six foot three, came rushing through the center of our quartet, knocking the stands over. We jumped out of the way and he raged like a madman for about twenty minutes telling us what fools we were. How could we believe this metronome mark? When he finally calmed down, we said, "Mr. Salmond, would you sing us the tempo that you believe is correct for the second movement?" The second movement is marked differently. He began singing and then we turned to Beethoven's metronome mark for that movement and it was exactly on that time.

We asked, "Why was he right for the slower movements and wrong for the fast movements." "Well" Salmond said, "if Beethoven had heard it (he was deaf) he would have understood that it was impossible."

I also want to mention another story about Beethoven's String Quartet Opus 59, No. 2. The trio in this work had a tune we all knew. What was this tune? It was the tune that Mussorgsky used for the coronation scene in *Boris Goudonov*.* But in Mussorgsky, the tune was played at a moderate pace. We were playing this tune a lot faster, as Beethoven intended, when we played our second Juilliard String Quartet concert at Juilliard. The violinist Joseph Fuchs was in the audience and he got up, all five foot two of him, and turned to the audience and said, "How can they play the Mussorgsky tune that fast?" He was outraged, you see.

IN 1946, THE BUDAPEST was the reigning quartet. As I mentioned, they played fabulously, beautifully. They played always in tune, and their ensemble was always perfect. However, they did not play much contemporary music and basically performed Haydn, Mozart, Schubert, and Beethoven. When the Juilliard String Quartet started to play concerts there were not many American quartets earning their living from playing concerts. At this time, the chamber music concerts in America were being given by almost all of the European quartets who were brought here to perform. On these tours, no quartet came without playing between thirty and fifty concerts. They traveled by

---

* Interestingly, there was a Swiss doctor who was an amateur cellist and had a lifelong hobby as a passionate researcher of all things Beethoven. His son printed a French memoranda that his father had found. He had a picture of the book that Prince Andrey Razumovsky had given to Beethoven. Razumovsky had commissioned the three Opus 59 quartets and had asked Beethoven to use a Russian tune in each of those works.

train in those days. Tickets to the concerts were affordable and the concert halls for string quartet concerts were mostly filled. One of the problems was that musical organizations paid minimal salaries for a string quartet. We would play concerts for $150. We would hope for $500, but we were playing wherever we were paid.

In our beginning days, the Juilliard String Quartet couldn't get jobs. The first year we had about a dozen concerts given to us from friends we knew. We also received commissions from friends who wanted their works played. In those early days, we were able to book concerts because we played contemporary music. Our manager would try to get us a job in, say, St. Louis, and say that we would like to play quartets by Haydn, Beethoven or Brahms, and the reply would be "No, we already have the Budapest or the Pro Arte quartet playing those pieces. We will only take the American quartet, the Juilliard String Quartet, if they play Bartók or another interesting piece that we don't know." If they had a commission or needed to have a contemporary work played, then we got called. When we played these concerts, we always sneaked in a Haydn or Beethoven quartet. Also, Claus Adam, the Juilliard String Quartet cellist between 1955 74, and I were both composers and we were open to the new expressions and techniques of contemporary music that were not part of the existing repertoire. Of course there were those pieces that we played once and then said, we don't ever want to play that piece again. But then there were the exceptions, such as Elliott Carter or Schoenberg. Each performance brought more and more fulfillment until we felt these pieces were as exciting and meaningful to play as Beethoven.

You have to understand, the Juilliard String Quartet had its own personality and its own involvement in the music we played. It received a lot of critical response, not only from the audiences but also from the music critics. Chamber music was considered by cultured people who loved it as the most beautiful and nonaggressive experience that you could have. You could come to a concert and on par with looking at a great painting you could contemplate the sounds of a Mozart, Haydn or Beethoven quartet. And then came along those damn Juilliards who were digging in and playing strong accents. We were much more aggressive in terms of drama. We wanted to play a calm phrase beautifully, and we did. We also felt, however, that Beethoven, for instance, was this absolutely dramatic, aggressive person who wasn't compromising his expression and so we played in a way that almost none of the great quartets played. A lot of the music we chose to play demanded that its power be uncompromising and not necessarily beautiful. So the critics didn't understand what we were doing.

We felt that you must have beauty, but you must also have dramatic strength. Strength is not beautiful. It is something else. We never avoided that dramatic strength and for that in the beginning, we were criticized. In the early days we were asked not to play Beethoven because we played it so aggressively. The most dramatic instance was in Amsterdam where for the first time we got boos as we left the stage. At later concerts, the Amsterdam audiences gave us standing ovations. I believe this change occurred because people began to realize that music is not just beautiful. It is also an arousing, meaningful expression that says many things.

Budapest String Quartet

Playing in a string quartet

You cannot be an outstanding chamber music player unless you hear all of the sounds and integrate them into your brain as one. You cannot be a person who just plays and hears your own sound more than the others. This requires years of experience. A quartet brings together four people who listen to each other's sounds and agree that they are amenable. As you start rehearsing, different personalities begin to open up and appear in the process of the rehearsal. One person may like almost all of the music played faster. Another person might genuinely like it slower. Now the differences may not be enormous, but they can be enough that you won't agree about the interpretation if you are stubborn. However, you always have to make compromises. You can't play only the way that you want.

The simplest way to explain differences in interpretations is to use as an example a Haydn quartet that begins piquantly and jovially. A quartet member says it should be played faster because in Haydn's day, the music was played faster than it is today. Another member prefers it slower. We now have a difference of opinion and we are playing the Haydn in concerts. What do we do? We compromise. The first night, we play it fast, as one member of the quartet suggested. The second night, we play it slower, the way the other person wanted it.

There are not only big decisions such as a tempo character, or how fast or slow you play, but also maybe the phrasing. One member wants to emphasize a harmony and another likes the rhythm to be a little different. Compromise means that there are different ways to look at decisions in musical interpretation. This is the most difficult thing for someone entering the quartet profession to learn how to deal with.

Another challenge is to concentrate on the music throughout the whole piece. At first I could think about a moment and then my mind would wander. I would think about the audience while I was playing, about the heat of the room, about the acoustics, and so on. It took me years before I could really concentrate on every note through a movement without interruption. That's inner concentration.

Also, one of the things that I've always contended is that notes do not exist in isolation and that all quartet members need to play each note in relation to the way the preceding note has been played. This means you will play the second note different every time because the first note is never played the same. This connection between notes needs to be true through a whole movement.

EACH TIME A NEW quartet member joins the group, dynamics change. I remember I had a meeting with Hillyer in 1955 and I said, "Now look, we have a chance to play with a wonderful, collegial new cellist, Claus Adam." We thought that once Arthur left the quartet that Rafe would be happy. Claus had previously been the cellist of the New Music Quartet in New Haven, with Walter Trampler, the violist. At the time we asked Claus to join us, he said that he didn't think he was ready to join another quartet. But then he finally decided that he wanted to. Hillyer, who was very fastidious in his playing, hadn't been

Juilliard String Quartet relaxing, c. 1955–58. Robert Koff, Claus Adam, Robert Mann, Raphael Hillyer

Juilliard String Quartet with Isidore Cohen and Claus Adam

happy with Arthur Winograd, but unfortunately, he also took a dislike to Claus.

One of Hillyer's problems with Claus, who was a magnificent cellist in his own way, was that he was not a natural cellist because he started studying so late. Claus wasn't always secure in the higher thumb position on the cello. Hillyer could be very insensitive, not because he was a bad person but because he was so uncomfortable with himself.

I was living on LaSalle Street and it was in September at the start of a new season. I got a call from Hillyer saying that he and Isidore (Izzy) Cohen, who had replaced Koff in 1958 as the Juilliard's second violinist, wanted to talk to me. They told me, "We can't stand playing with Claus Adam. We want another new cellist." I told them, as long as I was in the Juilliard String Quartet nobody was going to be kicked out. Of course, later on we would ask Izzy Cohen to leave the quartet[*], but at this point I resisted Hillyer's desire.

Later, when the Juilliard String Quartet was composed of myself, Claus Adam, Samuel Rhodes and Earl Carlyss, Claus said to us,

---

[*]   Isadore Cohen was asked to leave the quartet in 1988 because of his behavior during the Juilliard String Quartet's tour of Russia.

Juilliard String Quartet with Claus Adam, Raphael Hillyer, Earl Carlyss

"Look, it's been an absolutely wonderful experience to be part of the Juilliard Quartet. We have had a lot of successes and it's been a very important part of my life. Now I'm getting pretty old and I'm composing more and I want to do more teaching. I don't want to travel so much anymore." So we started looking for another cellist and Claus continued to teach cello at Juilliard.

When we wanted a new member for the quartet we didn't advertise. Each of us would provide a potential list of candidates and we would talk to a few friends to see who they might recommend. That's how we heard about Joel Krosnick. He had been the cellist of the Iowa Quartet.

The only reason we ever had a problem with Eugene Lehner was that he thought when a new person joined the quartet they should not get the same salary as the older members because they hadn't earned it yet. Our point of view was, if the new person was good enough to be in our quartet and play at the level that we did, they deserved the same salary as the rest of us.

At the time that Claus was leaving the quartet and Joel was joining as our new cellist, Bob Freeman, who headed Eastman, tried to entice the quartet to move from Juilliard to Eastman. Earl, Sammy and myself met with Bob without Joel. He offered us a million dollars and jobs for all our wives. But we knew we would have to change our name, and I wasn't about to do that. We didn't take the offer and Joel joined the Juilliard String Quartet.

With this new Juilliard String Quartet (1974) of myself, Earl Carlyss, Samuel Rhodes, and Joel Krosnick—three of the members were young enough to be my sons. I had not even thought about the fact that Claus and I had balanced out the younger members of the quartet. And now, I was the old fellow with strong ideas and three young guys. It wasn't that I didn't accept or open myself up to other people's opinions. But when I felt strongly, I felt very strongly.

I also was a little like Claus. I was never as secure as most of the other members of the quartet. In the early days, I had a lot of trouble playing truly in tune. And throughout my professional life some people thought that I was a superb player, and others felt that I played a little out of tune, or that I had a stiff bow arm, and so on. But basically, people responded very well to my playing.

However, with this new young Juilliard String Quartet, we were learning the repertoire over again. Most people would say to me, "How can you stand it? Here you are with another change in the quartet and you have to learn all of the Beethoven quartets over again. Aren't you tired?" My answer was, "My God, are you kidding? This is a chance for us to begin to explore the piece with a fresh ear, a fresh mind, and a fresh point of view." The reality, however, was hard at first.

We had to learn a lot of new music and we were on our first tour with Joel Krosnick in the United States. We were in our hotel room in Denver, Colorado, under pressure to learn Beethoven's Opus 135, practicing the slow movement. Sammy said, "You know, we have played this before in a particular way. Could we consider a different relation between the variations than the way we are playing it now?"

What Sammy was suggesting wasn't an assault on how I wanted the piece played, but it meant giving up my ideas about the slow movement.

This was a moment in the music that I really loved. There weren't many moments in music where I wasn't flexible. But I was being very resistant in my fashion, which was one of my flaws.

All of a sudden, Earl, who was very religious and the son of a Lutheran minister, exploded. He said, "Bobby, if you don't open yourself up to the things we are trying to find out, I can't stay in this quartet." He actually got up to leave. I said, "Come on, Earl, stay here." So we had a big talk, and I realized that although these three young men were less experienced than I was in terms of playing in a quartet, they were as intelligent, or more intelligent, than I was. I had two paths that I could follow. One was to continue to be the kind of person I was with my strengths and weaknesses. This would result in either their or my leaving. Or, while I was not as young as they were, I could be as open and allow us to fully explore what they wanted in the music. Also, I could accept the fact that while I was the first violinist, I was only one participant out of four, with only one voice.

I won't say that I changed overnight, but I do believe that this struggle pushed my better instincts to take hold. I would say it took a few years before I could begin to look at a piece that I'd played, maybe fifty times, as if it were the first time. My quartet members bore with me, and I eventually became just as flexible and open as the rest of them. That wasn't easy to do. Playing in a quartet is teamwork. Whether it's a baseball team or a team of people doing research, everyone has to understand that certain people have strengths and weaknesses, and they are different from yours. The reason that a team is successful is because you know how best to reveal the strengths and hide the weaknesses.

Earl eventually left the quartet because he and his wife Ann Schein took wonderful positions at the Peabody Conservatory in Baltimore. As much as he loved the quartet, he wanted to make more of a life with his family. He gave us a year's notice so that we had plenty of time to search for a new second violinist.

By now we had learned and recorded all of the Elliott Carter quartets. We wanted somebody who had enormous virtuosity and an abil-

Juilliard String Quartet with Earl Carlyss, Claus Adam, and Samuel Rhodes

Juilliard String Quartet with Earl Carlyss, Joel Krosnick, and Samuel Rhodes

ity to adapt and to play without fear. We were lucky to find Joel Smirnoff, who fit in marvelously. Smirnoff was very different than I was. He was colorful and a radical. He'd given up violin for a while and attended the University of Chicago as a non-music major. During this period he studied dancing and played jazz violin.

After we became established, the Juilliard String Quartet played between 100 and 150 concerts a year (that's over 6,000 concerts during my fifty-one years in the Quartet). In retrospect, I can say that the first twenty-five years of the quartet life were pure hell. The next years were purgatory, but the last years were pure heaven.

Juilliard String Quartet with Joel Smirnoff, Joel Krosnick, and Samuel Rhodes

[MENTORS]

Felix Salmond (1888–1952)

One of the first important musical mentors of mine during my Institute years was the eminent cello teacher Felix Salmond. Salmond taught at both the Juilliard Graduate School and at Curtis, and had taught everyone from Leonard Rose to Frank Miller, and all of the up-and-coming young American cellists. He was a great musician in the old-fashioned sense. Anyway, he fell in love with me. I was in many chamber music groups that Mr. Salmond coached. I remember playing trios with the duo-pianists Arthur Gold and Bob Fizdale. I also played in quintets and sextets. Under Salmond we were inspired to play way beyond our abilities. It was Felix Salmond who was inspiring us to play. Salmond also recommended me to play the Beethoven concerto with the Juilliard School orchestra. He played trios with the Lhévinnes—Rosina or Josef—and he invited me to be the violinist. We even played an evening concert in someone's house, and that was wonderful.

My piano is Salmond's. When he died, Salmond's widow knew how much he loved me and I loved him and offered his piano to me at the bottom price instead of just selling it to anyone. So I bought it. I still have it to this day.

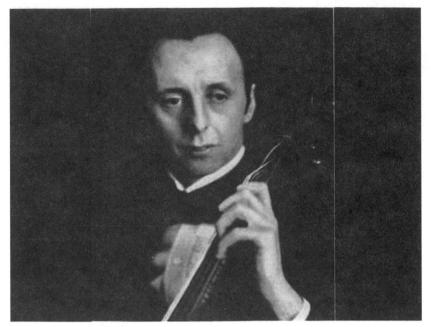

Felix Salmond

I learned from Salmond what is important about teaching and what is not important about teaching. You have to draw the people out on their own. You have to learn how to inspire people so they can light their own fires rather than be put on fire by you. That is a very important basis for teaching and I learned this from Felix Salmond.

Eugene Lehner (1906–1997)

Eugene Lehner was a heavenly force. No person shaped so many others in chamber music art as did this man. Multitudes of musicians, young and old, will respond "amen." This beloved legend—husband, father, violist, mentor, philosopher, vegetarian, curmudgeon, self-doubting, ego-strong, frail Hungarian giant arrived on the tide bearing marvelous musicians fleeing the Nazi terror. With his beautiful Danish wife, Lucca, and son Andreas, he chose to live in the Boston community when offered a position in the Boston Symphony. Playing in an orchestra was a very small part of an extraordinarily meaningful music life. His own coming of age was shaped by the master musicians of the Liszt Conservatory in Budapest (Leo Weiner, Zoltán Kodály, and Béla Bartók) and later, his life in Vienna with the Kolisch String Quartet where he participated in the creative musical ferment led by Arnold Schoenberg, Alban Berg, Anton Webern, Rudolph Kolisch, Edward Steuermann and a large group of believers. This profound background, which was tempered by thirteen years in the Kolisch ensemble performing the quartet literature from Haydn through Schoenberg without benefit of music in front of him*, was what he brought to Boston and Tanglewood, inspiring as a teacher and friend, all of us who were lucky to come under his sway. He was the greatest musician I've ever known and he always made little of himself.

I remember vividly my first encounter with this musical oracle. I was not quite twenty-six years old. Robert Koff, Arthur Winograd, and I were desperately searching for a violist to complete the quartet. After a number of unsuccessful sessions with a number of violists, Winograd suggested this fellow in the Boston orchestra who he had studied chamber music with at Tanglewood. He was older than we, said Winograd, but a fabulous musician and person: Eugene Lehner.

On the occasion of a Boston Symphony concert in New York, Mr. Lehner joined us for an afternoon of quartet reading. He specifically requested that we play Opus 130 Beethoven with the Grosse Fugue, the second Bartók and the third Schoenberg quartets. It was love at first hearing. This magician of the musical art captured us totally without trying. I begged him to become a member of our quartet. Soon after he wrote a "dear Bob" letter. He confessed that he loved playing music with us, but he dwelt on his thirteen-year age difference

---

* Lehner wanted the Juilliard String Quartet to memorize all of our pieces the way the Kolisch Quartet had done. The Kolisch Quartet was famous for playing everything from memory. Finally, probably in our second year as a quartet, we decided to try it for one concert. I remember that Beethoven's Opus 59, No. 2 was on the program. Hans Letts, who was Juilliard's major quartet teacher, had a wealthy friend, a businessman who owned instruments. We played Opus 59, No. 2 at his home without music. Winograd and I were comfortable doing this, but our two inner voices—Koff and Hillyer—felt that if you're playing classical repetoire, it's hard to play without sheet music. Unlike the Kolish Quartet, we never played any concert again from memory.

and how this change would be difficult for his wife and son. However, he did recommend Raphael Hillyer, then a 2nd violinist in the Boston Symphony who also played with him in the Stradivarius Quartet. Hillyer, like many of us, played viola as well as violin. Alas, we never got Eugene Lehner as a member of our quartet, but more importantly, we gained a mentor whose role in our development was immeasurable. Every composition that we studied during our early years was defined, illumined, and inspired by Lehner's unerring insight, imagination, and mysterious faculty of remaining open to new, provocative revelations not even thought of before by himself. In Eugene Lehner, I found my musical father. I was never with him a single time when some new or unexpected musical thought didn't surface. Unlike a mining operation, this musical resource was unending. His fame as a chamber music teacher spread like a prairie brush fire, but never burned out. He drew young musicians from all over the world. The music schools in Boston gloried in his ongoing attention. Ensembles such as the Schoenberg Quartet from Amsterdam and the Mendelssohn in New York grew very close to him as did the many students who coached with him every summer at Tanglewood.

Eugene Lehner was the real mentor and the meaningful basis for the growth of the Juilliard String Quartet. I remember once we were playing the Schubert A minor quartet. The minuet is a ghostly character, Schubert at his most distant and inner voice. There is something about it that rings bells if you keep it "inside" rather than play it "outside." Lehner sang that movement from beginning to end while lying on the floor. I'll never forget the sound of his voice. It taught us more than any words ever could. Another time at Tanglewood, he was teaching the very tragic Bartók Sixth Quartet. The quartet starts with a *mesto* or "deep sadness" which is an introduction to all of the movements. The rest of the quartet is very bitter and finally the last movement resolves into a complete *mesto*. He wasn't getting across what he wanted. All of a sudden, this tall, gaunt, marvelous man drops to the floor on his face, lying there like he was dead. The quartet got up and they didn't know whether they should call somebody; they think that he may have died from a heart attack.

Eugene Lehner

When they are thoroughly hysterical, Lehner turns his face and says, "Mesto! Mesto! Mesto!"

As Lehner grew older, he never faltered, never lost the enthusiasm or vigor of involvement with the musical scores or the ensembles mesmerized by his way with them. He was simultaneously the musician who knew everything while strenuously asserting that he knew nothing. He was indeed a reincarnation in music of Socrates. His lifelong attachment to music in no way isolated him from his passionate engagement with all art, culture, societal concerns, literature, science, philosophy, religion, and most of all family and dearest friends.

[FAMILY]

Lucy

September 1947, the second year that the Juilliard String Quartet rehearses together, fights one another, performs wherever it's invited, I am wandering up and down the halls of the sixth floor Juilliard building I have spent precious time in since I came to New York from Portland, Oregon in 1938. Next to the main entrance is a small, cozy room where all concert details for the school and the students are managed. As I pass by this particular, sun brilliant morning, I see a new, unfamiliar face in the concert office, seated behind a desk. Not only unfamiliar, but strikingly profiled with a beauty that a painter searches for. How do I know about painters? Well, I paint on a musical canvas with many colors of tones and intensities. This young woman is not only beautiful but magnetic. I simply have to meet her. I'm not totally incapable but the direct invitation to come with me to visit Stefan Wolpe, my composition teacher, takes time and courage to maneuver. To my surprise and delight she says yes.

The night arrives and on the walk to Wolpe's place, Lucy informs me that she is not a musician and knows little about classical or contemporary music. Juilliard has hired her because of her talent for running complicated activities. Many of Wolpe's students and friends will crowd the large piano room where David Tudor, a phenomenal pianist

Lucy, in her late twenties

of contemporary music will perform Wolpe's 30 minute, raging ava-
lanche of tonal sound titled "Battle Piece." When the excited crowd
settles down as David begins to play, one part of my brain feels uneasy.
How will my new date respond to this atonal onslaught? Everyone
else, including me, travels this acoustical ride; on and on each minute
passes by, with bursting excitement and finally when David roars to
the thunderous end, the room explodes with shouting, standing listeners, all of us in a state of musical and fraternal ecstasy. Little do I
guess at this fervent moment that the young woman next to me, still
sitting, is confused and wondering how she has allowed herself to be
trapped in such an unpleasant and unending situation. She is determined to end it as quickly as possible. At this very moment, one young
woman yells over the audience, "David, David—play it again!" Rap-
turously the whole group with one notable exception joins in, "David,
play it again!" With the innocence of a protected child, I am unaware
that this beautiful, lively, interesting, enchanting person next to me is
not only silently cursing but fully determined never to spend another
moment with that nut, Robert Mann.

Family travels

In the early Juilliard String Quartet days, we were asked to play a
concert at the Ojai Festival near the coast of Los Angeles. The Quartet had bought a Jeep station wagon and I bought it from the Quartet,
so it was mine. I wanted to drive my station wagon across the country
and I was going to take my parents with me, as well as Winograd, our
cellist. So we went on this trip with my parents. You have to know,
my mother was one of the most persevering people in the world. She
was also a health nut. She had bought six beautiful Arizona grapefruit.
When we got to the border between Arizona and California, the man
at the border asked, "Do you have any food with you?" And my
mother said, "Yes, beautiful grapefruit." The man answered, "You
can't take them into California. And, that's the law." We all said,
"Come on, Mom, you've gotta leave them. There's a trash can there
so you can just dump them and we'll go on." Her reply was, "No, we

are going to eat them right now, before we cross the border to California." We all started laughing, even my father. We all said, "No, we just had breakfast and we don't want any more grapefruit." I'm not exaggerating. My mother ate six grapefruit right in front of us while we all howled with laughter. And, she got madder and madder, but she was damned that she was not throwing those grapefruit away!

At the same time, Lucy had never been out of New York, so I induced her to fly to Los Angeles. I picked Lucy up and together we drove to the Ojai Music Festival. We didn't get paid much money for the festival, but they put us up. They learned that we were not married and they wouldn't let Lucy stay with me. Lucy ended up staying with Bobby Koff's mother and was thrilled because she could reach her hand out the window and pluck an orange from a tree.

Then I decided that I was going to show Lucy the United States. Our first trip was up to the Sequoias. I wanted to show her the mountains, then onto Yosemite, to all the mountains in California, and to Crater Lake in Southern Oregon. I even brought her to Eugene where my dear friend Max Felde's parents were. I remember Lucy's absolute amazement when Mrs. Felde took Lucy out to pick vegetables for dinner. Lucy had never seen vegetables grow in the ground before.

I also wanted her to see Tillamook, but when we arrived at Tillamook I didn't recognize a single thing. It had been thirty years since I left and it wasn't the same town at all. I was very disappointed. We went on to Portland where I saw my friend Izzy Tinkleman who was running a music school there. He went with us on a drive around Mt. Hood and then we left him and Lucy and I went on to Glacier National Park.

Lucy was a city girl, and for our Glacier Park hike I had gone to Abercrombie and Fitch and bought all the equipment, boots, and clothes. It was about a five mile hike up to just under the Continental Divide. This was about my third trip to Glacier, so I knew the rangers from previous visits. I went to the ranger at St. Mary's station and asked, "How are the paths going up to the lake? I want to take Lucy up to the little lake underneath the Continental Divide." He said, "Well, you know, there was a lot of snow last winter and I haven't sent

Robert and Lucy hiking with Robert's sister, Rosalind

the trail boys up to figure it out. If you go there, please report to me how the conditions are." Here I was, dragging Lucy through tons of snow. I mean, literally, it was a minimum of two feet all of the way. It was just picking your foot up and putting it ahead, and being wet and icy. Finally, we get to Gunsight Lake. It's a beautiful little lake and one of my favorites. There was snow everywhere except just around the gravel near where the water goes into the stream and this is where I set up our camp spot. In the middle of the night she wasn't sleeping. Maybe when you're lying on the ground for the first time, you don't sleep. All of a sudden she was screaming bloody murder.

I woke up and she was looking outside. I had put a lot of empty logs around us. I hadn't realized how many Rocky Mountain porcupines lived around there, and how happy they would be that this gentleman had brought them fresh logs that they didn't have to dig through the snow to eat. They were munching the bark. There were at least three or four of them. Lucy had never seen a porcupine in her life. I took a frying pan and batted them away. I wanted to make her more comfortable, but that was impossible. At the first sign of light Lucy said, "I have to get out of here." So we went down, and it was all downhill from there. It warmed up that day so there was enough sun and the snow was melting. We walked down through flooding ice water. Lucy had blisters on her feet from the boots and mosquitoes were everywhere. She was probably thinking the end of life was coming. She sat on a rock and pulled off the boots and threw them at me and said, "Fuck you. Fuck Glacier Park and I hope that I never see either of you again." I thought that was the end of our relationship. I brought her back home and I was able to get her back. I never took her on an overnight, extended camping trip again!

Traveling with children

In the early days when the Juilliards were trying to make a career of giving concerts we played a few concerts in New York, and then in other cities like Chicago and Philadelphia where we knew people. Finally, we were asked to travel to Europe. At that time, our violist Raphael Hillyer had two children and he didn't want to leave them for a month and a half and asked if we could hire another violist for the tour. I told him that we couldn't do that. A quartet means four people who know each other and live and play together. We were not going to have a substitute violist. It's not like a baseball team. So we refused to go to Europe at that time.

Later, Isidore Cohen, a wonderful violinist, became our second violinist. When we asked him to join the quartet he said, "I can't join the quartet if it goes on tours longer than two weeks. I don't want to be away from my family any longer than two weeks." This was difficult. A tour to Europe or Asia had to last at least a month to make ends meet. We compromised and Isidore agreed to tour with us, but at the longest for three weeks.

Tours were difficult. It was hard to bring the family along since often during a tour we would be flying every day to a different city. However, when our children became school age, my family would accompany us wherever we played during the summer. For many

Mann family in Paris, early 1960s

Juilliard String Quartet children on tour with the Quartet (Hillyers, Cohens, Hansi Adam, Manns), Dartington, England, 1960

Mann family in Hawaii, 1960s

Quartet "family" fun; Earl Carlyss and Robert on the island of Moorea, 1966

years, every other year we were in Aspen, Colorado, at the Music Festival, with the alternate years spent traveling abroad during the summer. During these years, our children traveled many times to Europe, to Russia and south to Azerbaijan, to Taiwan, Japan and Korea. Traveling could be very tiring, but it was a wonderful family time.

Family concerts

LYRIC TRIO

I have been composing music since the age of thirteen. While I have composed for orchestra, chamber ensembles, and voice, I have always been fascinated by the combination of spoken word and music. Thus it was natural when I met Lucy, a talented actress, that I would be inspired to write many works in this medium. Initially, I set some of the Hans Christian Anderson fairy tales and Rudyard Kipling *Just So Stories* to music for violin, piano, and narrator. Our first recording was informal and just sent to friends. It was well received and it was Isaac Stern who encouraged us to begin performing these works for audiences. Thus The Lyric Trio was born, giving its first performance at the Norwalk Museum of Arts and Sciences in 1951, and then our first New York concert at the Carnegie Recital Hall in 1952. Our first pianist was Leonid Hambro, but over the years we have been lucky to include many wonderful pianists in this group and have given many performances, even at the Saito Kinen Festival in Japan. Lucy is still performing to this day, with my son Nicholas taking my place as the violinist.

Lyric Trio with Brooks Smith, piano

LYRIC TRIO + TWO

My inspiration for giving children's concerts came from having children. Lucy and I became friends with the main music librarian at the Free Library in Philadelphia. She asked if we would give a children's concert. We already had the Lyric Trio. We decided to make it the Lyric Trio + Two for this occasion.

We planned a concert showing the instruments I had collected, and demonstrating them. I was always buying instruments—drums, rat-

Robert blowing a Tibetan horn

Family practicing for a children's concert

tles, bamboo flutes that you would blow through and make all kinds
of fascinating sounds. I put this together with a program talking about
how music came about by knocking rocks together with rhythms and
dances. Lisa sang and Nicholas played the violin. Lucy narrated one of
the fairy tales and we all played the instruments during story lectures
that I wrote on different musical themes. We had kids from the audience come up and bang the drums. It was such a success that for many
years, every year after, we gave a children's concert at the library in
Philadelphia. These concerts lasted for fifteen years. We even recorded
a children's concert for PBS television.

One of our favorite traditions was visiting our friend, the architect
Louis Kahn, after these children's concerts. He lived with his wife in
a wonderful historic house in Philadelphia. Conversations in his home
were always something we looked forward to. We loved listening to
him talk about buildings and light. He was a remarkable architect and
intellect.

[MUSICAL JOURNEYS]

Germany and Hanns Eisler

I had never met the composer Hanns Eisler, but I did like his music. Eisler was born in Leipzig, Germany, the same year as my mother in 1898, and his family moved to Vienna in 1901. He eventually studied composition with Arnold Schoenberg and Anton Webern. In 1925 he moved to Berlin where he began to work closely in the theater with Bertolt Brecht. His left-leaning political views estranged him from his Vienna teachers but their influence remained ingrained in his marvelously crafted compositions. He later composed for film as well as the anthem for the German Democratic Republic. Hitler came into power and Eisler moved to the United States, first to New York City and then in 1942 to Southern California where he worked again with Brecht and taught composition.

Hanns had one hell of a problem, not of his own making. His brother, Gerhardt, ran the United States Communist Party. Don't forget Joseph "Savonarola" McCarthy and his witch hunt for "communists" in the United States. Gerhardt was going to be prosecuted and he jumped onto a London bound ship and then onto a Polish boat and escaped before he could be arrested and brought back to America. He was just steps ahead of justice department officials, escaping arrest and trial. Hanns wasn't a U.S. citizen and lived silently in the California hills. No matter where he went, he was legal game and the government wanted him to leave. The ruling—because of his brother, Hanns Eisler must leave the United States.

A number of Eisler's friends wished to send him off with a meaningful gift—a New York concert of his compositions in Town Hall. On the program was a string quartet played by our colleagues, the New Music Quartet. We admired the work and went backstage after the concert to tell Eisler. "You naughty boys," he remonstrated. "Why Hanns, what have we done?" we asked. "The Juilliard String Quartet refused to play my work! Why did you refuse to play my quartet?" We didn't know anything about it and said, "But Hanns, we haven't the slightest notion of what you are referring to." Later our quartet learned that the organizers of this evening's concert had approached the Juilliard School asking for our participation. Without telling us, Mark Schubart, Juilliard's dean at the time responded, "Absolutely not!" I was outraged and apologized to Hanns profusely. "Good luck, Hanns, in your new life." He was returning to Germany and I had no idea if it was East or West. He smiled and said, "If you ever come to Berlin be sure to look me up."

One year later, it was the early 1950s, the Juilliard String Quartet was rehearsing in our room at Juilliard across from Grant's Tomb when the door quietly opened. A tall, thin, arabesque of a fellow glided in without knocking. His voice was ghostly soft. "My name is Matteo Lettuni. I am the cultural affairs officer in West Berlin." At this time, Berlin had different sectors. There was the American sector, the Russian sector, and so on. We waited silently and he continued, "The three Western powers—England, France and the United States—have committed themselves to producing a West Berlin cultural festival. Each nation will send its best artistic, cultural representatives to take part. For the first time in our country's history, a United States president (Mr. Eisenhower) would designate presidential funds to send our nation's artists to this festival. We listened and wondered. This is 1951, nobody knows us. Why do they want us?

Mr. Lettuni read our questioning faces. "Those of us organizing the U.S. participants are well aware of your great success with the

BaLrtók string quartets at Tanglewood. We would like you to represent the chamber music for the festival and include some concerts by your quartet. We will also be having Judith Anderson in a company doing *Medea* and Celeste Holm in *Oklahoma*.

All four of us were performing silent cartwheels of happiness—our first opportunity to play in Europe! And to think, what a prestigious circumstance! We had never been to Europe. Our acceptance was in unison and word soon spread through Juilliard about this wonderful invitation.

And then all the Israeli kids heard about us going to Berlin. There was a big clamor and one of our favorite chamber music students came up to us shyly, speaking in a most distressed and uncomfortable fashion. She said, "You know that there are about 35 of us Israelis at Juilliard and all of us are very upset that you are going to Germany. Can we meet with you?" Not one of us had given any thought to non-musical implications. Here we were, four American Jews excited about playing our music for audiences who just a few years previously had been clapping for Nazi-approved music played by Nazi-accepted musicians. To the young Israeli student we replied, "Yes, we will meet with all of you."

Our studio was packed, standing room only. A young man spoke, "You must know that you four members of the Juilliard String Quartet are amongst our most favorite teachers. We are horrified that you are going to a land where many of us escaped with our lives and many of our families did not make it. My parents died in the Dachau camp. How can you good persons, even Jews, consider playing for those people?"

The following discussion was pure agony. Not one of us had any answer for the group of young people whom we loved. Lamely, we countered their protest. "You know, we aren't going to make music for the German people. We are representing our own country, the United States."

It was a long and painful meeting. We ourselves had doubts but the students made it crystal clear. More than half of them declared, "As much as we treasure our relationship with you, if you choose to go, we will have nothing more to do with you." We were conflicted and torn in two directions. We rationalized and finally decided to make the trip. True to their word about half of the Israeli kids turned their backs on us and quit our classes. And, also angry at us was one of the leading cello teachers, Uzi Weisel. Interesting enough, I later received a letter from Weisel apologizing for his behavior because he had since traveled with the Israel Philharmonic and had played in Germany.

Still troubled, but bursting with curiosity and the opportunity to play in such auspicious company, we now happily settled into a big, West Berlin hotel. I was with my love, Lucy; Winograd, our cellist, brought his girl, Betty. Dying to make some connection to this new world, Lucy asked, "Doesn't Hanns Eisler live here?" We stared at each other. "But doesn't he live in East Berlin?" "Yes, he does and I think he is teaching composition in the East Berlin Hochschule fur Musik." (Remember this is 1952 and there was no Berlin Wall.) "Well, how would we find him, get in touch?" Lucy, always the practical one, suggested the telephone book. Slowly, slowly we turned pages and sure enough in small print—Hanns Eisler—with a telephone number and address. Shall we call? We were on an adrenalin high. After three rings a female voice barked, "Hello." I responded, "Herr Hanns Eisler?" "Ein moment." Twenty seconds later I was talking to Hanns Eisler.

"How wonderful that you are here in Berlin. Why don't you come over for a visit?"

"That would be great, but Hanns, we are in West Berlin and you are in East Berlin."

"No problem," said Hanns. "Take the Ubann across the border and then grab a taxi to this address."

"But Hanns, the East German marks are different."

"Oh don't worry, East Berlin taxi drivers love West German marks."

Without thinking and full of anticipation, Lucy, Arthur, Betty and I took the subway and arrived at a square in East Berlin. Sure enough, there was no difficulty. The four of us were conveyed in a somewhat dilapidated Mercedes through a quiet, green foliaged section of Berlin, one stately mansion after the next. Time stood still. Had there really been a devastating war destroying many countries for many years? We reached the tall old world house surrounded by century old trees, a well-cared lawn and profusions of flowers, where Hanns Eisler and his wife lived. Hanns answered the doorbell. Hugs and warm communications filled out the time and space of our visit. "Hanns, you and your wife seem to be living the good life." He laughed with his whole body. "Couldn't be better. I teach serious composers at the Hochschule, I live here with a maid, a gardener and any extra help I need." (I wondered to myself—this is communism?) It was getting late and we should have been going back. The doorbell rang. In came a couple, the man looking very much like his brother. It is Gerhardt Eisler, the Propaganda Minister for all of East Germany.

My guess is that all four of us were a little uneasy. We were introduced. Hann's brother was not a diplomatic personality. We hardly met and he was accusing the four of us, "You support General Marshall. You are enemies of the people." We got into a political argument with this man, at which point, he was talking and getting very red in the face. We finally got a moment between angry breathing and Arthur Winograd asked, "You know they're reporting that in China there have been ten thousand people killed because they are anti-communist or anti-Revolutionary. What about the thousands of Chinese being executed for anti-government bias?" (Communist Russia was at this moment buddies with Communist China.) Long silence—then with a lion's roar, Gerhardt Eisler shouted, "We are trying to create a world where all people count and even if more than thousands resist our action, we must persevere! We're trying to do something good for the people. If it means we have to get rid of some people, we have to. We'll kill fifty thousand people if we have to."

Total, lengthy silence—"would anybody like some tea?" timidly offered Mrs. Hanns Eisler. As soon as we could, a taxi took us back to West Berlin. We were not very presentable, unshaven and wearing jeans. We were greeted by an urgent telephone call from our friend and sponsor Matteo Lettuni. "Where the hell have you been? Everybody, and I mean everybody—English, French, Americans and Germans are over at this other hotel for a big news conference. Get over there without delay!" "Yes, Matteo." Not bothering to change clothes or shave we anxiously hurried over to this new hotel. Completely out of place, looking like bums, we saw Matteo and like delinquents, we apologized. He looked as if he would send us back to America on the spot. "Where have you been?" I cannot explain to you, the reader, how dumb or naïve was the reply. I say, "Matteo, you will never guess who we were visiting." I told him the entire escapade and add terror and confusion to his already raging facial expression. A full minute elapsed before he opened his mouth. "Let me warn you, that the money that brought you here from the president's fund is with con-gressional approval. If anyone in our government hears about this, there will never be another cent spent by the president for such an occasion again." And, he added, "Quite possibly you might be accused of traitorous behavior." Sorry Hanns, but we weren't so clever. How-ever, all good compositions, happy or sad, or neither, have a coda:

Winograd and I, with our loves, had just come out of the audito-rium onto the street. We were thrilled with a performance of Bee-thoven's Ninth Symphony played by the Berlin Philharmonic under the great conductor Wilhelm Furtwangler, assisted by wonderful singers and a rousing trium-phant chorus celebrating the brotherhood of human beings. We stood on a Berlin street corner sobbing our hearts out, uncontrollably.

Hanns Eisler

Frankfurt

After we played our Berlin concerts we arranged to play a number of
concerts in what in those days were called America Hauses in Germany. We played in Frankfurt and other cities. Claus Adam had a
friend who was the Consul General for the United States in Frankfurt
and after we played in Frankfurt we were given a party. We were
taken around in a big Volkswagen station wagon. I had Juilliard's
Guadagnini violin and the other three quartet members also had very
good instruments with them. A man was charged to take us up to the
party and said to us, "You don't have to worry, the driver will stay
down here the whole time and watch your instruments." So we went
up and when we came down after the party all of the instruments
were there except for my Guadagnini. It was gone. So I looked at the
driver and asked, "What happened? Where is my instrument?" He
sheepishly admitted that the wife of the Consul General came down
to check on him and invited him to come up and have a sandwich. So
he went and someone had stolen my violin. What was I to do? It was
a Juilliard Guadagnini. We wanted the theft to be reported in the
American and German newspapers. We went to the military policeman who wasn't interested in a stolen Guadagnini violin at all, because he was a homicide man. Then he heard that it was worth $10,000
and had it printed in the newspapers.

The next place we were going to was Stuttgart and in Stuttgart
there was a very famous violin dealer by the name of Hamma. He was
called and it was arranged that he could loan me an instrument, a
Strad. So we went on to Stuttgart. The violin dealer said that the
Germans, and therefore he, had been bombed by the Americans and
he showed me charred pieces of great instruments that were in a big
box that had been collected. I played the Stuttgart concert on my
loaned Strad and we went back to Frankfurt. And, all of a sudden, my
Guadagnini appeared. Many black marketeers were operating in
downtown Frankfurt. I was told that a German man was walking
with a little boy, carrying a violin case. A soldier went up to him and

said, "You know I'm leaving back for the States and I don't want to take my violin with me. What will you give me for it?" So he sold it to the German man and the German man had read the story about my stolen violin in the newspaper. He turned out to be honest and when he inquired, it was, in fact, my violin. He did get a reward for giving it back to me.

Italy

Following these German house concerts we had a month off and Lucy and I decided to drive to Italy. We rented a little Volkswagen Beetle. Rafe's wife, Gerda, was Austrian and she told us that when we went through Austria we had to see Franz Josef's glacier. On this trip, Lucy and I made a book. Wherever we visited, Lucy would paint a picture of the place and I would draw a picture of the place. We did go to Franz Josef Glacier and it was marvelous. We ate sausage and fried potatoes and walked on the glacier. It was on Grossglockner, which is Austria's highest mountain, nearly 12,500 feet. We drove across Austria and went into Italy over Brenner Pass. We were having an argument—whether we should have brought two cameras and not just one so that we could have had one for black and white film and another for color film. I saw a truck in front of me driving very slowly and I decided to pass the truck. To my horror, it was a long truck and I saw he was turning left into a little side road. I had to make a quick decision—either slam on the brakes and maybe crash into him or go faster and escape him, which is what I did. The Beetle was small, and the truck's tire fender caught the Beetle and literally threw us through the air. We flew into the field about 15 to 20 feet away, and landed on our tires. The cover in the back of the car, where the motor was located, had completely ripped off, the motor revealed, and all four tires completely burst. But we were alive and everything with us was safe, including my violin. The crash was so loud that the entire neighborhood, farming people, came out to see what had happened. The police arrived too. What a way for us to enter Italy.

Russia and Gerda

There were a number of difficulties surrounding Raphael Hillyer's joining the Juilliard String Quartet. One of the foremost involved his wife,
Gerda. She was a most sensitive and tough young woman who had fled
the Nazis in Austria and arrived in America with her family. When Rafe
joined the Juilliard String Quartet, the family had to relocate to New
York and Gerda gave up her medical career that she had established in
Massachusetts. I found her to be a wonderful and intelligent friend.

After a number of years, the quartet received an offer to make its
first visit to Russia. Our first group discussion began in a context of
excitement, but all of a sudden Hillyer said very quietly, "I am very
sorry, but if the quartet must go, I will have to stay here because my
wife is not well and I cannot leave her." He continued, "However, if
you must go, get another violist for the trip." We were flabbergasted
and I was in no doubt as to my answer. I told Hillyer, "We are a real
quartet, and we go as we are now or we don't go." And that was the
end of our meeting.

Two days later, when the four of us gathered together for a rehearsal, Hillyer said without preamble, "If the offer of a Russian tour
is still on, I can go with one condition. I consulted Gerda's doctor and
he felt that if I took her with me on the trip, I could agree to go. It
will not be easy, but I am eager to try." The rest of us were grateful
and the cultural affairs officer in Moscow was contacted.

Hard to believe, the quartet with Mrs. Hillyer arrived in Moscow.
The cultural affairs officer plotted the scenario of the coming events
with happy hopes. Even Gerda quietly smiled.

In Moscow we were invited to play for the students at the Moscow
Conservatory, which was old and had a venerable history. I remember
two things that happened at that visit. First we had tea in the director's
office. Then a quartet of young women, I think they were the Prokofiev Quartet, were brought in to perform for us in the director's office.
We were sitting there, and I remember they were offering Shostakovich and Gaydn (Haydn is Gaydn in Russia). We asked for Gaydn and
they started to play Prokofiev. Their teacher shouted at them, "Your

guests wanted your Gaydn not Prokofiev." The other thing that happened was that a timid little man was allowed to come into the room. He was introduced and he handed us a program. What was the program? It was the great violin teacher, Galamian's graduation program from the Moscow Conservatory—this man had been Galamian's teacher.

The next day we took the train to Leningrad and by afternoon we were planning our schedule for the next day's concert. We agreed to meet for lunch. Then, a strange moment occurred. Hillyer appeared at the restaurant without Gerda. Immediately we all asked, "Where is she?" He replied somewhat hesitantly, "Gerda has not felt well from the moment of landing in Moscow and finally when we arrived in Leningrad, she and I decided that she should fly to London and stay with friends while I finish the tour and then I will join her in London." The three of us were surprised and thanked Hillyer for joining us on the tour. After a most successful concert in Leningrad the four of us flew to Odessa for our second concert.

That same afternoon, we were taken by our Russian hosts to many fascinating places, returning to the hotel late at night, happy, tired and looking forward to the next day's concert. It was midnight. I was slowly calming down in a full tub of hot water in my little hotel room when the phone rang. Who in Odessa would be calling at midnight? I somehow got out of the tub, there was no bath towel, and rushed to the phone. I wrapped a window drape around me and asked, "Who is this?" The voice of the cultural affairs officer came through the phone static, "Robert, how is it going?" I thought to myself, he's crazy. Why call me now? He continued, "Robert, are you still there?" I replied somewhat irritated, "Why call me this late?" Then slowly he went on, "Can you tell me if Hillyer's wife's first name is Gerda?" My heart sank, "Yes." "Well, I'm sorry to tell you, we have just received word that she arrived in London, went to a hotel, and has fallen to her death.

The silence between us was endless. I finally cried, "My God!" How can I handle this? At least I began to speak and think, "Of course, the rest of the tour is out. We have to immediately get back to Moscow and then to London. When is the next flight from here?" He replied, "Again I'm sorry, but the earliest you can fly is at 11am tomorrow." When the conversation ended, I was in a state of shock and realized that the next step was to tell Hillyer.

How? I knew he couldn't move until the next morning. At this moment I made one of the worst decisions in my life. I would not tell him until the next day before we would leave on another sightseeing trip. In my room was a full bottle of whiskey. Between crying and swallowing, the longest possible night in my life ended at 6am when I found myself outside Hillyer's door. Somehow, knocking, I entered and told him what had occurred. "What now?" When the group assembled and we finally found ourselves at the embassy, Hillyer must immediately fly to London. I elected to go with him. The other two Juilliard members remained in Mosow.

The trip to London with Hillyer was a long wave of silence and somehow we arrived for the funeral. It was after the cremation that Hillyer finally spoke quietly. "Let's return to Moscow. I wish to finish our concerts in Gerda's memory." I couldn't believe what I was hearing. I had also already spoken to Lucy in New York and she had gathered the Hillyer children together. When I told her of Hillyer's intention, she emotionally called William Schuman, Juilliard's president, who ordered the quartet back home without delay. No other instance in the fifty-one years of Juilliard Quartet life was so deeply wounding as the end of this wonderful, beautiful woman's life. The radiant, shy touching smile of Gerda Sgalitzer Hillyer hides in the depth of my memories. I wish it to remain forever.

South America and Lucy

In the 1970s the Juilliard String Quartet was poised to begin an extended concert tour of South America. The first stop: Bogotá, Colombia. We had never before experienced the musical climate in this part of the world. Our first concert surprisingly was a stunning success. In the audience was a young, attractive woman, the curator of the famous Gold Museum. The following day was unscheduled and this curator invited us for a guided tour of her domain. As we walked the halls of the museum, Lucy could not wait to ask where she might find examples of the folk art of this region, not the commercial offerings found in airports and tourist centers. The curator was taken aback, "That is not my field of expertise," she replied, "However, when we are finished here at the museum, if you cross the avenue behind the museum you will find an antique shop that may offer what you are interested in."

The objects displayed in the Gold Museum were dramatic and astonishing but immediately afterward Lucy crossed the avenue with unstoppable determination. I meekly followed. The shop we entered was very quiet and the objects displayed were indeed breathtaking. The owner of the shop appeared. He was not a native Colombian but spoke English with a strong Hungarian accent. "What a wonderful concert you performed last night. I was especially moved by Beethoven's quartet that ended with the formidable 'Grosse Fugue.'" Lucy interrupted his praise to describe what she was looking for. The man became quietly thoughtful and ushered us into a spacious backroom containing various paintings, sculptures, ornaments and jewelry. From a far corner he retrieved a medium size canvas painting. At once we recognized that it was charming and offbeat. The painting contained the expected plaza and cathedral. However, what captured Lucy's interest were two towering columns on each side of the church entrance. The columns were not of stone, but an amalgamation of birds. Tiny birds upon tiny birds rising endlessly into the sky above the church. Our music-loving proprietor hesitated then explained, "When Pizzaro came from Spain to this region in the sixteenth century, he brought many priests with him whose prime objective was to convert the 'heathens' to Christianity. One missionary priest lived for a time in a place now known as Cochabamba, Bolivia. In addition to his religious duties he taught a number of young men how to paint a picture. One particular youth possessed an arresting ability to create the picture you are now looking at." Lucy was totally captivated. Out of her mouth sounded the words, "I love it, I want it and I must have it. How expensive is it?" The Hungarian modulated with utmost sympathy, "It truly is worth a lot of money, but I was moved by your husband's music and your overwhelming desire. I can see how much the painting means to you. For that reason only, I will sell it to you for the amount I paid for it, US $800 dollars." To us that was a lot of money but I could not keep Lucy from her newfound love.

Leaving Colombia, I triumphantly carried the painting along with my Stradivarius violin into the huge Braniff plane flying south to Santiago, Chile, where a number of concerts were scheduled. After landing, Lucy and I approached the customs counter with our luggage including my Strad and Lucy's newly acquired painting. The situation in Chile at this time was dire: continuous street demonstrations, rioting with police and civilians literally battling for spaces between the buildings. Little did we anticipate what was to happen ten days later— the assassination of Chile's President Salvador Allende.

In front of us stood a stiffly erect customs agent in a sparkling, fresh uniform. His handsome features and trim mustache were dominated by a stern facial expression. He ignored my violin case and our luggage. His English was curt and unfriendly. "You cannot bring this painting into the country." No amount of entreaty prevailed. "Leave the painting here," he demanded. "Take a receipt and when leaving Chile present your receipt. We will give back your painting." What should we do? Leave the painting or cancel our concerts. Of course, play the concerts!

Minus Lucy's painting we entered the country. Everywhere was chaos and tumult that played havoc with our nerves. Obviously the situation was deteriorating. It did not help to suspect that these happenings were being instigated with U.S. State Department help. We played our concerts and then we were back at the airport intending to fly to Buenos Aires, Argentina. We approached customs with our receipt. A soldier, uniformed, with a holstered gun asks, "Si?" We give him the receipt. His immediately replied in broken English, "Sorry, no painting here." No amount of argument succeeds. Finally the soldier threatened, "Get on the plane. We will try to find your painting before your plane leaves." Lucy was then assisted into the cabin of another Braniff plane nearly two stories high by two military policemen. Lucy sat in her seat distraught. Time was ticking and departure was imminent. Suddenly Lucy bolted upright into the aisle and before anyone could react, jumped out of the exit door and practically fell down the stairs attached to the plane. She rushed to the front of the plane and stood facing the front with hands outstretched, shouting, "I am not moving until I get my painting."

Everyone on board was astonished—the pilots, the stewardesses, the passengers, and crew working on the runways. Even I, who have learned to expect almost anything from my beloved Lucia. Impasse? Forceful eviction? Not at all. In the distance on the edge of the runway, barely noticeable, was a man on a bicycle carrying a large, square package. As he neared the plane, Lucy saw that he was carrying her treasured painting. The man dismounted his bike and entered the cabin still carrying his unwieldy package, followed by Lucy. The tense moment relaxed. Breathing became normal. Lucy was not shot and we were soon soaring above the majestic peaks of the Andes on our way to Buenos Aires, our high spirits restored.

We arrived in the city where classical, western music is an important cultural activity. Even concerts by visiting string quartets are greatly appreciated. However, before our concert, we have the luxury of a free day, nothing scheduled. Lucy and I, happily hand in hand, wandered around the great open space in the center of the city, Plaza Major. The displays in the shops surrounding the plaza appeared wondrously inviting. Suddenly Lucy jerked my hand, "Look," she cries. I dumbly follow her stare. In a little art shop below the store level we could not believe what we saw. She dragged me down steps to the shop. In the window were not one but two Cochabamba paintings exactly like ours—the columns of birds with the cathedral and all. Fantastic! How did the paintings get to this place? We hurried into the shop. Inside was a calm atmosphere and a single young lady, watching our tumultuous entrance. "Where, where, where did you get those two paintings in the window?" we simultaneously cried. "What?" she responded in English. "Those two paintings? Oh yes, you mean the Bolivian Indian paintings." She smiled a warm, friendly smile. "You are interested, no?" We pleaded, "Please, how did you obtain them?" She laughed disarmingly and proceeds, "It is quite a story." She appeared somewhat nervous but continued, "There are two brothers who live in Cochabamba, Bolivia. They are very talented and every year they send us a few of their paintings." Lucy was confused by the use of the present tense. "They send you these paintings now?" The girl answered, "Of course. They have been doing this for years." I blurted out, "How much do you sell them for?" She says disarmingly, "They are not very expensive, about $150 each." Lucy gasped, "Are these brothers still living?" She responds, "Oh, very much so. We hope they continue a long time because their work is very popular."

Lucy turns to me and orders, "back to the hotel." When my wife orders, I do not resist. In our hotel room we were silent. Lucy did not take off her coat, deliberately picking up the telephone she dialed a New York phone number, her bank. With hardly an opening sentence she inquired, "Has an $800 check made out in Bogotá, Colombia, been cashed?" She was told no. She answers, "Good and cancel the check right away." At last we were saved. The deceptive Hungarian émigré in Colombia would not get away with this fraudulent enrichment.

Lucy and Eleanor Adam shopping for artwork on a tour

Finally, this long, exhausting South American tour is finished and we unpack our bags in our New York apartment. In the following days our collective guilt about keeping the "criminal" painting grows. A friend, the pianist Horatio Gutierrez is about to embark on his foray into the southern hemisphere. We ask him if he will be playing in Bogotá and he is. We tell him that we wish him to return a painting to a shop owner in Bogotá and he agrees. Later, there remains a nagging and somewhat haunting shadow. Lucy and I both agree, it was a refreshing painting and we miss it.

Aspen, Colorado

In 1949, a very unusual man, Walter Paepcke, was responsible for the revival of a ghost town named Aspen. At that time, there was nothing there except for mines and old miners. The mines were defunct and no one was mining anymore. He started to bring people to visit. He brought Albert Schweitzer, the Nobel prize winning philosopher physician from Africa. He brought Mitropoulos, the internationally famous conductor and composer, and the Minneapolis Orchestra to come and play. And, they celebrated the great human writer, Goethe, on a centennial of his birthday.

So, the Juilliard String Quartet was practicing in our Juilliard studio and the door opened, as it did on many occasions. And this time it was a fellow, he looked like a businessman, and he asked us, "What are you doing this summer?" We told him that we hadn't made plans yet. He said, "I'm Walter Paepcke and you might have heard about the music festival that I started in 1949. It

Walter Paepcke,
Founder of Aspen Institute

Aspen Music Festival tent, early days

isn't just music but a mixture of the arts including playwrights, philosophers and everything. It is an institute. And, we are going to continue it. I have plans for the future and have already asked the Paginini Quartet to return for five weeks. I'd like for you to also come for five weeks and dovetail so that you can play the Mendelssohn Octet and the two Darius Milhaud quartets that are supposed to be played separately and together. Would you come?"

We accepted Mr. Paepcke's invitation and that began our connection to the Aspen scene. Lucy and I drove my Jeep station wagon and we had a little shack at the top of Red Mountain. Vronsky and Babin were there. They were a famous piano team and Babin started the Cleveland Conservatory. Thornton Wilder who wrote *Our Town* was there and so was Isaac Stern. We had an absolutely wonderful time.

One night for fun we played all six Mozart viola quintets with the wonderful violist William Primrose.

Another time, Jennie Tourel, the wonderful mezzo-soprano, was there singing and we had our four-year-old daughter Lisa with us at the concert. We always sat in the top row of the open air tent where all the concerts were played, so we could leave easily in case Lisa got noisy. Lisa was in dress up clothes and high heel shoes and we went backstage. All of sudden Lisa went over on her own to Jennie Tourel and started pulling on her dress. Jennie was annoyed but Lisa continued. Finally Jennie turned around and said, "And little girl, who are you?" Lisa looked at her and replied, "I am Jennie Tourel." From that moment on, they were fast friends.

We spent many wonderful summers in Aspen. I had my mountains and I hiked all over. We also went and played at the monastery at Aspen every summer, where we made deep friendships. When we first visited the monastery all the monks except Peter, who was in the gift shop, had taken a vow of silence. Through Peter we offered to bring music to the monastery since they could not accept our invitation to

St. Benedict's monastery, Aspen

attend a concert at the Aspen Music Festival tent. They were thrilled, and we brought the first music concert to be played in that remarkable place. Over the years we became friends with several of the monks, Father Joseph, Brother Benedict (who made wonderful sculptures out of nails and bolts and later became a dentist!), and Brother Peter. The monastery has a special place in the heart of our family.

Jennie Tourel, mezzo soprano

We also became connected to the Aspen Institute, which is dedicated to intellectual exploration and dialogue of all kinds. Leaders in all different fields come to give lectures and participate in seminars. Lucy and I both participated and I would give lectures. We were very close to Joseph Slater, the man who ran the Aspen Institute from 1969–86. Slater was a passionate lover of music. One time he asked me,

PHOTO CREDIT: BERKO STUDIO

Robert and Nicholas playing for an Aspen Institute Seminar

"Bobby, give me a one sentence definition of a true musician, a really great musician." I thought a moment and finally said, "The simplest thing I can say is a really great musician is someone who knows how to connect two tones." Joseph Slater said, "That's interesting that you say that because that is exactly what Isaac Stern told me, too."

That is what Bartók and Hindemith used to say about great pianism, or producing great tones on the piano. Hindemith said, "It is of no importance whether a single tone is produced by Franz Liszt or by Mr. Smith's umbrella. A single tone, as we have stated repeatedly, has no musical significance, and the keyboard does not provide any exception to this rule. The tones released by the keyboard receive musical value only if brought into temporal and spatial relations with each other. Then the infinitely subtle gradation in the application of pressure, the never-ceasing interplay of minutest dynamic hues and temporal length proportions, all the bewitching attractions of good piano playing—only the artist can produce them convincingly; and it certainly is not his hand that reigns within the microcosm of musical diversity but his musical intellect as the master of his playing hand. Even the application of the world's most perfect umbrellas could never cope with this diversity, gradation, and interplay."[*]

Bartók used to say the same thing about the connection between notes.[**]

Years later, Slater came to me and said, "You know, I'm setting up in another place in Baca, Colorado, a similar thing to the Aspen Institute. It will be an extension, but I want to add a music program. I just can't have it without a music program." We suggested that we form a group, using myself, my son Nicholas, Lucy narrating, and in addition a violist, cellist and pianist (our dear friends Bonnie Hampton and Nathan Schwartz). He liked the idea and we succeeded. The group was called the Baca Ensemble, and for about six glorious summers we lived up in

---

[*]   Paul Hindemith, "Some Thoughts on Instruments" in *A Composer's World: Horizons and Limitations* (Cambridge: Harvard University Press, 1952), 189-90.
[**]   "Mechanical Music," in *Béla Bartók Essays*, ed. Benjamin Suchoff (New York: St. Martin's Press, 1976), 290.

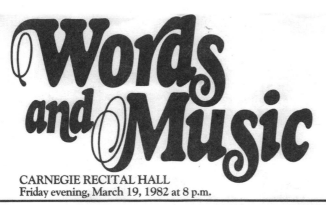

Words and Music

CARNEGIE RECITAL HALL
Friday evening, March 19, 1982 at 8 p.m.

BACA ENSEMBLE

Lucy Rowan, narrator
Robert Mann, Nicholas Mann, violins;
Maureen Gallagher, viola;

Bonnie Hampton, cello
Nathan Schwartz, piano

BACA Ensemble flyer, 1982

the mountains (nestled under the Sangre de Cristo range), in the middle of nowhere. Total freedom to prepare two concerts a week for the participants at this program, with repertoire of our choice. It couldn't have been a more wonderful experience.

Playing in the Aspen mountains, later years

[TOOLS OF THE TRADE]

ONE OF THE MOST WONDERFUL PEOPLE IN THIS WORLD WAS REMBERT Wurlitzer, who came from the famous family that made organs. He also had a big violin shop. In fact, René Morel, the famous instrument restorer, worked in his shop with a man named Sacconi. I was desperate for a violin and so I went to Rembert and he helped me. He found for me what he believed to be an early Del Gesu Guarneri. It was a good instrument and I remember it cost either $12,000 or $14,000. He allowed me any number of years to pay for it. That's how I got my first important instrument and I was quite happy with it. It didn't have a very big tone but it had a beautiful sound.

The Strad

Tony Swarowsky was the son of Hans Swarowsky, who was a big conductor in Europe and also the conducting teacher of Zubin Mehta. He taught a lot of young conductors. Tony was not a musician. He could sort of conduct, he could play the cello, but most importantly, he was a dear friend. He married a French woman, settled in Paris and was studying to be a psychiatrist, although his passionate hobby was photography. At the time, he was treating Robin Lehman, the son of the man who gave many of the great paintings to the Metropolitan

Museum of Art. Robin was training to be a musician and even studied composition. He was a very strange young man who kept busy collecting manuscripts and instruments. Tony also acted as Robin's agent. One time they went to visit the daughter of Alma Mahler who lived in New York to see if they could buy the manuscript of Mahler's Seventh Symphony.

Robin had composed a string quartet and I proposed to Tony that the Juilliard String Quartet play it. Robin was at loggerheads with his father, who was exceedingly wealthy. We ended up playing Robin's quartet for his father and became quite friendly with Robin Lehman. One day, Tony called me up. I remember we were living on Morningside Drive. Tony was bickering with a famous engineer named Lewis who built bridges all over the world and owned a quartet of Stradivarius instruments. Robin wanted me to come to the Hampshire House on Central Park South where he was staying, and look at this violin collection. Of course, I went. I looked at all of the instruments. I couldn't play the cello but I could still get a general idea of how it sounded. I thought the cello was beautiful. I told Robin not to buy the viola.

I thought that one of the violins was terrific. It was very famous and had been owned by an early Italian violinist. It had been played by Arnold Rosé, who was concertmaster of the Vienna Philharmonic for more than fifty years, so was known as the Rosé Strad. Rosé sold it to Lewis, the engineer. From my recommendations, Robin took out his checkbook and said he would buy the cello and one of the violins. He made out two separate checks, and I remember he made out a check for the violin for something like $36,000 or $37,000. Then Robin thanked me for helping him and said, "Wait a minute. Let's go have a drink." Finally he asked, "Would you like to play this instrument?" Well, I was thrilled and suggested that I would try to pay the instrument's insurance. He said, "Oh, no, no. I have other Strads in Paris and other instruments. I want you just to play it."

I played the Rosé Strad for about a year and was in heaven. I got a call from Tony and he asks, "How do you like the Strad?" I answered, "Are you kidding? It's fantastic." He said, "Well, why don't you buy it? I'm sure that Robin would let you buy it." I laughed and said, "You must be joking. How could I afford it?" Tony said, "I think he would sell it to you for $35,000." I told him that I didn't have that kind of money. Tony answered, "Now let's be practical. First of all, I'll bet you he would take the instrument you paid off, which is $12,000 or $13,000. He'll take it as part of your payment. He doesn't need the money."

Tony also told me Robin was buying manuscripts. I had been given Webern's own copy of his Piano Variations by a friend of Eugene Lehner, Dr. Rudy Kurtzman, who was an amateur pianist. Kurtzman had also been a friend of Anton Webern and he got this manuscript from the composer as a gift. So Tony said to me, "I'll bet you that Robin would buy your copy of Anton Webern's Piano Variations." We called Robin up in Paris and he said, "Well, yes. I'm willing to sell the Strad if you can manage it." He also wanted to know how good the instrument was for me. I called Isaac Stern and said, "You have got to help me." Tony, Lucy and I met Isaac at Carnegie Hall, which he had just saved from demolition. The hall was empty and first Isaac got onstage and played my Guarneri. Then he played the Strad. I thought he sounded wonderful on both instruments, so that was not a problem. Now it was my turn to play both instruments on the Carnegie Hall stage. Everyone said, "You sound so much better on the Strad." Isaac told me that I should buy it. Robin said he would take my instrument as partial payment but wanted to have the Strad evaluated by the top luthier in France. So Isaac called him for me and told him that Robin wanted him to evaluate the violin.

Robin had one condition. He said, "I will take your violin as partial payment for the Strad only if you will let your beautiful wife Lucy bring it over to Paris. And, I will buy her ticket." So, Lucy went over and stayed in one of Robin's fantastic homes on the Right Bank. The French luthier gave Lucy an evaluation of $60,000 for the violin. Robin had agreed that I could buy the Strad for $36,000. He gave me five or six thousand for the Webern manuscript and my parents gave me six or seven thousand dollars. Lee Hambro gave me one or two

Lucy in Paris with Robin Lehman
PHOTO CREDIT: ANTON SWAROWSKY

thousand and even Hillyer loaned me a thousand. I somehow had the money for the violin and all of a sudden I was the owner of a beautiful Stradivarius.

There are two things about Strads. There are instruments that do what you try to have them do. And they are wonderful. There are also instruments that are wonderful but you have to play them a certain way. The Rosé Stradivarius is the kind of instrument that, if I played it the way that it wanted me to play it, sounded wonderful. It was a hard lesson to learn over the years, but I finally did learn it and I love the instrument and have played it for many, many years.

PART III

Relationships

Arnold Schoenberg
116 N. Rockingham Ave.
Los Angeles 24, California.

April 22, 1949.

Mr Robert Mann
103 La Salle Street
New York, N.Y.

Dear Mr Mann:

I have already been informed by the
Ojai Festival Committee that you will play
my String Quartet at this occasion. I was
very pleased to learn this.

I am sure I will be there at this time and not
only see you again, but also to hear you for
the first time. I am very glad about this.

I am, with cordial greetings,

Sincerely yours,

Arnold Schoenberg

Krzysztof Penderecki   1 Berlin 37 (Zehlendorf)
                          Kleiststrasse 26

Mr. Robert Mann
Juilliard String Quartet
Juilliard School of Music
130 Claremont Avenue
New York, N.Y. 10027
U.S.A.

Berlin, November 4, 1968

Dear Mr. Mann:

At our meeting in Mérida we discussed the possibility of my
writing a work for String Quartet which you and your quartet
would perform at Juilliard's opening at Lincoln Center for the
Performing Arts. I regret to have to inform you that I have
changed my mind and have returned to the plan I had originally,
that of writing a work for orchestra. Since I wrote a work for
String Quartet a few months ago, I find it impossible to write
another one within one half year. I really am most sorry for
disappointing your expectations and hope you will find understanding for my view in this matter.

I will be sending you the work for String Quartet which I recently wrote and would feel most honored if you chose to perform it at some convenient date.

I remain, with best greetings,

Sincerely yours,

Krzysztof Penderecki

P.S. Permit me to call your attention to the fact that I have
     a new address in Berlin.

[COMPOSERS AND RECORDINGS]

Arnold Schoenberg

It was 1947 and the quartet had just started. Because of our connection to Eugene Lehner, we loved the music of Arnold Schoenberg, who was living in California. I also was a composer. So, on a trip to Glacier, lasting about two weeks, I took along my camping equipment and my own compositions, leaving them at a place along the way. When I left Glacier, I flew from a city near Glacier Park, through Reno, Nevada, and down to Los Angeles, where my family was now living. My brother lived in Los Angeles, and my quartet had given me the task of contacting Schoenberg. We knew that he had composed four string quartets and we wanted to know if he would write a fifth quartet for the Juilliard String Quartet.

Dimitri Mitropoulos, a friend of mine and of the Juilliard String Quartet, was the great conductor, pianist and composer. He told us that he would help to pay for a fifth Schoenberg string quartet. We thought that we could raise about a thousand dollars for the commission. I arrived in Los Angeles and I called Arnold Schoenberg and he agreed to see me. I went to his home in Westwood and as I remember it, I brought along five or six of my own compositions. I asked if he would take a look at them, and he did. We sat on the same sofa and he didn't look at the score very carefully. He just sort of turned the pages to see what I had written. And then he said, "Young man, if you want to be a composer, I give you only one piece of advice. Whether you like it or not, whether you are sick or not, no matter what, you must write at least fifty bars of music every day. It doesn't matter if it's good or bad. If you do this every day long enough, you will be a composer."

Then I came to the point to ask what I needed to. I said, "You know, Mr. Schoenberg, I started the Juilliard String Quartet and we are a young quartet. We really love your music enormously. Would it be possible, if we can raise the money, to commission a fifth quartet?" I remember during this conversation that Schoenberg had very bad eyesight. However, he was still composing. He showed me in his bedroom that he had a wall where he had composed a big work on the wall. He was composing on the wall because his eyesight was so bad. He told me that he hated to compose now and would put off his composing until it was almost upon him. Then like torture, he would start composing and get into it and write quickly and be done with it. He was that kind of a genius.

I also remember that Kolisch, the violinist who had been so involved in publicizing the original metronome markings in Beethoven scores, was walking in and out. At one point, Kolisch took me aside and he whispered to me, "Well, how much money would you think the Juilliard String Quartet could give for a commission?" I was embarrassed because I didn't think we had enough money and we didn't. I told Kolisch that Mitropoulos would help us out with one thousand dollars. This was a lot of money for us. After all, we were each only receiving $2,500 for the entire year. Kolisch said, "Mr. Schoenberg could not do that for such a small amount. Really, don't even bother asking him anymore. He needs much more money than that." He was right of course and we didn't have the money. That was the end of the Juilliard String Quartet's attempt to commission a Schoenberg Fifth String Quartet.

However, this did set the
ground for something that
happened a few years later, I
think in 1950, our third
summer as a quartet, right
before Schoenberg died. We
got in touch with him again
and asked if we could play
his quartets for him. We
were invited to his house to
play. There were many people in attendance that night,
including the composer David Diamond who took
notes, though I didn't know
him at the time. I remember

Arnold Schoenberg

that Schoenberg's daughter Nuria was there. We told him that we
would like to play the first, third and fourth quartets for him. We
didn't play the second quartet because it involves a singer. We were
confident about playing the quartets because Eugene Lehner had
coached us on the Schoenberg quartets. We had played for Edward
Stuermann, who was one of Schoenberg's close colleagues, and I think
we even played one of the quartets for Kolisch. We asked Schoenberg
which quartet he wanted to hear first. I remember that he was a small
man, with a humorous smile. He told us in a raspy voice, "The first
quartet. I haven't heard the first quartet in a long time. Please play
that."

The first quartet of Schoenberg is in four movements lasting 45 to
50 minutes without a pause, depending on your tempi. When we
finished it, I said, "You know Mr. Schoenberg, the people who were
playing Beethoven for Beethoven could have the response of Beethoven. We can't do that. But now we have the chance to find out what
Arnold Schoenberg thinks of the way we play his string quartets."
Schoenberg was quiet for a long time and then he started chuckling.

He said, "You know, you played this quartet in a way that I never imagined it." We thought, *My God, what have we done wrong?* So I said, "Well, Mr. Schoenberg, please don't spare our feelings. Tell us how we should go about playing the quartet the way you like it." He didn't say anything for some time and then he said, "No, I like the way you play it. I want you to continue to play it this way." And that was that*.

Elliott Carter

*(written as the preface to the score for the complete
Carter String Quartets, at the request of Elliott Carter)*

Two violins, a viola and a cello. What is it about this non-exotic string foursome encompassing the range of the human voice that for more than 250 years has motivated composers to create such a compelling repertoire? The pantheon of great string quartet literature is illuminated with inspirations from Haydn, Mozart, Beethoven and Schubert on through the nineteenth and twentieth centuries to the present.

After a lifelong involvement with this repertoire, I cannot escape the conclusion that Elliott Carter in his five quartets has created a musical world that, for its boldness of design, integrity of form, polyphonic interplay of voices, virtuosic use of instruments and profound emotional expressiveness, is as fulfilling as any in the entire string quartet literature.

---

* I remember when we played the Fourth Quartet we had a couple of problems in the realization, especially in the last movement. In the second movement there is a place where the main voice is played by the second violin. It is marked very softly, and the other parts are marked louder. We asked Schoenberg, "How will the main voice come through?" His answer was that it will come through if you play it with the right kind of tone. In another place he asks some of the instruments to play double artificial harmonics. To do this, you have to keep one finger down and then a fourth higher, and double, meaning two notes of harmonics on two different strings. It is possible. However, then Schoenberg said, "You should play it ponticello" That means you play really on the bridge and it sounds squeaky. Schoenberg liked playing on the bridge. Not near the bridge but on the bridge. Even that's possible. On top of that, he wanted col legno tratto, which means not with the hair of the bow on the bridge, but with the wood of the bow and drawing it. We said, "We can't make any sound out of this. How can we do it?" Kolisch was there and Schoenberg said to Kolisch, "Rudy, can we do this?" And, of course we did, and played it.

Juilliard String Quartet with Elliott Carter

My experiences with Carter's quartets parallel my earlier encounters with the late quartets of Beethoven. Some critics may question the validity of Carter's tonal language, just as many nineteenth-century critics questioned the language of Beethoven's last quartets. Although my musical ear had already expanded through diligent study of Bartók and Schoenberg, I could not believe what my ears took in on hearing Carter's *First Quartet* (1951). Here was a soaring musical spirit anchored in a traditional path but bristling with amazing new colors, vital and mysteriously shifting rhythmic pulses, emotional highs and lows that transported me for over 40 minutes. I knew then that I must play this man's compositions.

I vividly remember the Juilliard String Quartet's struggle to play the notes contained in all the passages, to feel naturally the startling rhythmic modulations—like shifting gears—and the struggle to hear as well as comprehend the quick-passing vertical sonorities. When rehearsing late Beethoven quartets, string ensembles are astonished at the clash of non-related notes in many passages when played in slow motion. But like distance in viewing a painting, such detailed aural confusions become magically clear when played at the proper tempo. This is also true for much of Carter's polyphonic writing.

Carter's *Second Quartet*, first composed in 1959 (later revised), was not premiered for some time, and finally the Juilliard was given permission to play the first performance. In this work was a truly new scoring for string quartet. The four voices were isolated not only by a singular character and tonal base for each instrument, but also by physical space. The tonal and rhythmic dimensions of this music were powerfully concentrated, and the discourse between instruments even more liberating and evocative than in the *First Quartet*. A sure test of the value of this music lies in the hundreds of hours required to overcome its difficulties. I've never begrudged that time working on Carter. The rewards became more and more satisfying with each new performance. It is important to acknowledge here that complexity in music is not in itself good or bad. Only when such unusual relationships of vertical sounds combine with linear motion to forge a strong musical effect can one appreciate the value of that complexity.

While the challenges of learning the first two Quartets were extraordinary, the difficulties in preparing the *Third Quartet* (1971) were monumental. Again there were new rhythmic relationships to master, but additionally there was a whole new domain of instrumental coordination. The *Third Quartet* is in reality two duos, one of violin and cello, the other, violin and viola. I chose to play "Duo II" with the viola. Earl Carlyss, our second violinist, played a part in "Duo I" that explodes with all kinds of pizzicato derring-do. He is probably the only violinist who has ever practiced scales and arpeggios pizzicato (no bow) to develop his technique for the *Third Quartet*. It took the Juilliard String Quartet two full rehearsals just to be able to get through the first measure of the piece. In this measure "Duo II' has the violin playing six triplet beats that can be divided into two or three larger pulses. The violist relates to three of those pulses with groups of five notes in each pulse. "Duo I," while harmonically connected to "Duo II," relates only to a four-beat pulse that coincides with "Duo II" at the end of the bar, a bar that lasts just under three and a half seconds.

Robert Mann *performs* Elliott Carter

Wednesday, March 28   8:00 p.m.   at Merkin Concert Hall

PHOTO CREDITS: E. CARTER/KATHY CHAPMAN, R. MANN/CHARLES ABBOTT
Publicity, concert at Merkin Hall, New York City

Complicated? Yes, but when negotiated successfully, the sensation is similar to catapulting over a roaring waterfall at the start of a white-water journey. I believe that performances of this work have resulted in some of the exhilarating moments of my life. There is a timekeeping device called a click track that can be a great aid in ensuring the accuracy of the performance, but somehow the Juilliard String Quartet always preferred to take its chances without it.

I first heard the Fourth Quartet (1986) played by the Composers String Quartet. Here again was a new lyricism, fascinating colors, and an almost Mozartean transparency. I couldn't wait to begin work on this piece. What I was not prepared for was the skill with which Carter wove together the individual textures and rhythmic figures. While he had separated the tonal and emotional character of each instrument in the first three quartets, he now assigned a unique rhythmic character to each of the four voices (violin I, "the square;" violin II, "master of triplets;" viola, "external fives;" cello, "tormented sevens"). The miracle is that this exotic aural kaleidoscope produced a coherent, powerful musical statement.

I would like to share with the reader one personal observation. In earlier days, it seemed that Elliott Carter's major focus was on the hierarchical rhythmic realization of the performance. Many years later there was no question that the composer's ultimate desire was for an interpretation replete with expressive, surging intensity.

Is there no end to this man's creativity? Of course not! A stream of arresting new works flowed from his pen until his passing, and the Fifth Quartet (1995) is among them. Like the previous quartets, I find the Fifth Quartet ever fresh and open-ended. I first heard it played by the Arditti Quartet. In 331 measures of music, more than a third of these are scored for only one or two parts. Here we see the need to communicate with a more inner-orientated voice, as with Beethoven, Bartók, and Shostakovich in their last quartets. Structural and emotional continuity is simplified. Six contrasting movements are connected by five interludes, where four voices speak to and with each other as in a recitative.

The *Adagio sereno* obtains a heavenly musical purchase by the ingenious use of harmonics. And the final three and one half measures achieve a *ludus tonalis* signature that brings the *Fifth Quartet* to a perfect, cadential end. I confess, as a long-time string quartet addict, that performing this brief denouement with the other three players—expiring after a last double-stop ends, sotto voce—alone provides me with the answer to why string quartets are still written after 250 years.

I know that the five works will be ever present wherever music is important. I am grateful to have experienced them and to have known Elliott Carter, just as in an earlier time Ignaz Schuppanzigh knew Ludwig van Beethoven.

Aaron Copland and Lukas Foss

We also played with, and loved being with, Aaron Copland. He was one of America's best composers and was also a magnificent human being. He was warm, supportive, and vulnerable, and we had the greatest time with him. When he played piano, he would always get very nervous in performance. We recorded the sextet (the famous clarinet, piano and string quartet piece) and the piano quartet. Once Copland called me and said, "Bobby do you know a good violinist who could make a transcription of my duo for flute and piano for violin and piano." I said, "I certainly do, me!" So Copland came over and gave me the music and told me what he had in mind. I transcribed it and he accepted everything that I did. I think he changed one spot where I'd gone an octave higher. He liked the lower register and lowered it.

Another pianist/composer we played with was Lukas Foss. We had a wonderful time with Lukas at the Library of Congress where we played both Mozart piano quartets.

Béla Bartók and Peter Bartók

I have to say, one of my great regrets is that I never met Béla Bartók. He was busy at Columbia during the time I was at Juilliard in graduate school. He was working on all of his recordings of the folk music that he collected on his field trips. He had the music on all of these old Edisons. He was busy transcribing them onto more contemporary equipment. I loved Bartók's music and was trying like mad to learn some of the quartets. I was too intimidated to try to get in touch with him in hopes of playing for him. He was known to be not too impressed with performances of his music. Once, two sisters played the First Sonata for him on piano. They were expecting a great deal of help from him after he heard them, and he all he said was, "You know, the first movement was a little too slow. The second movement was too fast and you have to practice more." Bartók also didn't believe in teaching composition. And yet there is a wonderful book written in which people who studied with him write their memories about him. It really is quite illuminating.

I did learn something firsthand about Bartók from a young composer from Hawaii that I knew at Juilliard by the name of Dae Kom Lee. Somehow, he wrangled a session with Bartók. He went over to Columbia to show Bartók his compositions. Dae Kom told me that Bartók looked at his music and then asked him, "Do you ever play

Beethoven piano sonatas?" He answered, "Of course I do." Bartók answered, "Well, I want to show you something." He took one of Beethoven's most cryptic scherzos, minuets or whatever. Dae Kom told me that they spent three hours dissecting it with Bartók showing how he thought Beethoven put it together. That was Dae Kom's lesson with Bartók.

When Peter Bartók, Béla Bartók's son, lived in New York we became very good friends. During the recordings of Bartók's music that Peter produced, he would ask me to look at the music and to make a decision to put a flat or sharp in a particular spot where there was a debate because there were different versions in Bartók's handwriting. Peter had trouble deciding which version to use and would ask me for help.

Béla Bartók wasn't making any money with his compositions and he was very ill while living in America. He spent some time at Black Mountain College in North Carolina where there was an ex-Hungarian community. One of the people who lived there was an international copyright lawyer by the name of Victor Bator.

Bator convinced Bartók, who was on his death bed, that Admiral Miklós Horthy was in league with the Nazis and had taken over Hungary. Of course Bartók hated the Nazis and fascism. Bator said, "You know your will is such that if you die probably a lot of things that you want to give your wife or your son or to this or that will end up in Horthy's regime's control. So I want you to make a new will." So Bartók made a new will and named Bator to be its executor, the head of the trust. The will was worded the way that Bator told him to word it. After Bartók died, it turned out that Bator really had used his role as executor to get all of Bartók's manuscripts, and correspondence given to the Bartók estate, not the family members. This meant that family members received no money from the sales of his work. When Bela Bartók was alive he didn't receive much income for the performances of his pieces. After he died, however, they generated more and more money.

Peter Bartók was a fantastic recording engineer. In the early days, he only worked in monaural. However, people claim that the sound he got was one of the most wonderful sounds that anybody ever re-

corded. Peter had a company, and Béla Bartók put in his will that the
estate should help Peter to keep the recording company going and, of
course, one of the major missions was to record all of Bartók's works.
And, Bator was doing this.

Bator was also doing many things that were not helpful to Peter and
they started a long lawsuit that lasted for many years. Peter's mother,
who was Bartók's second wife, was a little unstable and she had gone
back to Hungary. Bator would give her money so she wouldn't support Peter in the lawsuit. It was a terrible situation. Peter was getting
into thousands of dollars of debt to pay the lawyers. By now Bator was
a communist. He would go to the American court and say, "if you
give a ruling and take this away from me it's going to be against the
communist government in Hungary." Peter was losing all of the bat-
tles. Finally, long after Bartók died, Peter finally won and got all of his
father's manuscripts. Letters too. Finally, he got everything and had
control.

In any event, we were very good friends and Peter had an idea. He
wanted to record his father's violin and piano sonatas; his father had
given him the privilege of being the first to record the first piano
concerto. Peter asked me to record the solo sonata for him. He asked
me, "Do you have a copy of that score? If you don't we will have to
get you one. I'm going to give you the original. I've transferred it but
the original is nice to have." I have to say that I am not a great violinist. I'm not being overly humble. But that was the best that I have ever
played in my life. Joseph Szigeti wrote to me saying how tremendously
impressed he was with the recording. I treasure that.

We also did the first recording of the first violin and piano sonata.
We followed that recording with the second violin and piano sonata,
and by that time Peter was recording in stereo. Peter wanted to have
the piano concerto recorded and he asked Lee Hambro to play it. He
said to me, "Bobby, you and Lee are such great friends and I need a
conductor and you're a conductor so I want you to conduct."

I loved, loved this idea. Peter had a very unusual arrangement.
There was a cellist in the Boston Symphony, Josef Zimbler. who
played with a group in the summer that he called the Zimbler String

JOSEPH SZIGETI

·LE CRÉPON·
BAUGY S/CLARENS (SUISSE)

September 9th, 1963.

Dear Robert Mann,

Now that I have a little more leisure to listen to the recordings in my collection, I was at last able to give sufficient time to your recording of the Bartok Solo Sonata.

I have been wanting to tell you for several months now how tremendously impressed I am with your superb idiomatic playing of this challenging work. It is a sad reflection on the state of the phonographic industry that a recording of such authenticity should be practically unobtainable.

Of course your performance was no surprise to me, having owned and listened to your six Bartok quartets for several years now.

Do give my best regards to Rafael and to your other colleagues and try and look us up here when next year you are playing in Switzerland.

With all good wishes,

Cordially,

Joseph Szigeti

Szigeti letter to Robert

Sinfonietta. It was made up of musicians from the Boston Symphony who he paid to play concerts when they weren't playing in the Symphony. So, Peter had the Zimbler Sinfonietta hired for the recording. When Bator heard about this he said, "Absolutely not. Robert Mann. Who ever heard of Robert Mann as a conductor?" Bator went to his Hungarian friends, such as Fritz Reiner and Eugene Ormandy, who were all busy. Bator said that he would have Lee Hambro as the pianist. That was okay. But, for the conductor he said, "I want Tibor Serly." Tibor Serly was a fairly decent composer and musician who tried to be close to Bartók during his last days. So Bator felt that he was the right person to conduct since he understood Bartók very well.

The story continues. I wasn't there. I heard it from Eugene Lehner who was in the orchestra and from Leonid Hambro. Eugene and Lee went up to Boston for three recording sessions, and I was in New York. I got a call from Peter Bartók who said, "It's a disaster. We haven't got a recording." You know, recording, especially with an orchestra, is very expensive. You record for 45 minutes and then you take 15 minutes off. I learned later that Serly got in front of the Boston Symphony and talked for most of the 45 minutes. He told the orchestra what a difficult piece it was and how he's the only person that understood the music. He wanted to impress the orchestra, and went on and on.

So Peter asked me to visit him at his home in Riverdale to listen to the recording. Sure enough it was very sloppy. None of the tempi were any of the tempi that Bartók suggested on the parts. I said, "Well, I don't know what you can do. That's it." I got a call from Victor Bator who says, "I want to see you."

I went to see Bator and in his office he told me that they had already spent $9,000 (which was an enormous sum of money in those days) and the recording was way over budget. He said, "What we would like you to do is to listen very carefully to the tapes, and those places that are the worst, I want you to go up to Boston and have a session with the Boston Symphony members and re-record those spots so that we can make the splices." I said, "Excuse me, but I'm not going to do that. I'm sorry, Mr. Bator. That's not my interest and I don't want to do that." Then I left. A week later he called me back. He said, "First of all I have to tell you. I asked Fritz Reiner, Joseph Szigeti, and Yehudi Menuhin, what kind of a conductor you are. They all said that they didn't know, but they did know that you are a fine musician. They also all agreed that you could do it and that I could trust that you would get the record done. So, will you go up to Boston now? I'll give you two sessions, and record it." I was now in a bargaining position. I told Bator that I couldn't do that. I told him that he would have to postpone the recording for at least a month so that I would have time to study the score. I also would have to have his guarantee that if I needed a third session that he would give it to me.

So, I went to work and learned the entire orchestral score, one of the few orchestral scores that I memorized every note of. I went even farther. I got all of the parts and I remarked them. Everyone argues about what's written in the score. I had heard a lot of Bartók and I knew that the orchestra, for instance, wasn't making certain kinds of accents that Bartók wanted. The notes were either too short or too long. So I marked all of the parts. I also went to see my conductor friends, such as Jorge Mester. I asked him, "What should I do?" I told him what I was doing to prepare and wanted him to tell me what else I needed to do.

Finally, before I went to Boston, I talked to my friend Leon Barzin, who had been Toscanini's assistant. Leon was a very talented, marvelous conductor who really should have had much more recognition for what he did. He led the National Orchestral Association, which was a training orchestra for really marvelous young professionals who hadn't found jobs yet. I asked Leon if he could give me half a rehearsal to conduct this group to try out my conducting skills and to hear how the music that I had re-marked sounded. Lee went with me and we were given an hour and then it was time for a break. I got ready to leave and I thanked Leon and said, "This was just wonderful. I really learned a lot." Leon wanted to talk to me and he called me into his little Green Room. Then he blasted me, "Why? You're stupid. Why did you do this? Why did you do that?" He gave me hell and pointed out many places where he thought I had gotten it wrong. I told him thank you and got ready to leave again. He said, "Oh, no, no, no, no. I've decided that you should take the rest of the rehearsal. I want to see if you understand what I'm telling you." He was that kind of a guy. So I finished the rehearsal.

I went up to Boston and I took Rafe Hillyer, and also Jorge Mester. Rafe and I had gone through the score together. When we got to Boston to do the recording, Peter told me that there wasn't a place on stage where he could put his equipment. The orchestra was on the stage of Boston's Symphony Hall, not set up like they would be play-

Peter Bartók in his recording studio

ing a concert but sitting in a rectangle. The Boston Symphony members that I was going to conduct knew me from Tanglewood as a violinist and a quartet member. So when they saw me coming to conduct them, they thought, "Oh God, we have another amateur. We've already had an awful experience recording this piece." The first thing that I did when I got to the podium was to ask them to put my music stand away. I knew the score by heart and didn't need a score in front of me. I told the orchestra, "Now listen, you don't know me as a conductor. I've listened to the tapes and you know that they are really terrible. I really know what to do. I want to rehearse certain sections." So we started right off with the first movement. Within five minutes they knew that I not only was a good conductor, but that I knew what I was doing with the piece. I had Rafe and Jorge, who were in the recording room with Peter, alerted to what I wanted to accomplish. So we wouldn't waste time, I would say over the microphone, "Have I got what I talked about, or do we need to do it again?" They would answer yes or no. We recorded it in two days and the results were phenomenal.

When I went up to the recording booth, I was still holding my batons. Rafe looked morose and said, "I suppose we have to start looking for a new first fiddler for the Juilliard Quartet." And what I did was to break the batons and throw them out a window.

By the way, the sound Peter achieved in his recordings, acoustically, was very strange but fantastic. When I recorded the *Contrasts* with Stanley Drucker and Lee Hambro at Washington Irving High School downtown, he didn't have us on the stage but had us take our seats on the floor of the auditorium. And, when I recorded the solo sonata at the Pequod Library in Connecticut near Bridgeport, he would turn some seats over so that the wood was there and on other seats would leave the cushions on top of the seats. He was always listening to the sound.

Columbia Records

The Juilliard String Quartet had a recording relationship throughout our years with Columbia Records. The first great quartet to record with Columbia was the Budapest Quartet. So, in the early years the Juilliard String Quartet could only record those pieces that the Budapest would let us record. After all, the Budapest Quartet was the top dog. They weren't going to play Berg, so we recorded Berg. Goddard Lieberson, who was the president at Columbia Records, was very interested in American music, and so we also recorded all kinds of American composers. Much later, after Lieberson resigned from Columbia, we were asked to record the two Charles Ives quartets. At that moment, it wasn't the time for us to make a recording of Ives quartets. It wasn't that we didn't want to, but we had other things on our mind. Columbia came back to us and said that they needed to have those quartets recorded. We made a counter suggestion. We proposed if we were to record the two Ives quartets, would they let us re-record the Schoenberg quartets? We had recorded them much earlier in our career.

Lieberson had agreed and then left Columbia. We were told by Columbia that they would not agree to the arrangement and that it had all been Lieberson. Now he was gone and they wouldn't do it. I was very upset and at Lucy's suggestion, I called his son, the composer Peter Lieberson. I was sort of embarrassed, but I pleaded with him. I said, "Even though your father no longer works at Columbia, could you ask him to help us and to tell Columbia to honor their promise for us to record? He's a respected man." Peter's first response was no, "Don't lay it on me, Bobby." However, he finally did it. He went to his father and his father spoke to Columbia. And, very begrudgingly, Columbia allowed us to record the Schoenberg quartets again. For some absolutely weird reason, those Schoenberg quartets won the Grammy Award for chamber music that year. That usually doesn't happen, and the Grammy tends to be given to something more popular, like Perlman playing a Brahms trio or something. It was unbelievable.

We recorded about 150 pieces of music. I can't remember half of the recordings we made. We recorded many little weird works such as a little cantata by Milhaud, narrated by Madame Milhaud, as well as a sextet by Ellis Kohs, both for Columbia. I also remember that on our first trip to Europe, we recorded an early string quartet by Irving Fine, and a twelve-tone Norwegian composer. We recorded and performed in Oslo. That actually was one of the ways we were able to go to Europe that first time, by agreeing to record the Norwegian composer.

One time, Columbia Records wanted us to record Shubert's Trout Quintet, one of the greatest pieces of all time. They wanted us to use the pianist Murray Perahia and he refused to record with us. He said that the Juilliard String Quartet changes tempo when they play, for example, a melodic tune. In other words, he was saying that we, the Juilliards, didn't keep the tempo going from beginning to end. Well, we did admit that this was true.

Later we did play the Trout Quintet with Claudio Arrau at the Library of Congress. We also played the Franck and Dvořák quintets with him. He would never allow us to skip one repeat. He said every repeat was sacred. Once, when we were taking a break in a rehearsal at the Library of Congress in Coolidge Auditorium, we were sitting where the audience sits, just resting and talking to him. One of us asked him, "Claudio, why don't you ever play any contemporary music?" He answered that he just didn't feel comfortable playing music by contemporary composers. He said, "I'll show you." He got up on the stage and he played a Stockhausen piece from memory, about 21 minutes, and it was fantastic. When he was finished he came down and said, "You see, I don't really feel this music." But he was capable. He preferred to play contemporary music only at home for his own interest and curiosity.

And later, we played the Trout Quintet with a Naumburg winner, the Cuban-born American pianist Jorge Bolet. Bolet was a marvelous gentleman and a fantastic pianist who learned in a very interesting fashion.

We were scheduled to play our first performance with Bolet in London. Then we were going to play at the Library of Congress in Washington, D.C., followed by a performance in Alice Tully Hall. We had three performances scheduled. When he arrived in London to rehearse with us, it wasn't that he hadn't practiced the piece but he was completely ill at ease playing it. His genius was that after three rehearsals he played it beautifully. By the time we got to the Library of Congress, it was magnificent and by the time we played at Alice Tully Hall, I just wish that we had recorded that performance. It was one of the great performances of my life. It was fantastic.

Glenn Gould

We played with Glenn Gould, who we met through a Montreal-based critic friend of his. Glenn, of course, lived in Toronto. I don't know how Columbia got us together but the first thing we ever played with him was the Schoenberg *Ode to Napoleon* for narrator, piano and string quartet. He brought an actor friend of his down from Canada. The recording sessions were fascinating. He tried to show his actor friend how to do the narrations. I thought Glenn Gould was better than the actor friend. I remember whenever we took a break he would immediately start playing his own arrangements of Richard Strauss operas. He knew every note that Richard Strauss wrote and he would play and sing. He would say, "Now, here's this phrase from this opera, this act." He was just amazing.

The next recording we played with Glenn Gould was a Christmas record, for which he'd written a funny little oratorio. I can't remember the name of it but it involved a string quartet. He wanted very much for us to play it. He'd also written a long, serious string quartet that sounded a little like the composer Franck's language. In fact, he came to Bobby Koff's apartment to show us his piece. It was late at night and he was playing and singing his quartet very loudly and all of a sudden there was a knock on the door and a policeman was there and said, "You'd better stop this yakking or else we're going to have to do something about it."

We were happy with Glenn on most occasions when we were together. Columbia came to us again and said, "We want to put out an album of all Schumann. We want his three string quartets and you already played the quintet with Leonard Bernstein." Of course we wanted to do it. They asked, "Would you record the piano quartet with Glenn Gould?" Yes of course, that would be wonderful.

We arranged one rehearsal with Glenn during which the sound engineers would set up. By the second rehearsal they wanted to start recording. We didn't have a performance plan. Glenn was coming from Toronto by train; he never flew. He met us at the old Columbia recording studio which was located on the East Side. When he arrived, the first thing he said to us after we greeted each other was, "I hate the music of Robert Schumann." We started laughing and said, "Glenn, why are you doing this then?" His answer was, "Well, it's a challenge. We'll try to figure out a way to make it work."

He was very perverse. Where the score said legato, he played staccato; where it said crescendo he would make a diminuendo. I remember at one point, the scherzo has very quick eighth notes which are marked *pianissimo*, as soft as possible. Glenn said, "I am not going to play it that way. The recording equipment is perfect and I want to play it the way I play it. The sound engineers can bring the sound down in the control room. They can bring it down to pianissimo.

Glenn had great faith in technology. I remember another incident when we were listening in the recording room as a group and the telephone rang for Glenn. It was Jamie Laredo and they agreed to record all the Bach works for violin and clavier, also for Columbia. They were talking about arranging rehearsals and it seemed that whenever one was free the other was busy. We were listening to the entire conversation only hearing Glenn's side. Finally we hear Glenn say, "Well I have a suggestion—we really can do this. We will both get a room that has an amplifier for connections to telephone wires and I will play in Toronto with the piano and we can rehearse by telephone.

The Juilliard String Quartet was at Aspen when Columbia sent us the recording for our approval. We were outraged. Even though we loved Glenn Gould and it was fantastic playing, we thought that in the slow movement instead of hearing the beautiful cello solo all we heard was the *boom boom boom* on the piano. So, it was my job to call the head of Columbia Records' classical division and tell him that they couldn't release the record. He said, "Now look, I'm going to speak to you in terms you have to accept. First, Glenn Gould is one of our best classical sellers in the entire market. And, he means more to us than the Juilliard Quartet, even though we like the Juilliard Quartet. Secondly, besides playing this one piece you are playing three quartets by yourselves and also playing with Lenny. It's going to be a big album. I will make a vow to you. If you let it be released and it gets a bad review, I will take your wives or your girlfriends to the most expensive French restaurant in New York City. You will have a fantastic dinner if you get one bad review." Well, you know something. We never got a bad review. So we never got a meal.

I have to say something about that recording. I don't listen to my records at all, but every once in a while someone will tell me that they listened to that Schumann recording. Then I will go and listen to it myself. And when I do, I feel schizophrenic. It's one of the most thrilling performances you could ever listen to. But as a purist I don't like it.

Grammy Awards

In all, the Juilliard String Quartet won three or four Grammys and was nominated many, many times. We won a Grammy for our Ravel/

Debussy recording and also for our Bartóks. Actually, the Recording Academy has a Hall of Fame of Recording and our Bartók quartets are in that. In 2011 the Juilliard String Quartet itself was given a Lifetime Achievement award. That was quite a moment. Sitting next to Julie Andrews, who was also being given a Lifetime Achievement award, I thought about how lucky I have been to be successful doing what I love.

Past and present members of the Juilliard String Quartet at the Lifetime Achievement Awards ceremony, 2011

Robert and Julie Andrews at the Lifetime Achievement Award ceremony

[LUMINARIES]

Oscar Kokoschka

The summer after we played the Bartóks at Tanglewood, we stayed on South Mountain. I brought Lucy with me. At the same time, Oscar Kokoschka, the great expressionistic painter, had been hired by the people who ran South Mountain to teach an enormous class of painters. He immediately heard that the Juilliard String Quartet was studying and practicing and playing Schoenberg's third and fourth quartets. He was a great friend to Schoenberg and a lover of music and he asked permission to attend our rehearsal. That's how Kokoschka became a great friend to both Lucy and myself.

Later on, wherever the Juilliards played and Kokoschka was near us, he would show up with his wife Ann Ilda. For instance, when we played in Switzerland or Lausanne, he was there. I remember once we were invited by the daughter of Queen Elizabeth of Belgium, who had married the exiled king of Italy and ended up moving to Portugal for the rest of his life. In any event, the daughter had set up a chateau near Geneva. She wanted to emulate her mother, who had set up the Queen Elizabeth prize and competition and who had also played chamber music. The daughter wanted to start a contemporary music series in her chateau, about 18 kilometers east of Geneva. The Juilliard

Drawing of Robert by Oscar Kokoschka

String Quartet was invited to open the series and our program would be the five pieces of Webern, the first and third Schoenberg string quartets, and then the five Webern pieces repeated. She invited critics, musicians and friends from Paris, Berlin and all over. And, Oscar Kokoschka came to this concert too.

Anyway, our second violinist Bobby Koff had an irrepressible sense of black humor. We were shown a corner of an enormous grand room where we were going to play. And, when we were practicing all of a sudden a tall, thin gentleman wearing medals came up to us and said, "La Reine, the queen would like to meet you." So, the Queen approached us and we all stood up. The Queen was holding the score of the third Schoenberg string quartet. She said to us, very politely in English, "You know I've been studying this quartet that you are going to play tonight and I wonder if you can show me something about it that will help me appreciate it more when you play it tonight." Bobby Koff goes up to her, takes her score out of her hand, turns it upside down and says, "If you read it this way it might make more sense." She excused herself and left. We nearly died of embarrassment at Koff's black humor.

After the concert an enormous room was set up for a reception with all kinds of little card tables topped with the most delicious appetizers. Kokoschka came and sat down with us as well as a friend of his, an Italian woman who was married to a very famous European conductor named Igor Markevich. She was introduced to us as a Duchess or something. I said to her, "You know, the quartet has just made one of its first tours of Italy." I told her that when we were headed to Trieste, our violist, Rafe Hillyer, had arrived one day early. When we joined him, he told us, "Last night I went to a concert played by the La Scala Opera Orchestra and they wouldn't let them go. They had to play encore after encore after encore." He said, "We better have all kinds of encores ready because they are nuts for music." Hearing this we got ready and prepared a few encores. For that concert, first we played a Haydn quartet and there was hardly any applause as we left the stage. Then we played a Bartók quartet and there was even less applause. Then we played the Schubert "Death of a Maiden." We took a bow, got off the stage and the applause stopped. I said to the Duchess, "You are Italian, can you explain this to me? I thought and was told that the Italians love music. They didn't like us at all." The Italian Duchess said, "You have to understand something about us. People think we love music. We don't. We love words and that's why we love opera. I mean we just literally hang on to singing words. But chamber music, only a very small group of people like chamber music." Actually she was wrong. We played in lots of Italian cities and they loved chamber music.

In June of 1972, Lucy and I found ourselves in Switzerland with some time off. Knowing that Oscar Kokoschka was living nearby we contacted him by phone. He told us that he was delighted that we had called and proceeded to tell us that he would love to draw a portrait of me. He asked "When can you come by?" To which Lucy immediately responded, "how about tonight!" And sure enough, we had a dinner date that evening. With violin in hand, we showed up at his house. After a most enjoyable meal with Oscar and his wife, Oscar invited Lucy and me into the living room. His wife excused herself. Oscar brought out a bottle of Chivas and I took out my violin. I proceeded to play Bach while Oscar, seated in a chair, began sketching me using charcoal on large paper. The evening was full of music, scotch, painting, and friendship, with all of us getting quite drunk as the evening wore on. Time after time, Lucy and I would watch in horror as Oscar would tear up what looked like a wonderfully prom-

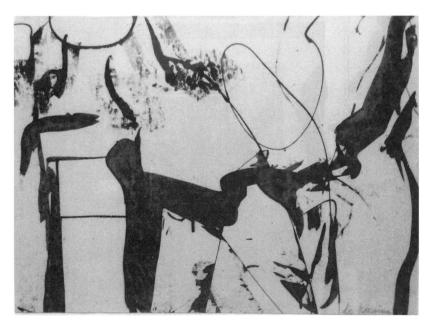

Ink drawing given to Robert by Willem de Kooning

ising sketch. Finally, late into the evening, he called into the other room for his wife. She came in, looked at the drawing he had in hand, and nodded her head in approval. Oscar proceeded to sign the drawing and handed it to Lucy and me. This portrait of me remains, to this day, one of my favorite possessions.

Willem de Kooning

At Juilliard there were some very interesting musicians and artists who had fled the Nazis. One of the most important was an architect, painter and sculptor by the name of Frederick Kiesler, who was friendly with the Juilliard String Quartet. One day he called us and said, "You know, we have a group, who are colleagues, painters, sculptors and we meet once a month down on Eighth Street. We call ourselves the Eighth Street Group. We like to invite guests who are related in the arts, and we would like to have you come and play for us." Well of course we were thrilled. After we played Kiesler apolozied for not being able to offer us a fee. We told him that we were not expecting to be paid. We were in for a big surprise. Kiesler then introduced us to a young blond artist who said, "I really enjoyed the evening. I have painted all black enamel on white paintings, and I'd like to give each of you one." That was Willem de Kooning and his painting is on the wall of my apartment. The other three quartet members sold their paintings over the years, but I wouldn't sell mine. I remember that Rafe didn't like the de Kooning painting at all and asked Bobby Koff if he liked it and wanted his. He gave it to Koff, and then changed his mind and took it back.

Albert Einstein

In 1952, the Juilliard String Quartet spent an evening with Dr. Albert Einstein in Princeton, following a Sunday afternoon concert at the university. Aware of Dr. Einstein's lifelong devotion to chamber music both as a listener and participant, we offered to play for him at his home. He graciously accepted. A fervent hope inspired a devious plan

Albert Einstein

that necessitated our bringing along an extra viola and the music of
Mozart's two viola quintets. He received us in a genial mood and
wearing extremely comfortable attire. As we played both Beethoven
and Bartók, he listened a room removed (not wishing for a visual dis-
traction), and, while he did not seem to share the general aversion to
twentieth-century music that seemed to infect his fellow physicists, it
was evident that Dr. Einstein's heart belonged to the earlier music.

After the Bartók we launched our surprise attack. Producing the
Mozart score and the extra viola, we said, "It would give us great joy
to make music with you." He protested that he had not played for
years due to a hand injury. With the insensitive exuberance of youth
we persisted, and he, the true scientist recognizing an irresistible force
versus immovable object contretemps, gently acceded to the inevita-
ble. Our second violinist handed his violin to Dr. Einstein, and picked
up the extra viola himself. Dr. Einstein without hesitation chose the
great, brooding G minor quintet.

Supersensitive to the great man's remark that he had not played in
seven years, from the very first sounds we regrouped around Dr. Ein-

stein in complete rapport with his deliberate but purposeful momentum: basking in the warm glow of making Mozart's music with this disarmingly unassuming human being. Slow, slower, and slowest crept each successive movement. In direct reaction to the slow tempi, the intensity of our manic happiness grew. Dr. Einstein hardly referred to the notes on the musical score (notes in his mind were never to be forgotten), and, while his out-of-practice hands were fragile, his coordination, sense of pitch, and concentration were awesome. The mood of the Juilliard String Quartet as we finished the Mozart was beatific. Time was late; we gathered instruments and reluctantly bid him goodbye.

At the door he, obviously satisfied that we had coerced him to join us, seemed to want to say more than just a thank you for the music. Finally, he remarked, "I love America and American musicians. They are wonderful. My only complaint is that like the tempo of life here in this country, American musicians tend to play their music too fast." I replied, "You know, Dr. Einstein, I am sorry to report that the Juilliard String Quartet is also accused of this indiscretion." He was silent—one could sense his thoughts touching on the evening's Mozart, so unhurried, so lovingly respectful of his own tempo desires. "You are criticized for playing too fast?" He shook his head and said, "I don't understand why."

Dudley Moore

The Juilliard String Quartet was first invited to the Edinburgh Festival in 1960 to play the Bartók quartets. It was memorable in a few ways. First of all, Isaac Stern was there with us. He had married a wife who didn't like him to be close to all of his former friends. So we would spend time together in other cities when we could. He flew in early so that he could spend a day with me in Edinburgh. He was also performing, but playing later than the Juilliard String Quartet. He came and we had a wonderful day, and that evening he said, "You know what we have to do? We have to go to something that has just opened, called Beyond the Fringe." They were a young bunch of boys,

Robert and Dudley, after their concert recital, 1981

two were from Cambridge and two were from Oxford, who were called Beyond the Fringe because their theatrical revue was considered fringe entertainment. Isaac wanted to go hear them because he had heard that they were just terrific. We went and they were fantastic. The audience was just delighted.

After, I went backstage to tell them how enchanted I was. Dudley Moore had played the piano in the show. He was very sweet and he asked me what I did. I told him that I was in the Juilliard String Quartet and we were at the Festival playing Bartók. He told me that he loved Bartók. So I said, "Well, would you like to come to our Bartók concerts?" His answer was yes and that began our relationship that lasted for many, many years. He even played the piano for my daughter's wedding. Beyond the Fringe was one of the most successful shows in all of theater history. They played in London, New York and worldwide. I used to stay with him in his London house and when he finally moved to America he visited us often. When he moved to Venice, California, I would stay there with him too.

When I visited him, we would spend every single minute that we weren't eating, reading every single piece of music that was written. We especially loved Bach and would play all of the Bach sonatas for clavier and violin. We played lots of Mozart and many other composers as well. Dudley could sight read anything. An interesting thing about Dudley's playing was that he never practiced with enormous vigor. Most pianists develop a lot of muscles to have weight and to be able to play strongly on the piano. That he couldn't do. Therefore, if you asked him to play a Brahms sonata, he'd play all of the notes, but it wouldn't have the depth of playing. If you picked the right piece for him he was fantastic. He could play Bach and Delius wonderfully.

He didn't play classical music in concert, however. At one point I said, "Dudley you have to play a concert." It took a lot of arm twisting and he finally said, "All right, let's pick a special program." So we concocted one and I got Hildy Lemogian from the Metropolitan Museum to present the concert on a Sunday morning. We opened with Bach and played a Delius sonata. I also got Joel Krosnick to play with us and all of the press came. That was the first time that Dudley ever played classical music in public, and he was scared silly. It was quite a triumph on every level.

One evening I invited Itzhak Perlman, Walter Trampler, Zara Nelsova, and Ani Kafavian to my apartment for an evening of chamber music. That same night, Dudley was performing his show *Good Evening* with Peter Cooke. They had a television show in England that was as famous there as the most successful television shows were in the United States. Anyway, after he was finished with the show he was coming over to be with us. When he arrived, I said to the group, "Would you like to play something with Dudley?" Itzhak Perlman, who is very humorous and likes to poke fun at things said, "What can he do? He plays musical jokes, how could he play classical music?" So I replied, "Well, what would you like to play with Dudley? We looked at the group and which instruments we had, and Itzhak said, "Do you have the music for the Chausson concerto for violin, piano and string quartet? I did. Itzhak said, "Well, ask Dudley if he'd like to play it with us."

Jorge Bolet said playing Chausson honestly is very, very difficult. Dudley looked at the score for about 5 minutes, flipping the pages and said, "I'll give it a try." He sat down at the piano and sight read it, note perfect. He had never seen it before, never even knew the piece existed. I saw every one of the musicians with their mouths dropping. After that, everybody was after Dudley to play with them.

I also played a concert with Dudley in Los Angeles that was a big success. My friend, Gerard Schwarz, who was the conductor of the Los Angeles Chamber Orchestra, was conducting a benefit concert in L.A. and I suggested that Dudley play for him. I said, "You know Dudley's terrific and he is a big person in California. Why don't we play the Beethoven Triple Concerto?" And so we did, with the Los Angeles Chamber Orchestra and cellist Nathaniel Rosen joining us. It was also suggested that we play the Beethoven Triple with the St. Paul Chamber Orchestra. They only wanted Dudley and suggested that the Triple Concerto be played with Yo-Yo Ma, however Dudley insisted that I and Nathaniel play the concert with him.

Lenny at recording session with the Juilliard String Quartet, 1959

As time went on, Dudley played more classical music in public, play-ing with musicians such as Lynn Harrell, the cellist. One of the pieces he began to play was Gershwin's *Rhapsody in Blue*. He was one of the most remarkable musical minds that I have ever known. Absolutely.

Leonard Bernstein

In the early 1980s, we played with Leonard Bernstein. We recorded the Schumann quintet and the Mozart G Minor piano quartet with him. The first time we played with him was at the Library of Congress. I remember at one point he asked me where he could find a post office. He had something important that he had to mail. I told him about the post office across the street from the Library of Congress and we walked over. He went up to the teller, a little old lady, and he mailed his letter. She looked up and she saw Leonard Bernstein. She said, "You know you're a very pleasant looking young man. I hope you have as much success as your famous namesake." Lenny was wonderful and of course we kept in close touch with him throughout the years, especially when he was giving his famous television lectures on music. I remember studying one of the Bach Brandenburg concertos with him. He would illustrate things. I also remember when he did a contemporary music evening. My God, it was an enormous barn of a studio and it had a full orchestra, a jazz orchestra, a children's chorus, and he wanted the Juilliard String Quartet. He asked us to play an Anton Webern bagatelle. We got ready to play and we were quietly sitting in our corner and there was all of this pandemonium going on until we approached the live performance of the broadcast. There were four or five minutes left before we were supposed to play. All of a sudden he started clapping and calling for silence. I mean it's enormous, maybe 300 people in this huge room. Everyone was silent and he said, "All right, Juilliard Quartet, I want to hear Webern before the program starts." We had chosen the one that starts with three instruments playing from almost no sound slowly growing into a crescendo. All of a sudden he said, "My God, I'll lose my entire audience. Out." So we didn't play Webern. We played Schoenberg instead.

Lenny was a very affable guy but he did have certain attitudes towards tempi. When we played the Mozart with him, he was very strong about the last movement rondo being somewhat slower than we liked to play it. We felt it was because he wanted to protect his playing, and didn't always have enough time to practice his piano part. But the recording is very good and the quintet is wonderful. Lenny was magnificent.

Menuhin, Ricci, and Stern

Three star violinists began their musical lives in San Francisco: Yehudi Menuhin was born first in 1916, then Ruggiero Ricci, in 1918, and finally, Isaac Stern in 1920. These three stars were recognized in their earliest years, even before grade school, by their parents and teachers as possessing unique gifts. These young men didn't understand their own abilities even as they began playing their instruments.

Roger, as we called Ricci, possessed the spirit of Paganini: small of stature, with giant hands that encompassed the greatest command of violin playing I have ever known. He played Paganini's caprices in his sleep. A composer named Vitorio Gianini wrote super athletic variations on the Paganini *24 Variation Caprice*, reinventing not just fingered tenths but fingered twelfths. The rest of us were in awe of Roger's ability to do this. We were jealous.

Yehudi was different. I first heard him in recital in Portland, Oregon. We were both young teenagers. He could move an audience to tears, as he did then with Bach's *Ciaccona*. At age 10 he played a masterful Beethoven violin concerto with an orchestra. I was equally talented, but my realm of accomplishment was catching rainbow trout with a fly-rod in Oregon coastal streams.

Many, many years later, I boarded an airplane to Buffalo, New York and found my seat next to Mr. Menuhin, as I called him. Ensuing conversation involved Béla Bartók's solo violin sonata, which I wanted to learn. I had become passionate about Bartók's music. Menuhin had commissioned this particular work from Bartók and his recording of it was marvelous. I told him that I had heard he had made a lot of changes that were not in the printed edition. He was very nice about it and said, "I'll make a copy of the manuscript and send it to you." In those days you didn't have Xerox machines. And he did that for me.

To my amazement, I discovered many differences in the manuscript Menhuin sent me. Besides the fact that there were quite a few changes in the first two movements, I found that in the last movement Bartók wrote microtones—in other words, quarter tones. Instead of going chromatically up half tones he went chromatically up using quarter tones and even used some third tones and so on. It had a completely different quality when I looked at it. Menuhin explained that he had suggested changes to the composer and Bartók had complied with alternate passages, the most consequential being the elimination of those micro-quarter tones in the last movement. So, that's the way I recorded it. After that, everyone in the entire musical world who played the violin said, "Where did you get that version? You know we don't know anything about that version. It wasn't in the edition that Menuhin released." Bartók's son Peter published it with the original notes and I was teaching those microtones changes to every violinist who wanted to play the piece in its original form. When Peter asked me to record the original version with the microtones, I could not say no. After the record's release many violinists including Joseph Szigeti asked: "where did you find this different version?"

My acquaintance and friendship with Isaac Stern began in a totally different fashion. I first heard him play in Portland as a kid. I was two days older then he was. We were both born in 1920. I was born on July 19th and he was born on the 21st. He came from San Francisco and as a young violinist played the Saint-Saens B Minor Concerto. I remember how he played it. I didn't know him, but I remember I went backstage and shook his hand because my teacher was the concertmaster of the Portland Symphony.

In 1939, at age nineteen, while I was attending the Juilliard Graduate School in New York City I developed an extremely painful stomach ulcer. The prescribed treatment was drinking a lot of milk, which I did every day in the school's student lounge after a class or practicing session, and I would schmooze with people who came in and out. One day a stranger was sitting in that space. He was somewhat older, and didn't appear to be a musician. After some conversation about the state of chamber music, he said, "You know, I am not a musician. My name is Hy Goldsmith. I'm a physicist who teaches at Columbia University and loves music." He wanted to know if I enjoyed playing string quartets

Musical discussion: Robert with Isaac Stern and Sasha Schneider, 1955

and I responded with a sweeping critique of what was wrong with most current chamber music performances. I knew everything, you see.

He looked amused and quietly said, "I have some musician friends who come to my apartment for informal string quartet evenings. Would you like to come sometime? You will have ample opportunity to demonstrate the proper approach to playing chamber music." I thought why not and said, 'when?' He replied "tomorrow night."

I took an elevator at the appointed time to the top of his building, the Oliver Cromwell on 72nd Street near Central Park. I landed on the 35th floor and knocked on the door and who should open it but Isaac Stern. I was taken a little aback because I knew that Isaac was a good player. Seeing him, my ulcer cried out, but I entered this physicist's penthouse domain overlooking major portions of Manhattan to the north, south, east, and west. Quite a few people were already assembled at one end of the large room; they turned out to be a mix of scientists, doctors, professors, and other chamber music lovers all ready to listen. At the other end of the room were four music stands and chairs. The next knock at the door produced William Primrose, the great violist. Now I'm thinking, "What did I get myself into?" A few moments later, in walks the six foot, three-inch Gregor Piatigorsky holding his cello case with one hand.

After some introductory social interplay I quietly sat down with my violin in the second violin chair, waiting for my eminent new colleagues to produce music on the stands and join me for an evening's reading of Haydn, Mozart, Beethoven and Brahms. We slowly tuned up to the 440A pitch given by Isaac. Just as we were about to start, Hy Goldsmith, my scientific host and new friend, leaned down and whispered into my ear, "Okay, Bob, show us what chamber music is all about." Chamber music is a different medium than concertos and virtuosic athletic show-off pieces. This was the music that I had cut my teeth on from an early age. Surprisingly, and much to my relief, I could easily hold my own place with the eminent others.

Robert with Dorothy Delay and Itzhak Perlman, Perlman Master Class, Juilliard, 1989

Itzhak Perlman

I first heard about Itzhak Perlman from Dorothy Delay, who was at that time Ivan Galamian's assistant at Juilliard. She told me that I had to hear this young violinist who was only thirteen years old, studying with them and an amazing talent. Later, when Itzhak was a bit older, he would come and play for me in our apartment north of Juilliard, which was then on 123rd Street and Broadway. It was actually Toby, Itzhak's girlfriend (and future wife) who pushed him to do so, because, she said, I was one of the few people who would tell him the truth about his playing! Toby, herself a violinist, was studying chamber music with me at the time and loved how I challenged them to think about the music. She wanted Itzhak to have that experience too. Toby and Itzhak would also come just to visit Lucy, me, and the kids, and Toby would help our son Nicholas to practice. We would hang out, enjoy each other's company, and became close friends.

Through the years I have seen Itzhak become a superstar. My respect for his musical ability is profound. Our collaborations have taken many forms, including his premiering (with Sam Sanders) a composition, Chiaroscuro, I wrote especially for him, at a Carnegie Hall recital in 1975. Our friendship is a history filled with tremendous memories and shared experiences.

Seiji Ozawa

There is no one, besides my quartet colleagues, with whom I have a more deeply meaningful musical relationship than the conductor, Seiji Ozawa. I first heard of Seiji's remarkable talents from his teacher and my friend, Hideo Saito, at the Toho School in Japan. Over the span of the next fifty years, I had the joy to collaborate and work with Seiji on numerous occasions.

I have many fond memories of teaching at Seiji's International Academy for quartets in Switzerland, and have performed, conducted, and taught over the years at his Matsumoto Festival in Japan. My bond with Seiji is both personal and musical, but at the heart of it lies our

Robert with Seiji at his International Academy
PHOTO CREDIT: TANIMICHI OKUBO

shared set of core musical values. It was only fitting that my very last concert with the Juilliard String Quartet took place in Tanglewood, in the Ozawa Hall, with Seiji in the audience.

Modern Jazz Quartet, John Lewis, Billy Taylor

In the early days the Juilliard String Quartet played with the Modern Jazz Quartet. John Lewis and his quartet were marvelous guys. I don't know how we got together but we played quite a few concerts with them. We were even invited to play a joint concert in Carnegie Hall.

We played first, I think it was Schubert's "Death and the Maiden." Then the Modern Jazz Quartet played, and then we played arrangements that John Lewis made for us to play together. Of course the audience was absolutely wild, and we had to go out and play encores. We had rehearsed John Lewis's version of the D Major Suite for string orchestra. Right when we were ready to go out on the stage, I realized that I didn't have my music—and we had only gone through it once. So in front of almost three thousand people I improvised my part, and John Lewis was smiling at me the entire time.

We also later played with Billy Taylor and his Trio. We even received a commission in Wisconsin for Billy Taylor to write a piece for string quartet and jazz trio, Homage.

The Smothers Brothers Television Show

The Juilliard String Quartet was asked to play on the *Smothers Brothers Comedy Hour* television show in 1968. Although some people said we shouldn't do it and then criticized us for "stooping so low," Josef Gingold, one of the great violin teachers said "More people watched you on that show than all the people in the audiences in the history of the Juilliard String Quartet combined."

PART IV

Looking Back

[RENAISSANCE MANN]

Teaching

In the early Juilliard String Quartet days, we were not given the role at Juilliard to teach chamber music. Hans Letz, a German violinist who had been concertmaster of the Chicago Symphony and played with the Kneisel Quartet, was still very alive and teaching quartets at Juilliard. I was given the job of teaching sonatas with a class of ten violinists and three pianists. At first, I was very frightened because most of the players could play rings around me as instrumentalists. After I heard them play I realized that their technique was built for Paganini and show-off music. When it came time to play Beethoven and Mozart I knew more about the technique of producing the sound and the phrasing than they did. I was very relieved. I was also very free-wheeling. If it was a beautiful day, I would suggest to all of the students in my class to take a nice hike. So we would walk down to the ferry on 125th Street, and I would pay the five cents each that it would cost to go over to New Jersey. Then we would walk on the trails along the Hudson River. There were no buildings on the other side. We would walk to the George Washington Bridge which wasn't finished yet, and climb on the bridge and walk back to New York.

In the mid-1980s, the Juilliard String Quartet taught at Michigan State University in East Lansing (see Part V). One of the quartets we taught was from China, brought over to Michigan State by Walter Verdhr. I was coaching this quartet, and the violist seemed very uncomfortable. He didn't seem to be a natural violist and I mentioned this to the interpreter. The interpreter told me that a few months earlier an order came from Beijing that fifty violinists would have to become violists. That is how he began playing the viola.

When I left the Juilliard String Quartet, I still was a strong teacher of chamber music at both Manhattan School of Music and Juilliard. I love teaching chamber music. I think that everyone who has spent an enormous amount of time and involvement in their art form

Robert coaching at Seiji Ozawa's International Academy, Switzerland

Robert coaching at the Robert Mann String Quartet Institute, Manhattan School of Music, 2012

doesn't want to just impart those things through a single performance to an audience. I always found that getting young people to play the way I felt about the music was one of the most fulfilling things in my life. There is nothing more important than imparting your knowledge and inspiring the next generation with your passion. Every year since the early days I have taught about five or six quartets. After retiring from the Juilliard String Quartet in 2012, I began The String Quartet Institute at the Manhattan School of Music. A week of intensive quartet coaching, with daily master classes, streamed live, has been a highlight of my teaching life. Numerous young talented quartets have participated, too many to name. There is nothing I find more rewarding than exploring the world of quartets with the young,

Robert at Seiji Ozawa's International Academy, Switzerland, 2009

bold, and adventurous groups of today. Taking in what we give them, the quartets that we have taught then develop an equally meaningful way to perform the music. Hearing them find their own voice gives me the greatest pleasure of anything.

Conducting

I had a talent for conducting. People said that I was a good conductor and for a short time I began to contemplate maybe being a conductor rather than a violinist. I always found that for me playing the violin was a struggle and I didn't find that with conducting. The main problem with conducting isn't how you physically move your body in relationship to the players you conduct, but is knowing the score. I mean you really have to know the score backwards and forwards. I would memorize the score. In the end, however, I couldn't give up playing chamber music.

Robert conducting the International Academy student orchestra, Switzerland

Composing*

IN THE WORDS OF NICHOLAS MANN (1992):

At Juilliard my father studied composition with Wagenaar, who opened his eyes to Schoenberg and Berg. He also met Stefan Wolpe, who took an interest in his compositions and greatly influenced his compositional development. He also benefited from his role as arranger, transcribing everything from *Rhapsody in Blue* to *Scheherazade*, to even the Brahms *Double* for piano trio.

Very early on my father became interested in setting words to music. When he met my mother he had an added inspiration—she was an actress. He began to put the fairy tales of Hans Christian Anderson and *Just So Stories* by Kipling to music for violin, piano, and narrator. One year my parents made a tape of them to send to friends for a Christmas present. They were so well received that the Lyric Trio was born, and my father began composing for narrator in earnest. There are probably more than thirty works he has written in this genre. Several of them are recorded on Bartók Records and the Baca Ensemble on Musical

---

*   Robert Mann's compositions are published by Peer Music.

Heritage. My sister, Lisa, and I began to join in giving children's concerts that centered around these works (we became the Lyric Trio + Two). Recently my father has set both Native American and Chinese poetry to music.

One of my father's first major successes as a composer came as a result of the conductor Dimitri Mitropoulos, who was an early supporter of the Juilliard String Quartet. Mitropoulos saw a narration work of my father's entitled "The Terrible Tempered Conductor." He was very impressed with the work but was bothered by the humorously negative image of a conductor. He asked my father to write another piece for him to perform. This was the origin of "Fantasy for Orchestra." On finishing the work my father brought it to Mitropoulos during the intermission of a New York Philharmonic concert. Mitropoulos noticed that the work ended softly. "Couldn't you bring back a climactic moment to end the work? Soft endings are so problematic." Unhappy, but not wishing to lose a unique opportunity to have his piece performed, my father agreed to the suggestion. Elliott Carter, Pierre Boulez and Peter Mennin came to hear the New York Philharmonic at the dress rehearsal. Carter turned to my father: "very good but it sounds like you tacked on the ending." My father's respect for Carter as a composer immediately grew greater. But maybe Mitropoulos was correct. The work was a success and Mitropoulos took it on tour to Vienna and Salzburg with the Vienna Philharmonic*.

----

* **Eleanor Roosevelt, "My Day" column**
NEW YORK—Saturday night I heard a most delightful concert by the New York Philharmonic conducted by Dimitri Mitropoulos at Carnegie Hall. The soloist was a pianist, Mr. Jean Casadesus, and of course I confused him with his father and was surprised to see such a young man coming on the stage. He played beautifully and I enjoyed his performance very much. The orchestra played a Fantasy for Orchestra by Robert Mann. Mr. Mann is the leader of the Juilliard String Quartet but I had never heard one of his compositions before. I found it interesting but I am not sure that modern music is easy for me to understand on the first hearing . . .

Eleanor Roosevelt, "My Day, February 27, 1957," *The Eleanor Roosevelt Papers Digital Edition* (2008), accessed 1/15/2017, https://www2.gwu.edu/~erpapers/myday/displaydoc.cfm?_y=1957&_f=md003734a.

Those people who are unaware of my father's life as a composer are always surprised by the large output of his compositions. The La Salle and Concord String Quartets performed his "Five Movements for String Quartet." Itzhak Perlman commissioned a duo and premiered it with Sam Sanders in Carnegie Hall. My father has also written a duo for cello and piano for Joel Krosnick and Gil Kalish. This past December the Juilliard Symphony premiered his "Concerto for Orchestra" in Alice Tully Hall, with the composer also serving as conductor—another of his little-known but often performed roles.

Those who have worked with my father as teacher are aware of how strongly he feels that to truly understand the creative process the performer, or re-creator, should experience the world of creation. For my father though, composing is not just a hobby but a real passion and an important part of his musical life. He has never pursued the political necessities of furthering his career as composer. He simply loves to compose and has something special to offer the musical world.

[MUSINGS]

My mother always loved to sing. She sang in the Portland Symphony Chorus throughout the time she lived in Portland. When she came to New York she immediately looked around and found out that they needed singers in the Brooklyn Symphony Chorus, so she would go by subway to every rehearsal and concert. She sang for years with the Brooklyn Symphony Chorus until she became too old to take the subway, I think she was in her seventies by then, and then she joined the YMHA chorus. The interesting thing is that they didn't only perform ordinary music. She sang everything from Bach to Stravinsky and even Copland. In her way she developed her own musical repertoire and attitude towards music.

My mother was inordinately proud of what I accomplished. All mothers are proud, but she loved the fact that I had made a success playing the violin. She lived until she was 93. Although my father died in his late 60s, he also knew I had become a successful violinist and that my sister was a pianist. What is too bad is that he didn't live long enough to see my brother's success as well.

I remember when we first moved to Tillamook I was nine, and my brother, Alfred, who was five years younger, was four, and my sister, Roz, was eight years younger. Rozzie started to study piano when she was four or five and we still lived in Tillamook. I have a wonderful

Alfred, Rosalind, and Robert, c. 1943–45

memory of the three of us from those days taken at a parade. We had a scooter and Rozie is dressed in a princess outfit and one of us was wearing a dog suit. The main thing that I remember from this time is that my brother was always tagging after me and I didn't like it.

My brother was a very good student but music wasn't his thing. He did try playing the cello, then a bassoon and the oboe, but none of them took. I went off to study music in New York but Alfred stayed in Oregon. He went to Oregon State as I remember and went into science. But my father bought a lemon grove in California and he took the family down and Alfred transferred to UCLA as a physics major while helping my father with the lemon grove. World War II started and Alfred went into the Air Corps and was a navigator. After the war he went back to Los Angeles and completed his studies. He got married and went to work in the experimental research department of Technicolor, which was part of the film industry. He was always causing his superiors trouble because he was discovering mistakes in their

Anna and Charles Mann with Lisa, c. 1953–54   Anna Mann, later years

projects. Finally, he became disgusted and announced to the family
that he had some ideas of his own that he'd like to develop but he
needed some capital. I remember Lucy and I gave him $2000, and my
mother and father gave him $6000. He got a few other thousand from
other people. He started in his garage to work with solar cells, refrac-
tion of light. This was his interest at that time and he worked very
hard, day and night, to create his own company. He was a fantastic
worker, much more than I am. The company that he started won a
national contract to build an environment on the earth with the hottest light that could be thrown on the outsides of space capsules, to see
how they would resist the heat. He won that contract against companies such as Bausch and Lomb. Next, he presented his approach to
outfitting space shuttles with power-generating solar cells. Again, he
won the national contract beating out all the major companies. I'm
telling you the truth—his solar cells powered our spacecraft to the
moon. Eventually, his company was bought out by Textron, a big
corporation, and he became a vice president of Textron, the company.
Later he presented an idea to build a twenty-square-mile solar cell
farm in southern New Mexico and Arizona to produce cost-effective
power for the United States. He became a lobbyist for big companies
but eventually became disgusted with politics. Having made many

contacts in the medical profession, he decided to put his energy into medical technology. I'll be brief. He developed many companies and made enough money that he has now given $100 million each to both USC and Johns Hopkins University, as well as similar donations to Technion University in Israel. He was named businessman of the year in Business Newsweek. As I write this, he has eight companies and is considered one of the great entrepreneurs of our time. I wish my father could have seen his accomplishments*.

PHOTO CREDIT: CHRISTINE BUTLER COURTESY OF MANHATTAN SCHOOL OF MUSIC ARVHIVES

Robert with his sister, Rosalind, his brother, Alfred, and Alfred's wife, Claude, 2009

---

*   Alfred passed away on February 25, 2016.

[LEAVING THE JUILLIARD STRING] QUARTET AFTER 51 YEARS*

THERE ARE CERTAIN CHALLENGES WHEN YOU ARE EARNING A LIVING as a string quartet. You have to travel a lot. For instance, the Library of Congress was wonderful but we always had to travel to Washington from our home in New York. During that time, I would be away from my family in fall and spring at least eight times, each trip lasting three to five days. I finally came to the conclusion, after close to 6,000 chamber music concerts on every continent except Africa and Antarctica, that I'd had enough of chamber music as a profession. I didn't have to give up playing music. I could still get together with friends to read music. But I didn't want to work constantly for three-hour rehearsals every day.

My last concert with the Juilliard String Quartet took place at Tanglewood in July of 1997. We played Beethoven, including Opus 130 with the "Grosse fugue" and, following a number of curtain calls, the slow movement from Beethoven's Opus 135 that I dedicated to Lucy.

When I left the quartet it was my hope that the quartet would choose Joel Smirnoff to be the first violinist—luckily they did exactly that.

If people thought that leaving the Juilliard String Quartet was my move towards retirement, they obviously do not know me. More time

---

★   Written in 2009.

PHOTO CREDIT: *BOWING OUT,* A FILM BY ALAN MILLER, BROADCAST ON BRAVO
Bowing Out, *documentary of Robert's last performance with the Juilliard String Quartet*

to compose, still many opportunities to perform, and teaching, which has always been a pivotal part of my musical being, continues in full force. Coaching students, I'm just as involved as if I am playing it myself and I still get my musical addiction fix because I play a number of chamber music concerts a year with a makeup group, including my son Nicholas on viola. My ears are keen and my mind is active. I will continue to play and to teach as long as I can. My life has been a journey filled with deep conversation, musical, intellectual, and collaborative. And I have tried to live as I have counseled the many students who have graced my life and to whom I gave the commencement address in 2000, at the North Carolina School for the Arts:

"All my life I have operated on the principle that small is beautiful. Don't fear being a missionary in a small geographical area. There is the right time for expansion and gratification. Don't ever give up the search to discover that place and that opportunity which keeps your spiritual inside love alive . . . I still believe that the greater satisfaction lies in the effort and not the attainment . . . My wish is that when you reach my age, you can affirm as I do that this life of artistic involvement has been and still is *the best of all possible lives.*"

Robert Mann String Quartet Institute publicity

PART V

Remarks from Coaching Sessions

[MICHIGAN STATE UNIVERSITY]
Transcriptions from Coaching Sessions 1979-83

Development and Technique

DEVELOPMENT

. . . What happens in the beginning when we are learning to make music, we become kind of primitive computers—programmed to do certain things. In the beginning you have to be programmed. Put your finger down there. Put your finger down there. That's programming. The fascists and authoritarians get their roads built and their trains run on time. Everything is programmed. This reaches to a very deep point. Today you have more instrumentalists playing more perfectly all over the world. It's just incredible. I can name 200 violinists who can play every concerto perfectly right now. I can name them—their first names, even. The point is that out of those 200 there are maybe 3 1/2 who can say something or make me feel personalized about it. They are all programmed.There is no supreme way of doing something. You yourself change over the years. If you're that inflexible, you're going to die of rot. You have to be flexible. That's what growth is about.

. . . That's just the point. We are full of all kinds of mistakes and quibbling and things are imperfect, but when a crisis comes and we finally get it all together, we behave in a much more accomplished way. We are not programmed.

. . . Even if you make the wrong choices, that's good. That's what democracy is about.

. . . Everybody likes to be seduced. Everybody likes to be tickled, teased, and pleased. There is no doubt that the senses—the hedonistic senses, in the cheapest sense, are appealing to everybody.

. . . We learned something with our children, and it really worked. I only did it out of fanaticism, but I did it, and by God, it paid off fantastically. We never prevented our children from certain things. In other words, there are lots of "don'ts" in this world. We keep saying no. What we did: we even figured out symbolic ways to make it even more meaningful.

We would give each child a day once a year—not a birthday, but a day. And on that day, apart from taking a gun and pulling the trigger and killing their parents, they could do anything they wanted—from the time they were four years old. They could smoke cigarettes—as much as they wanted. They could drink whiskey or beer if they wanted—they didn't want it—they could drive a car—I would get them up on my seat. We could find a place where there was a parking lot or something. They could drive a car. They could stay up all night. . . . If they wanted as much candy—10 tons of candy . . . They could do anything. So from the age of four, they kept thinking. They would spend half a year preparing for what they were going to do on their day. They could even tear up clothes they didn't like. Anything they wanted.

And do you know—my kids are much more straight-laced than I am. They don't smoke. They don't drink. They would defend anybody's right to take marijuana or do anything like that, but they don't smoke it themselves. They are practically, I think, boring in that regard.

But the point is, it worked. The psychology of doing anything and letting yourself try everything ends up being more selective and more subjectively aesthetic and discriminating than if you say "I won't let myself do something." But your inner fuses are hankering for things you don't quite understand, because the interesting thing is that the cheaper things are cheaper, not by virtue of the fact that they are more available or something, but because if you keep doing them enough, they don't give you the same satisfaction. They are more shallow in terms of what they pay off in the end. They get more boring.

. . . The first step toward real development is recognition. For instance, putting it in terms of my own problems: I generally tend to over-energize too much of my music making and not lyricize —I'm very lyric when it's obvious—but to create lyric elements in areas where I maybe concentrate on rhythmic . . . The only way to grow on that level is first by recognizing it and not being defensive— "Well, that's what I'm about, and that's the way I'm going to make music."

. . . Recognition. You should hear yourself for what you are. There should be no false vanity. As a matter of fact, your ego is in better shape if you accept what's not good rather than trying to defend with some false defense because that's going to crumble anyway. It can't last if it's defending something that's bad by saying it's good. It's not going to last. That's why, for instance, I always feel that America, as a country, doesn't recognize its own self-interest into the future. It's always trying to think of the immediate future but thinking about it in a way that's going to be against it in the long run and eventually make it harder for us. If we don't see the Third World's health as being part of our health, we're in trouble.

. . . Let me tell you something: there is a rub in everybody's situation. If you live your exemplary lives and end up in heaven, you're going to find a rub there too—I know it—just to keep life interesting.

TECHNIQUE

. . . The true technique is what   it's like a pitcher in a baseball game. If you pitch an effective ball but it means that in six months your arm is torn to pieces and you can't pitch any more, that's not good technique. But if you happen to pitch in a crazy way, and it's all wrong, according to the books, and you can pitch that way for the rest of your life and nobody can hit the ball—that's technique. Isn't it? Right. I've never said that before. I think that's a good way to formulate what is technique.

In other words, I think it is good technique—whatever you're do-ing—if it produces the sound you want. What you're looking for is the sound—not a beautiful look. Because if the sound is lousy, what's the good of the look?

Rehearsal and Performance

REHEARSAL

. . . Quartets come to grief when they fight to the death about what they're going to do. No way. Take your ego and leave it at home. Try it different ways.

You're talking to someone who has been through seven quartet marriages, so I know what I'm talking about. I know where the grief comes. You have to keep all options open. That doesn't mean you don't have a preference. But you don't attach so much meaning as to which preference gets its day. What generally happens in a quartet is that when you live an idea long enough, you get used to it, and you like it, even though you were once diametrically opposed to it. That happens.

. . . I can only tell you what we do in our rehearsals. Our rehearsal is four people listening to their own sounds and to other people's sounds and feeling free to say anything about anybody's sound includ-ing their own. And the rehearsal is taken up about 50% in deciding which options we want to try and not talking but trying them. And the other is if they are not succeeding, is it because it's not such a good idea, or is it that technically something is in the way of what any one individual is doing? And then the minute we decide well, you're not really doing what we had in mind—what we think should happen there—the other three, as well as that person, say, "Would you try up bow, would you try down bow, would you try pressure, would you try different fingering? Everything is open. And I think that has to be in any kind of rehearsal technique. If you don't do that . . . I'm going to be much more pragmatic. It's like an oil search. You can look on the surface and your instincts say there's not enough oil there; but in a desperate circumstance you might come back and underneath you'll find there's an enormous amount of oil. There are sometimes enormous riches in places where you might not suspect them.

I've learned more about my own fiddle playing from my colleagues than I have from myself. And of the four people in the quartet, in terms of sheer technical know-how, I'm the most self-taught of the bunch because I do everything cockeyed wrong. They learned and rightly from the right teachers, so they know what I'm doing wrong when it doesn't sound right. So you've just got to get that in your system.

. . . Don't be constantly trying to find every single possibility. Find some that really hit you, but just know that your life is committed, in a way, to not stop because you happen to do a thing a certain way. You might find a better way tomorrow. The Juilliard String Quartet, we are still doing this with Beethoven. We are constantly working on things and changing shapes or feelings. I just want you to be aware that as your experience gathers, you will begin to eliminate. We have one advantage to you. We have done it so much that many of the possibilities are eliminated in our own minds, and usually the four of us come up with maybe a dozen possibilities of shaping a movement and every moment in it.

. . . My point is you're putting the cart before the horse. Don't get a concept and then find out whether the materials fit the concept. Get the materials into your blood stream and then you all of a sudden find a concept that is there in the material.

PERFORMANCE

. . . Everybody plays better in their own rooms than in the concert hall. Playing for your own pleasure and playing for other people as well is a real gauntlet. You have to decide early in your life—is this for me?

. . . Talent is a funny thing. I'm fairly cynical about talent. I've seen many hotshot talents come to our school. At 18 they are fantastic but 21 are they still growing and by their 30s, have they have become fabulous musicians?

My daughter, when she would dance—she was in the Metropolitan Opera ballet school—she was fantastic. When she played the piano, she was fantastic. When she would play a phrase, it would just melt everybody's heart out. But she was too anxious to become a performer.

My son, who is more shy, like you, is not so certain. But every time he gets up—we just played the Sinfonia Concertante by Mozart—and he played like I never heard him play before. He is a performer. It is just fabulous how he can get past this point. That takes a kind of courage—or maybe it's an element in the personality.

. . . Courage. There is a funny thing about courage. For instance, I have had a kind of cowardly courage. It could be something like driving a car—in a difficult place and all of a sudden you see something on a mountain road. There's no room on either side, and you're afraid you may slip. At the last moment you close your eyes. That's cowardly courage. You have to accept it. That kind of courage is bad on an instrument.

There's another kind of courage. Like last night I shifted at the end of Opus 18. I have often missed it. But last night I said what the hell, and I didn't miss it, I didn't close my eyes or my ears. That kind of courage follows through and keeps on top of things.

It's like cold water. You think you don't want to get in. But once you jump in, you discover it is pretty good, and then it's all right. You have to get in the habit of doing it.

. . . If you have an instinct for a direction, allow yourself to move. Let's just experiment and see if it works. If it doesn't, you can throw it out.

There are very few—I don't even know if they're lucky—individuals who have a kind hubris. They don't even know what nervousness or timidity or lack of confidence is. For the rest of us mortals, the challenging and the struggle is to do something positive and not worry too much about whether it is going to succeed or not.

I'm not asking you to go for broke in such a way that My God you start missing the bow and running out of bow and the fingers don't coordinate and all of those things. But I just urge you at every point—give a little more, give a little more.

. . . When somebody says, "How much does spontaneity play a part in your performance?" My first answer is, "A damn lot. It's constant." But the second qualifying answer is, "It's on a very minute level." In other words, somebody doesn't start a new tempo just all of a sudden or start playing much louder than you have expected, or phrasing it different, etc. You don't do that. But you have constantly a small amount of selectivity or options and you respond to somebody happening to play a certain note—and you play a little more—or you play a little less—or you play two notes a little bit closer together or a little bit farther apart. You spread them—you do this—you do that. You play a little more intense. You articulate just a little bit more or a little bit less. This constant spontaneity is part of what I want you to do in terms of selectivity of which notes you bring out. In other words, listen and "Ah, no, yes . . . "

. . . The tendency of all personalities is to reach high points and then to subside back into comfortable almost non-existence existence in which you don't have to put out much.

. . . Now let's talk about the direction of phrasing. The interesting thing is—one has a lot more flexibility before it sounds like you're actually running out or losing control—Most people . . . we all have a tendency to be static. You listen to . . . As a matter of fact, it's become almost part of the ideal of today's performance. You know why most of today's performances are more bland than in the past? Some critics like to use the word it's the "modern" approach—objective. Everything is more even-handed, everything is more perfect—but literally without flavors.

. . . The very concern with being in tune, making a beautiful sound, etc. is an inhibiting factor. The best performances "let go."

. . . Understating and overstating. An understatement must make you conscious of those nuances. If you play like a computer, you are inhuman. Exaggerate. Don't confuse the style with the events.

. . . This is a fascinating problem about quartets vs. playing quartets in string versions. All the conductors I've known and some I don't know die to conduct late Beethoven quartets in a string orchestra version. They even say that the Grosse Fugue is better. No way! Every time I've listened to it—and I mean good conductors, like Mitroupolos and Bernstein and others—they do it. But what happens is there's something about a group of strings, no matter how marvelous they are—and the most cohesive I've ever heard was Toscanini who used to love to do Opus 135, the slow movement and scherzo with the NBC String Orchestra—there's something that depersonalizes the intensities or the personal quivering expressive quality that four people struggling with the sound can get. The struggle is part of the message. They don't have to struggle. Twenty strings playing sound like that . . . instead of one guy practically killing himself and not succeeding—and making it sound absolutely triumphant because the struggle is part of the message. Mcluhan's motto—the medium is the message.

. . . What was missing in your performance was a sense of play. The greatest insights and discoveries come from a sense of playfulness.

. . . When you're younger and you're fired by what you want to do, and you've got ambition and you really want to get your message across and all that, you overdo everything. And it's good. That part of it is good, because it's genuine, it's passionate and there's commitment and involvement. But as you get older, first of all you start losing some of your power physically.

But the thing is that then you start looking around for the essence of what it is that makes music.

You don't have to do a lot if you all do the right thing. It comes through.

. . . Resonance is the name of the game. If you do the right thing, it resonates from the inside.

. . . People don't listen to their own sounds. You input and you say oh yes, I know what I want to do. But what comes out is not exactly what you've inputted. It behooves you when you play in public that you know what is coming out as well as what you're putting in.

. . . One other thing: If things don't go well as you're playing, don't feel like you've lost your parents. Don't get kind of uptight, "Oh my God! Oh my God! What's happening!" That's the first thing you have to drop like bad baggage on an airplane that's sinking. Drop it. Get a ballast going so the balloon goes up. Just divest yourself first of all of the intensity. I like intensity, but when things are getting uptight, don't try to play harder. Play more deliberately, more calmly.

Composers and Musical Context

. . . Plato and Aristotle point out that art comes from the word "artificial." Art is not natural. Artifice, artifact. They're "made," not "natural." Art is a reconstruction of elements in the world to something different. That is what every great composer is doing.

You frame it and the way you listen makes it all meaningful. Like Picasso's work—what made it art was his grasping this frame of reference. All art is artificial. You have to start being a musician who fabricates art.

But, like an instrument, you play on real emotions with psychological and philosophical gestures and relationships.

You have to decide whether something is even-tempered, impatient, eager, leaning back, going forward, intense, non-intense.

. . . People have no idea of how to make a scenario for music. Everything must fit together into some kind of totality of what has been set up by the composer.

You must: (1) understand the intention of the composer and (2) put it into action.

. . . How important is structure to one composer vis a vis another composer? Is the structure of a Debussy the same as the structure of a Beethoven?"

What is structure? It's like an architecture, or a vessel to hold something. It has to have a function and be able to help you say what you want to say. If you have, like in a Bach piece, sections, it begins to build up in a kind of Baroque architecture like a Gothic cathedral. By the time you finish having put all those blocks together you've got a magnificent structure.

. . . It is important to study the era of the composition and the life of the composer and his contemporaries. When you play a piece like this, you are taking something from another time, digesting it, and then presenting it to others. You are saying, "This is important to me and I want it to be important to others." You need to know what you are a conduit of.

. . . If you read about Haydn, or read the writings of Carl Phillip Emmanuel Bach, Quantz, Leopold Mozart, Rousseau (a philosopher, but also a music historian), you can discover other dimensions besides the mechanical and the instinctive approach.

. . . You need to truly understand the language of the composer, not just think you do. For example, I look at Chinese calligraphy, and I think, "Oh, that looks like water and that looks like that," and I make my thing, and then some Chinese scholar comes to me and says, "How can you say that? That's about how you should behave yourself ethically if you're a government employee in Confucian language." Do I say, "Oh, no no! I want it to be a star, and a language and poetry and music . . ."

. . . Music has two elements basically: (1) the scientific element. I don't mean scientific in terms of an active science, but the physical elements of music which science then attempts to analyze and (2) the expressive element of what is done with those elements that you communicate, one human being to another.

Now both parts from the very beginning have been very important. As a matter of fact, a whole religion was built by the followers of Pythagorus and the overtone series, a religion—a Greek religion—that was very strong, and the movement lasted for many, many years through Sicily and into Italy, almost up to the time of the Romans. When Greece was fading, the Pythagoreans were still going on about the order of the universe. It was a moral issue They used to believe that the relationships of the orbits of the planets—that between the various planets and the sun were tones.

Composers then began to develop out of you might say the almost natural materials—they developed expressively-wise—they began to develop systems, systematizing these expressions. For instance, we know that certain tone groups are the ones that occur in the most primitive systems of music. For instance, Hawaiian: do you know that they seldom used an interval larger than a major third? It was mostly a single monotone plus neighboring notes and then going up a third on either side and lower and with rhythms and rocks and different sound making machines. The Javanese people developed a certain scale which to us sounds out of tune. Most Asian scales are pentatonic. Now when the Greeks began to have a system of tones, their tones began to have spin-off of meaning. What do I mean by that? Many Greek philosophers would say that the Dorian mode, which is our C major scale was good for a law-abiding citizen to feel the proper emotions toward the state and toward his culture and society. But if you were to take one of those sensuous modes that came from the Phrygians or the Lydians or the people that came from Asia Minor and you played music using these modes that was considered absolutely almost like McCarthy—subversive—against the state. And the fight went on. When the Christian religion began, the business of ornamentation, and what fit a system and what didn't fit a system was a fight in terms of purity. Even Palestrina was censured by the church authorities for being too frivolous in his use of materials of making sounds and they kept fighting about this all the time.

Other composers and musicians are crazy about numbers. Berg, for instance composed by systems of numbers. To Berg the number 5 was almost awe-inspiringly mystical. He used it all throughout his compositional organization.

So the point is what you have to do, whether you study the score or don't study the score, is try to get a larger view of the material you're dealing with, to the best of your ability. You need to start by understanding the musical context of a piece. It's a good starting place for your musical journey.

Beethoven

. . . What you just played for me sounded like a Dittersdorf quartet. I don't know what's going on under the surface. But the surface is literally not interesting to me. And that is why I said you sounded like Dittersdorf. He wrote the kind of music that was "house music." He was a wonderful composer, but he composed what was expected of him. When Esterhazy needed something for an occasion for the duke or this or that, he produced a quartet.

. . . You are a very good quartet; the overall impression is one of a quartet that is going to play this while people are eating dinner. It's dolce, it's sweet, it's undisturbed, it's comfortable. It's—it's in the center of expression.

What do I mean by the center of expression? It's like a person who lives a life in which you don't risk extreme feeling. I'm not even saying that you don't feel the kinds of things that maybe inhabit the mind and spirit that was Beethoven. Beethoven was a very imperfect man. He was a genius, but he was an imperfect man. He was a bastard when it came to his nephew. I would hate to have been his housekeeper. There are all kinds of things that we know about Beethoven—his attitude toward money . . .

He was a man who was not rational in our nice bourgeois sense. But you play him very rationally.

. . . From the very beginning Beethoven disturbed his contemporaries. Now it's true that the people who played him at the beginning tried to make him sound like the others. The critics talked about it. As a matter of fact, Beethoven was really complaining about the critics,—"They don't really understand me." Until finally he wrote this wonderful comment in which he finally decided—he said: "I started to see the kinds of compositions (this was when he was writing Opus 18) that they are praising." He said, "I saw that they were just empty, vacuous niceties and then I didn't feel bad; because if that is what they think is wonderful, then they don't understand music."

. . . Now let's get down to specifics. It may be that is what you want. And by the way, I can even point out something else: You could play exactly this way—impeccably—in New York City, and the next night the Juilliard Quartet could be playing it—maybe not impeccably, but playing it differently. And I can even see the reviewer saying about us, as he said about our last quartet concert—this man who likes bland stuff—saying, "It was such a wonderful thing to hear this young, relatively unknown quartet play this music—with the wonderful dolce and the nice quality," and then use the terms he used when we played Opus 130 . . . He described our playing of that in one sentence in which he said, "Very exciting and incongruously violent." Those were the words he used. I'm sure he meant them.

Now you have to decide when I tell you these things, "Is he just a crazy guy on the fringe of what I don't want to know?" Or can I touch you about the thing I think about?

. . . Why don't you go from what Beethoven does first? Why don't we go from—what is the person . . . in other words, instead of taking

Beethoven and diminishing him and making him fit your life, why in the hell don't we get inspired to try and get into his life?

. . . The idea infuriates me—that we try to emasculate and to mortalize the greatness that exists in the human race. We do it with everybody. We do it with Jesus Christ. That is the first person that we do it with. And then after that we do it with everybody else. The whole approach is to cut everybody down to our size.

. . . I want to talk about Beethoven, who Beethoven was. People sort of forget that he was a sore thumb. In the nineteenth century, Beethoven's image had changed. It had become the noble Beethoven, the Beethoven who affirmed God, the Beethoven who was so majestic he was the pinnacle of western civilization. Not the radical—not the tempestuous—not the guy who got mad at a lot of people and said, when somebody complained about how his instrument sounded when he was trying to tackle something, "What do I care for your damned fiddles!" Not that man. But all of a sudden, you have musicians who start looking back and saying, "Was that really the real Beethoven? Is that the Beethoven we're talking about?" Mahler was one of the first musicians who started saying, "Is that the Beethoven we're all used to—this majestic, broad Beethoven . . .

Beethoven was a radical—a radical even politically. It took a lot of courage when the French soldiers were all around to say the things he said about Napoleon. It took a lot of courage. He was also a radical in terms of social change. There's this very famous and authenticated story of when he was walking with Goethe down the streets of a town where the Emperor and his court were, and a certain very important nobleman came and Goethe moved off of the curb and bowed and everything, and Beethoven just stood there on the sidewalk and said a curt greeting and walked on. Goethe was saying, "Why were you so rude? Why did you speak to this nobleman this way?" And Beethoven said, "The only reason you showed him obeisance is because of his birth. He hasn't earned it. I'm a person who has earned my right to be respected. This man was just born into a family and grew up. Nobility is nothing." So the order was changing for him, even in terms of human beings.

What I'm getting at is that he was after something in music that had never been composed before. There was a new element in the world, and that element was that tempo characters and intensities and structures were changing. Intensity was not a question of entertainment. It was a question of personal catharsis and involvement.

. . . Beethoven is a man of contrasts. The first fact that anybody is going to find out about Beethoven is that he is a manic depressive. He goes from the heights to the depths and that is what makes him slightly insane. That is what makes psychologists say that insanity isn't that far away from genius. A genius is a person who takes his insanity and is able to order it, whereas a poor person who is just schizophrenic and feeling all these fantastic things and can't understand it or have any rationale is lost. But the genius takes the same feelings that the other people have who let go without inhibitions and orders them.

I view Beethoven as not a "pretty" composer. Oh, he can be pretty—very pretty—but he is a person in whom all the qualities are, first of all, uncompromisingly what they are. Rhythm is essential, momentum is essential, harmonic understanding and relationships are essential, and dynamics.

Now you could say, "Oh, that is an ugly sound! I don't want it." You don't want an ugly sound. Right. But you don't always sprinkle the same amount of sugar on to every kind of similar piece of music.

Now I'll tell you exactly what I mean. At the beginning of the development section—to me, that is the most undolce spot in the whole work. That is like a storm. Have you ever been in a forest and the atmosphere is oppressive and it's going to be an eruption and you know it's going to happen? Nothing is happening. The insects are quiet and the birds have stopped. All of a sudden, RAHRRR! It's thunder and lightning! Boom! Like that!

That is this place, but you don't include that in your language. What you have done is always play—you played it just as pretty as you did that other phrase earlier which could take it much more. There's not enough variety in you expressive language for that. Again, I would want that to be more still, poised, absolutely . . .

I'm trying to get at a point—if Beethoven goes from fortissimo to pianissimo, why aren't you absolutely astonished to want to make that top to bottom alive and meaningful to you?

Mozart

. . . Think about the aesthetic of a man like Mozart. Mozart was completely different than Beethoven. You look at Mozart's dynamics. He has lots of pianos, lots of fortes—hardly any mezzo pianos, hardly any mezzo fortes—almost no diminuendos, very few pianissimos. Have you ever been to a lake when it's not clear in the sky and the water is very opaque and you see the surface of the water but you can't see any of the things that are down underneath? There's no clarity. There's no transparency. Mozart requires purity of vision as well as purity of sound.

Now what do I mean by those things underneath the surface?

Your performance is absolutely for me a passive performance. What do I mean by a passive performance? Mozart is cycling into you and what is coming out is, on the level of direction, or phrasing, or nuance, or even dynamics, or the atmosphere background—the psychological thing of what is happening—whether the music is lyric or very singing or whether it's dramatic and a little bit more exciting and interesting— all of it is laid back. I would call this performance very square.

How do I explain the difference between passive and active? Passive is doing what comes naturally with your instinct. A real musician who is actively sculpting the music is listening to every sound and fitting it into something. It doesn't matter whether he's up here (in the bow) or down here, or doing it with his foot. The point is that he's listening and shaping the sound.

Bartók (coaching Bartók No. 1)

. . . Lehner, our mentor, gave us great insight into Bartók. This quartet is the transition from the classic image of what the string quartet was and this kind of synthesis of folk material which is not folk material. By now it is abstracted, and by the time you get to the last movement

. . . for him, it is the first true abstract folk art that he has ever come across in music. It's not folk song any more. It is all the pain and all the emotions and all the simple, almost ugly way of saying deep things— that is what I want you to get at. Your ideal is too much beauty.

. . . Hungarian esthetic in classical music was always a very funny mixed bag, because it got very mixed up with gypsy music. They were really two cultures. Gypsy music is very definitely something that is worldwide. That's the first thing. And there is a relation to the music the gypsies play even in England to the way the gypsies play in say, Macedonia and southern Yugoslavia. The point is there were gypsies in Hungary, and the Austro-Hungarian Empire generally thought about gypsy music. They didn't think about Hungarian music. That was ridiculous. So when respected composers like Brahms and Liszt talked about Hungarian rhapsody they were giving you a gypsy rhapsody. As a matter of fact, I have been in a Budapest restaurant where they went through almost in structure and in harmony the same thing that two or three of the Hungarian Rhapsodies of Liszt go through— gypsy music.

Kodály and Bartók weren't joining any political parties, but they felt that this whole idea of the Hungarian language and the Hungarian ethos was different. That's why I want you to know where Bartók was at when he wrote this quartet.. He used to take very primitive recording equipment and go into the rural areas all over Hungary and then finally he began to go into Romania, into Yugoslavia, into Greece, and at one point he and Kodály got as far as North Africa. They would find a villager or farmer who played the flute. They didn't play it the way people play flutes today—nice, pretty tones and no breath . . .

Or they would sing, and they would sing "AAAAAAAgggghhh." Everybody would say, "My God! You call that singing!" But what they were doing—they would be singing folk songs with a glissando, rough sounds, expressive of human elements. In other words, you don't think of a perfumed picture on a screen as being the handsome idol or modern starlet. What you think of is full-bodied and has bodily smells and has passion.

Bartók was beginning to establish in his own mind what were the real folk elements that he was going to incorporate into his language. The main things were rhythm and certain kinds of intervallic approaches. The most obvious language pattern in Hungarian, as contrasted to French, is the strong accent on the first syllable "Tata, Papa, Papa, Papa."

The first thing to understand is that not only are the Hungarian language patterns Tata and Papa in their (singing). But the other thing is the language patterns of the romantics. Now what does that mean? You take the Tristan motive. It goes up. It yearns for something and then at some point it reaches an apex and resigns itself and collapses. Now the second half of that is this piece. The piece starts with a sigh. Until you think of it as a musical sigh—a musical gesture in which it expires, you're not going to even begin to start playing the piece with any kind of emotional affect that goes with the piece.

If I can cue you into this, if you're not cued in already, you'll be very far on the way to understanding not only the structure and material of music but also to understanding the emotional power of it. The music never loses its connection to language and musical affect. And the trouble with people like you—people like me when I was young—everybody—is that they begin to isolate musical sound, musical technique of playing an instrument from the thing that makes it meaningful: language and emotional affect.

Interpretation and Artistry

. . . I can only tell you what my life is dedicated to—at least in music. In music it's dedicated to trying to make those illuminating moments last longer and more continuous. I'm not able to; I'm not that kind of genius. But the point is that that is what I try to do.

. . . Every musician who is reinterpreting or trying to identify with a composer has to face a central problem. First of all, you have two opposing philosophies. Both agree that the composer is a genius but one philosophy says that the composer is saying something that is unique, that couldn't be said by anybody else and what he put down is fixed for all time.

The opposing point of view says that what the composer put down is a point of departure, and you must create something, and that is what makes the infinity of variety, and nobody's the same, and if you want to make an expressive crescendo, and it really is felt, and it's compelling, that that is important.

They say the composer put it down, but he was human. If he had lived twenty years later, and he was composing that piece, he may have done it differently himself. There are even examples of that where a composer like Hindemith began to recompose pieces he wrote in the earlier period which he then didn't agree with. Interestingly enough, in every single instance, I believe that it is less good composition than the original one. That is how I feel about it. But he didn't. He felt differently.

. . . Look at the end of Beethoven's variations of 131. If you ever have a chance to look in the Bonn Archives—they have the Photostats, I remember. All the pages that Beethoven scratched on for 131, including whole sections of scherzo crossed out and done differently, and so on, and then he goes on. Anyway, I don't remember how many versions there are of the last measures until the end. There are a whole bunch of versions, each one slightly different. Sometimes he puts the bass in the viola; sometimes be puts it in the cello. Sometimes he has one instrument . . . another instrument . . . It's wonderful to see how that mind was working, because there you have it laid out for you. It's like an autopsy. You don't feel it, but you see it. You say, "Jesus! He thought this and he thought this . . . Why did he choose the one he chose?" That is the interesting thing.

. . . I personally think that what you play should not be based all on logic or all on illogic. Adorno, the sociologist, said there is a role for the irrational in greatness. The important thing is that you should use all the information you have to make something more vivid, more meaningful, more experienced. This quartet creates an ambiance. You start very nicely, and you are doing things, but that very nicely continues. There is no wind, no rain, no change of climate—nothing happens to that dynamic. A little bit louder, a little bit softer, but it's all so comfortable that I don't feel anything.

I just want you to begin not letting one note be un-meaningful. And if it's supposed to be un-meaningful, make it meaningfully un-meaningful. How much music is neuter, neutral, nothing passive? There is always some moment in music that has that quality but it is made wonderful by being framed by things that are meaningful.

. . . Silence also must have meaning. Did you ever go to Noh plays? People who put on Noh plays are masters of sound and silence. Silence. In a Noh play the gesture with no sound is very important. What people don't realize is that western music truly has great use for silence. And the point is that you must understand the meaning silence plays in a piece of music.

. . . The theme of your life in music is variation. It isn't that you want to be different for difference's sake. But everything, once you start breathing, every moment is different. Every note is different. Every time you return to that note is different.

. . . Play all the half steps as if you are turning a corner. Each angle of a mountain range gives a new perspective.

. . . Play with "remembered vitality." How do you get vitality? By quicker motions. What is structure? It is "what is." You show how things are related. Without thinking of theatrics, think of genius ways that are surprising, imaginative, spontaneous.

. . . Where I feel you have to concentrate to make this piece much more meaningful—not only to the outside, but to yourselves—is on a couple of inner levels. Did you ever read Dr. Doolittle when you were kids? The man who talked with the animals? On his adventures he discovered an animal called the "Push me-Pull you." It was a mule that had two heads. They could never agree on which way they were going. That's just about what is happening with you with this piece. You really don't in any way tell yourselves—and therefore tell us—the priorities of what the beats are, and the structure of the rhythm is. You can't have emphasis at the beginning and end both. When you shape a phrase, and you shape it always the same way, there must be a purpose. There has to be some sense of intensification and relaxation in relation to those priorities.

. . . It's not just about playing notes. That's what you did. What's the character? What is it? Playful. Like fire flies in the sky. Or a guy goes and tickles all the girls but gets out of the way so they don't know who did it. Some kind of fun and bounce in it. You played it very sober. I understand why. Because it's hard. But that's the trouble with music. You need to separate how difficult it is from its character. Play every note as if you loved it. Every note. That's better. Now your children are beginning to feel that you love them. Yes.

. . . I don't care if you take some shepherd in the dessert before Christ playing to his goats, or a mass being constructed out of the language of God—out of the Latin text—or a minstrel singing about his love. It's like sniffing cocaine or hearing a gorgeous sensual thing. It's a high to feel the intensities. Now I'm not putting it on a shallow level. The point is that in all these examples you shouldn't just play notes. You're too good as a group and as individuals to just play notes and read a few crescendos and a few accents, and a few dynamics. If you go through this again, you can play on a much better level and communicate what the music is trying to say. Religion and music are how you feel inside first—not how you talk about it.

. . . Music has to be joy—not happiness in a stupid sense. It has to be like a mother with a child—a little baby—has to be pure love and response. This is most important of all is that you just say, "Nothing should be happening that isn't interesting . . ."

. . . Nuances are like the design of a Persian rug. Something strong is balanced by something weak. Every color and line and proportion, not the same. Too much sameness can be deadly. If you live with a person who is good, good, good all the time, you can go out of your mind—just as with a person who is bad all the time.

. . . Don't be even-tempered. MOVE! Nuance and momentum must be tied together. There is a breathing point and there is a focus.

. . . What you do is you play nicely and fully, but nothing ever grows to let you feel the climax. I never feel that you get over the hump. What does that mean? It doesn't mean playing harder and playing more grimly like a dog who bites the leg of somebody, and holds on—you can't get him loose. It isn't that kind of growth factor. No. Because if you bite through the leg then it's severed.

. . . If you have an ongoing, living, breathing quality you will take us on a trip of discovery of this piece. Don't think of it as "this thing we're going to try . . . this thing we're going to accomplish." I want you to be breathing. You have to control your breath. Take breath.

. . . What you really need is a sense of expansion. That means use more bow, use more vibrato, use more a feeling of energy.

. . . Change your direction. I'm asking you to do something on your own now. More is not always the answer.

. . . Playing in a quartet is like developing a sense of how you get into something and how you get out of something. It's like riding the carousel in Central Park with kids. Getting off and on. Don't get up-ended by the motion of what's going on. Get the muscles and the mind going before, so that at the moment all you have to do is open the spigot. The preparation is very important.

. . . In every action or sound or feeling or heartbeat, there is a cycle. When we talk about nuances or pulses or heartbeat or rhythm, we're talking about a cycle. And what does cycle mean? It means that there are different qualities to every moment and you have important moments of that quality and you have reaction to the important and then a gathering for another event and a reaction to it and another event.

. . . You have a child and you love them and you caress them, and then you pat them very quietly on the top, but there's more love in that gentle pat than there is in the first big hug.

. . . No matter whether you're a child or a grownup, an expert or an amateur, what you have to teach is a kind of paradox: there has to be an openness and respect for everything that you're not. At the same time, a questioning and a usage that makes it your own.

That doesn't mean you take it flippantly. You must study it and then ask yourself, "Do we dare to try something different?" Every action must be related to every other action. As every event occurred, it related to every event that had preceded.

Juilliard String Quartet at Michigan State University event

PART VI

Letters to Lisa

Asia Tour Spring 1961

THURSDAY & FRIDAY, MARCH 30 & 31, 1961

Dearest Lisa,

The Pacific Ocean is the largest ocean in the world and there are many wonders here to see. At this moment we are leaving Wake Island which is one of three little flat sand bars with a coral reef around them. And in a little while we will cross the imaginary date-line that is so hard to explain. But that means that I will jump from early morning Thursday right to the same time Friday.

But what I really want to write about is Hawaii. This is a magic land and our visit there was extraordinary. When you visit this summer you will see and hear what I mean. First let me send you greetings from your friend Joan Kagawa. Tell her friends at school that she misses them all.

She now lives in Honolulu, which is the only big city on all the islands. (There are about 250,000 people in Honolulu.) The name of the island (on which Honolulu is), is Oahu. There are many islands stretching out over a thousand miles. Some of them are just small rocks, the biggest perhaps the size of Rhode Island.

Now, you must know that these islands are our 50th state and were first settled by people who were Polynesian. The Polynesian people come from south of here. They traveled thousands of miles in big canoes. (Samoa, Tahiti, etc.) And they are a beautiful race of people. Also when they first came, hundreds of years ago, they saw that the islands were practically "living" volcanoes. (The islands are basically all lava rock, which crumbles on top and becomes dirt and thus, able to grow vegetation.) Many of these volcanoes are still erupting and the smoke and fire and ashes shoot out of the cone of the volcano and then lava (hot and molten) flows over the side and down the mountain till it reaches the sea and creates a steaming, awesome picture as hot lava hits the water.

The Polynesians were very fearful of these volcanoes and one of their gods was the goddess Pele, the goddess of the fiery volcanoes. After the god who created the world and one or two other gods, Pele was the most important and the religion of these people grew around Pele. The Polynesians are one of the most friendly and generous people in the world. That is the spirit of "aloha" which is a greeting and expression of love and friendship. When the early explorers such as Captains Cook and Vancouver came to the islands they were received with open arms. Unfortunately the white strangers were much inferior in their manners and behavior so that the islanders were hurt and confused, and in the instance of Captain Cook when his men stole and took away some of the island people, the islanders stoned him and killed him.

Over the years, many different races came to these islands: Portugese, English, Chinese, Americans, Japanese and most recently, Filipino. We speak of United States as a great melting pot, many different races marrying between themselves, but Hawaii is truly so. As a result, many of the people today are part one race, part another. And of many colors and the result is one of very beautiful people.

The land and water here are fascinating. Even though it is

very warm, there are always trade winds that blow and cool the air. Around most of the islands are many coral reefs (hard beautiful rock built by tiny, countless organisms). These reefs come almost out of the water and stop the waves and then long swells move in to the land (and one of the favorite sports is to take a long board, swim out to a long wave and ride on the board as the wave carries it to the beach). The mountains are not everywhere but they are beautiful and stop the clouds from reaching certain parts of the islands. This means that one side can be a very wet place and the other, a real barren desert. Where things grow, it is most beautiful and there are coconut palms (you must be careful because they fall off when ripe and can hit you on the head). There are bananas (these are not really trees but large plants). There are countless ferns and flowers. But, almost all of these, and even animals and bugs were brought in by all the people that have come here.

Sugar is the biggest industry, tourists are next, and pineapple after that. But now I come to the most remarkable of all. Do you remember Concha Hughes from Aspen? Well, this is her home and she is a true Hawaiian. She and her mother arranged an evening which I will always remember, and which I dearly wish you, Mommy and all your friends in your class could have attended. Most of the people who came were Polynesian but a few like ourselves were not. The home we came to had a garden filled with many types of exotic plants (orchids, ferns, hanging roots, etc.). Some of the guests were the finest present day musicians in Hawaii. And the evening consisted of warm talk, lots of music (at the end we went out and got our violins and played too), and a Hawaiian feast.

On our arrival we took off our shoes and left them outside the door. As we entered, the ladies brought us beautiful leis (wreathes of many colored flowers) and hung them around our necks, saying aloha and then rubbing our cheek with theirs (the ancient way of kissing). Actually not really rubbing, but softly touching the cheeks together.

The music was sung and played by guitars (not electric), ukuleles (brought here by the Portuguese) and a bass violin. In this music the words are most important. The Polynesian language is not written and all the legends, ideas, and ceremonies are contained in their chants. At first there were only chants. Concha performed one on her knees, dancing and singing, marking time with lava rocks (two in each hand, clicking them like castanets). When the missionaries came they introduced the melodies and harmonies of their hymns (not as beautiful), and these are the basis for today's Hawaiian melodies.

The food was wonderful. Raw fish, slightly pickled and seasoned, fried banana, transparent noodles with mushrooms, chicken, vegetables lightly cooked, salad and Poi. Poi is the ancient staple of the Polynesian people and is very healthy. Also, I don't think you would like it. The root of the Taro plant is pounded into pulp until it resembles a thick, gray paste. It tastes something like an unsweetened, gummy starch and most persons who try it for the first time don't like it. You eat it with your fingers (one for a man and two fingers for a lady).

And there was dancing. Not the kind we think of. The true hula was a very sacred dance. It was originally only danced at the new year and told the tales of these people and their gods. Later, these dances were danced on special occasions for their kings and now I come to the most extraordinary thing of all.

I fell in love with a most beautiful and unique lady. She is one of the most wonderful persons I have ever met. And she is 89 years old. She cannot walk (because of infirmity) except with help. But she also danced. With her hands, her face (eyes, mouth, head, muscles), her shoulders, her breasts and her heart. She is a great artist and more alive than all of us put together. She entered into the dance troupe of the last king of Hawaii at the age of 14 and in her is the true spirit of these people. She is acknowledged as the foremost authority in this art and in the ways of these people and besides she is delightfully, refreshingly frank and speaks her mind like few others do. She is gay, spontaneous, and true. I loved her and when she danced, all the grace, wit, love, awe, and joy of these people came out. Her name is Aunty Kini (all older women are called Aunty out of respect). When we said "aloha" at the end of the evening, we were very sad to leave.

I forgot to mention that Aunty Kini danced for Robert Louis Stevenson (as a child) and was the first woman to officially leave the island (with the King's permission) and she danced in the Chicago World's Fair, and before most of the royalty and presidents of the world (even the Tsar of Russia, Nicholas). When she came back she married a man who was a mayor of Honolulu for many years.

Well, we also drove about the island, swam in the wonderful salt water, practiced our violins and gave a concert. And now I am high up over the ocean. Night has passed and in two hours I will be in Japan and at three o'clock in the afternoon, I will be in Formosa. Lots of love, my best to Ms. Kreag, your schoolmates, and Dr. Camp.

Love, Daddy

MARCH 31, APRIL 1, 2, 3, 4, 5—1961

Dearest Lisa,

If I had thought that Hawaii was a climax and everything after that would be less exciting, I would have been wrong. Here I sit on a Chinese train on the island of Taiwan going from the biggest city of Taipei to the university city of Taiching (North to South) which is in the middle of the island and I must tell you that the last two days couldn't have been more exciting. How I wish you were here, for many things would thrill you.

We got on the plane in Honolulu after the concert (at 2:30 am) and we arrived in Tokyo, Japan at 8:30 am, 2 days later.

(Remember, when you go over the date-line you jump one whole day ahead. One minute it is Thursday, the next minute it is Friday.)

Tokyo airport is a "madhouse." Crowded, busy. Everybody rushing around. An American Embassy official met us and so did five young men who are our managers for our tour of Japan. They have a custom of bowing the neck at every moment that you speak or want to speak. It is a sign of politeness, but when I got on the airplane two hours later, my neck was stiff. And do you know what airline it was? The Thailand airline (once this country was called Siam) and the hostesses greet you with a sweet curtsey and their fingertips touching, altogether a most graceful picture. The pilot, however, was a Norwegian. This plane was not a jet and the trip to Taiwan took 6 and ½ hours, yet it went very fast. We saw the holiest mountain in Japan: Mt. Fujiyama—over 12,000 feet high and snowcapped, it towers above the landscape and is perfect. Also, as we flew south over the Southern Japanese islands, there were three smoking volcano craters. And then, after flying for over three hours above the China Sea we reached the island of Taiwan.

The first thing you see on Taiwan, (which was called Formosa or beautiful island by the Portuguese when they first came here) are the beautiful green squares and small terraces that hold the rice fields. Right now the rice is just coming out of the water (green plants) and each small field is closed in by a dike and all of them are on different levels to get the water to flow all over. When they want to get the water up higher they have two people step on a foot pump. The people who met us at the airport were both Chinese and Americans, and they were official people and just friends. Rafe's cousin teaches here at the Chinese Language Institute for Americans.

How can I describe this city of Taiwan to you? It is not beautiful, but it is fascinating as is every other city that we now (3 days later) have visited on this island.

Up in the mountains live tribes of very primitive people who were the first peoples on this island (which is only about 100 miles from Mainland China). Much, much later, the Chinese started to come over from the mainland of China and these are known as Taiwanese. China ruled this island until 1895 when the Japanese defeated the Chinese and ruled Taiwan for fifty years until the end of World War II. (Most people over 30 speak some Japanese). Then when the communists took over China, some 2 million Chinese came over to this land and live here with the Taiwanese.

In Taipei we saw all the strange sights of the Orient. Taiwan has the best standard of living in Asia, next to Japan, but it is still much poorer than our country. Everywhere people push and pull things and carry them hung on poles across their shoulders.

Also large oxen and water buffalo pull big carts filled with everything. Modern cars, barefoot children, mothers with babies strapped on their backs, old men, bicycles, pedicabs (carts connected to bicycles) all cross through the streets like ants, and horns are tooting, chickens squawking, children shouting, radios blaring. Wow! The shops are little holes in the wall, but they sell many things. One mustn't eat the food in the little shops (because we are not used to it and the conditions are far from clean). The shop signs are very colorful.

That first evening we went to a party given for us up on a mountain, in a Japanese type house (no chairs—only pillows to sit on). At dinner I sat next to the Ambassador (U.S.) and his wife and I am afraid that I was so tired that even Mrs. Drumwright (Mrs. Ambassador) noticed it, so we excused ourselves and went to our hotel to sleep. In the morning we walked around the town and visited a food market where everything looked like a fairytale but the smell was very strong.

And in the afternoon we went to two Chinese operas and a Buddhist temple. The operas were something just for you. The stories are from Chinese history, hundreds of years ago and the costumes are as colorful as can be. The makeup is amazing (a white streak from the nose to the forehead; reddish, purple

all over and heavy painted eyelids). The music is played by
percussion (drums, bells, gongs), a violin (Chinese type) and a
reed instrument (like a primitive oboe). The actors and actresses
and small children act, dance, sing, talk, shout, and the audience
also talks and shouts and moves around.

At one place we visited the back of the stage. And the actors
lived there. Each family had one little place curtained off (about
the size of half of your room) and there they cook, sleep, and
raise their families. The Buddhist temple is as fantastic as I can
imagine. Very colorful and inside are figures of Buddhas and
places to place sticks of incense to burn while praying.

And of course I rode my first pedicab (very bumpy) and
had my first real Chinese meal. Outside they were shooting
firecrackers in the Chinese manner (a long pole set upright and
hundreds of firecrackers in a string with the biggest on top). They
light the bottom one and an enormous barrage of explosions
is copped by a terrible big bang at the top (knocking the pole
down). The food is so marvelous that I want to describe it (you
know how much I like it). At one meal we had 12 dishes:

1. Roast pigeon
2. Abalone and milk soup
3. Fried prawns
4. Sweet and sour pork
5. Shredded cabbage with tomatoes
6. Beans and shrimp
7. Inside fried bread
8. Cucumbers with tomato paste
9. Chicken and egg
10. Fried pork
11. Papaya fruit
12. Eight treasure pudding made with rice base, raisins, lotus
    seed, beans, date mash, bean curd, pineapple and dragon
    eyes. All with host rice wine and the style of cooking was
    from Szechuan Province.

Then we gave our first concert in Taipei. 1200 people and more standing and after the concert they yelled and clapped hands. The next morning we went to hear a children's chorus. How I wish you could hear them sing in such a group. Children from 5 to 10 from all the schools of Taipei. The most musical are chosen and they sing and look like angels. Such musicians! We were moved beyond words and we played for them. See enclosed paper photo. Then we rushed to a train and traveled through the country to the middle university city of Taiching. We drove out to the imperial museum in a little town 9 miles away (driving here is like jumping off a cliff). Every minute you think you are going to hit somebody or something because everybody is running on the road in every direction. But the car driver just keeps blowing his horn the whole way. The museum was set in the middle of hundreds of banana trees.

There were beautiful scrolls, pottery, paintings and jewelry. After the concert some Chinese musicians played on their flutes and violins and sang their songs. The next day we flew to Taiwan and drove to Kaoching on the southern coast. The most wonderful thing here is the fish market. I took many pictures so you will see yourself but it is hard to describe. Early in the morning, the fishermen bring in the fish they just caught and put them under a gigantic shed (even sharks as well as tuna and many others). A man auctions them off and the hundreds of people who buy them to sell pull them away to another spot and cut them up. Thousands of fish and wild activity. We walked all over (fish, pieces of fish, pools of blood, and noise—what noise). The girls wear a strange costume while working in the fields. It is considered ugly to get sun tanned and they wear tight pants, jackets with long sleeves, in many colors, a conical hat and a cloth over the back of their necks and a cloth over their face up to their eyes. (They also are very shy and don't like to have their pictures taken.)

Today I bought some lovely things at the Taiwan handicraft shop, and at dinner we heard a Chinese classical orchestra and one of pieces they played was called "Flowers and Moonlight on the River in Springtime" and was written by Kang Kinlum about 616-907 AD (Tang Dynasty) over a thousand years ago.

Now we are approaching Hong Kong and we were very sad to say goodbye to our new Taiwanese friends.

Love, Daddy

APRIL 10, 1961

Dearest Lisa,

Our visit to Hong Kong is over and I sit in a hotel in Manila with just 15 minutes before going to a reception in our honor given by the United States ambassador to the Philippines. One of exciting facts of our trip for the State Department is that we meet all the people who are representing our country in the various places that we visit.

Hong Kong is not a country. But it is a very important place, and very beautiful. Many years ago the Chinese emperors would not let British (or any other European) merchants come and trade in China. Finally, over 100 years ago it was agreed that the British could settle on the island of Hong Kong just off the Chinese mainland and trade from there. So the city Hong Kong was founded around 1841. The island is spectacular with high ridges (mountains rising up the middle and all the roads are very steep and twisty. Many Chinese come to live with the British, (originally the people who lived by fishing were a race called Haks and they wear very colorful hats), and the population grew very fast and spilled onto the mainland which is called Kowloon and is a very ancient Chinese city. In 1898, Great Britain leased over 300 square miles "the new territories" (which are also mountainous with farming valleys) and this now is Hong Kong colony.

It is a crossroads of the orient and if you look at your map you will see that it is in the center of the area that contains Southeast Asia, the Philippines, China and Taiwan.

Today it is a city of 3,000,000 people and hundreds of big modern buildings and has some of the biggest shipping in its harbors. It is also a free port which means there are no taxes on products and one buys many things for less money here than anywhere else. (I bought a new movie camera.) But also there are hundreds of thousands of poor people. Especially those that fled from Communist China where life is very unhappy. These people live even on the streets and I saw many people sleeping on a small cot under a store awning and everywhere in the non-business district, mothers would cook rice on little fire pots right on the sidewalk and feed little babies while squatting on their haunches. Everybody is yelling and moving. Taipei was nothing like this. All the buildings have clothes hung on them to dry and everywhere children your age are studying how to read and write Chinese characters. Here is how your name looks in Chinese (and it means beautiful beach).

I think the most fantastic thing about Hong Kong is the floating population. There are people (over 30,000) who live their whole lives on boats. These boats are so crowded together that it is hard for them to move and they fish, they must travel over boats to get to the bigger junks (like our model Chinese boat) to go out to sea. Everything is on boats. Even small grocery stores sail around to the places where people can buy their food. And there is nothing more beautiful than a full sailing junk. Though most of them have motors today. We were given a 3 hour ride on a junk owned by one of the Americans and we sailed around one of the bays and islands. Here also, the American Consul (temporary) gave us a party and we met some lovely people. We were also invited to Dr. Chin's house for a fantastic Chinese meal at a fantastic house overlooking the sea and sent home in a Rolls Royce (my first ride). Dr. Chin has studied music and is very knowledgeable. We also heard music with all the Chinese instruments and singing. The Chinese violin is called an er-hu or ti-hu. They hold it up like a cello to play. Their lute is a very beautiful instrument and one boy played like a great virtuoso on a balloon guitar.

We went with a Professor and Mrs. Kirby. He is a great expert on Chinese communism. We gave two concerts. One for the community and one just for students. Rafe Hillyer has made a great hit because in Taipei he announced in almost perfect Mandarin Chinese and here in Hong Kong, he spoke in Cantonese which is the kind of Chinese most people speak here. The language has 9 tones and sounds very sing-song.

All the girls and ladies wear a dress hat has side slits which shows off their pretty legs and there are very many pretty girls in Hong Kong. One of the saddest things is that many of the refugees do not live on boats or in the new wonderful resettlement buildings (with play-grounds on the roof.) They live in terrible, poor shacks clinging to the mountainsides. The children there beg for money and we feel bad because the few cents we give them doesn't help much. But the government is improving conditions all the time.

Another thing, the smells in these cities are very strong but you get used to them very quickly.

After our student concert, Rafe and I went to a lady's house to hear some prizewinners in a big music competition. They were wonderful children and we had a marvelous time. Also two of them are very exciting talents. One, Davie Wei is only 9 years old and will be a great artist. Another, whose first name is Nancy, has music in her soul (and she is only 12).

The people in Hong Kong were so friendly that we were very unhappy to leave. But all Asian countries are like this.

It only took 2½ hours to fly to Manila in the Philippines and now I am finishing this letter after the reception and a dinner, where we not only met a lot of U.S. Embassy people, but the Ambassador to the Philippines from Viet Nam and England and

guess what? Also a young lady who came from Finland and was
"Miss Universe" some years ago.

Love,
Daddy

APRIL 22, 1961

Dearest Lisa, (and Lucy and Nicholas)

The propellers are starting and our airplane will fly from
Kyoto, Japan to Fukuoka, Japan and I do not want to wait any
longer to write you about our visit to the country of Southern
Korea. This country is the most unusual that I have ever visited
in my whole life.

As a young boy I read many books about strange lands and
when I dreamed about growing up, it was to dream of seeing
these places. Korea is such a place. Actually, we were in two
different cities in Korea. The first one was Seoul and this is the
largest city in the country. If you look on your map, you will see
that Korea is a peninsula jutting out from China (Manchuria).
The Korean people have a long history and have very definite
Mongolian features. Black hair, almond eyes, round faces, broad
cheek bones and very flat pug noses. They are not very tall,
but they are taller than many Japanese people. They have their
own language which is different than Chinese but, like Japanese
uses some Chinese characters mixed in with an alphabet. Their
alphabet which is quite new, has only 14 consonants but 10
vowels. One of the unhappy facts of Korean history is that they
have been under foreign rule for much of their countries time.
The most recent was Japanese and after the war there was a
tragic fight of Koreans in the South against those in the North
with the United Nations on the South side and the Chinese

Communists on the North. Today Korea is uneasily divided just above Seoul. (We only visited South Korea.) Seoul is a city of 1,300,000 and we arrived in the evening after flying from Japan. What we did see of the country were countless mountains and small valleys. It didn't look too promising. We were met at the airport by the American information officer, Mr. Henderson, and a number of Koreans including a former student of ours (Chung Chu Oh) and the head of the biggest newspaper in Korea which was sponsoring our concert in Seoul. The first thing we knew was that the roads are terrible. The ones that are paved are the worst of all. The holes are big and deep and after 45 minutes getting into Seoul (in a Jeep—most cars there are Jeeps) my insides were upside down. And the second thing was that our nerves were shot, because the roads are filled with people walking, riding bicycles, riding carts, riding cows, children and old people. And the drivers of the cars start honking their horns and don't stop. Every ten seconds we almost hit somebody or something. (I am told that there are many accidents and I will tell you about one, later in the letter.) We stayed that night at the Western hotel and we were very disappointed because we wanted to stay at a Korean style hotel. Why? I will tell you. In New York we live in apartments and houses—very solid houses. In Japan and Korea, people live in a very different way. The houses have wooden frames and made into sliding panels. In each room one can slide any panel wall so that it opens up to another room and even to the outside. Since Korea is very cold (we came from 100 degree heat in Manila to 40 degree cold in Seoul)—you think that such "paper" houses are too cold, not at all. They had the first kind of radiant heat. Under the floors are brick tunnels and charcoal fires send hot air under the floors. The result is that the floors are toasty warm, and this is important because you always must take your shoes off in a Korean (or Japanese or Chinese) house and also—you sleep on a mat on the floor. (This is not too hard but the pillow is a hard roll and that can cause a stiff neck) and when you eat you sit on a pillow on the floor and of course, you always eat with chopsticks.

Anyway, the next morning we got up early and had another harrowing ride out to the airport to fly south to the city of Teagu. Here we were to play our first Korean concert and this is the place that I refer to when speaking of a strange land. The farmer in the country lives exactly like his ancestors did 2,000 years ago. When he tills his small piece of land, his wife or sons pull the plow and he stands behind and directs it. They live in huts of mud and straw with thatch roofs and when a typhoon (hurricane) comes, many of these huts are blown down. Their main food is called Kim Chi (sour cabbage made in big Kim Chi pots). The people are poor. Every spring there is a shortage of rice and people live on one meal a day until the next crop is ripe. The roads are crowded with activity and the costumes are very clean. The women wear a flowing wide gown and have a small little jacket over their shoulders. The men wear white pants or robes. I was told the flowering gowns made it easier for the women to sit on the floor. (Japanese women wear a tight Kimona but they don't sit, they kneel.) Cows, chickens, dogs, children, people carrying everything; little Mongolian ponies pulling big cart loads—and the old men in their white robes and the funny horse hair, black hat which young people don't wear anymore (in the cities).

The Mayor of Taegu gave us a lunch and he arranged for us to be entertained by Kisaeng girls. These are like Japanese Geisha girls and they spend all their lives training for this. They dance, play instruments, sing and even light your cigarettes. At this dinner were three lovely girls in their twenties. The songs would sound funny to you because they make strange tones in their larynx (throat) and have strange melodies, but the dancing is indescribably beautiful as is the Korean lute and drum playing. I hope my movie is of the dancing and playing come out because you would love to see this. One dance was with a large

yellow handkerchief and was one of the most graceful dances
I have ever seen. We also met General and Mrs. Edson at the
lunch. (He is the commander of the U.S. Forces in this part of
Korea.) At night the shops all stay open with candlelight (most
of them don't have electricity). There was a big anti-government
demonstration scheduled for the day of the concert, but the
United States information office appealed to the newspaper to
avoid a dangerous crowd for the sake of the concert and we
understand that they did prevent the demonstration from getting
out of hand. After the concert where the lights went out during
one piece (but we finished it in the dark) we were invited to
a Korean dinner (also with more Kisaeng girls). The food was
interesting but not as good as Chinese food, but there was lots of
sake (rice wine). My legs were tired after so much squatting on
the floor.

The next day Mr. Inman, the information officer took us
50 miles through the country to a very famous shrine called
Kyung-ju. I felt as the early travelers, like Marco Polo must
have felt. Such strange sights. At one market I could believe that
somebody had taken me back to the ancient days. I had an old
pipe maker make me a long bamboo pipe for Nicholas and we
saw an old man and a young boy of about 10, dance and play
music. (They were selling medicine herbs.) The little boy had
on a most colorful costume and a hat with many long tassels
which he twirled by shaking his head. At the shrine were many
students and at a picnic place there were families dancing to
drums. In the Orient, women are not very well treated. (Even
their husbands are picked for them—today! Even our students
from Juilliard who go back to Korea—they are not very happy
about this.) But at the family dances everyone gets a little drunk
on rice wine and they have a wonderful time. On the way back
we stopped by an ancient observatory for looking at the stars
and in the fields we picked up numerous pieces of pots, some of
which were over 1,000 years old! We saw the big burial mounds
where kings were buried, some as big as hills and we also took

part in a lucky but terrible accident. A jeep tried to pass us and even though they had lots of room they went into a ditch and turned over, landing on the top of the car (no roof). We jumped down and with some farmers lifted the whole car up and seven people crawled out! Four men and three women. We thought they might be badly hurt, but they seemed alright after a while and we took them into the next big town. The plane taking us back to Seoul was cancelled because of snow and we spent a night in a poor Korean hotel. We were unhappy because we were supposed to be guests that night at a truly remarkable dinner with dancing and playing of Korean instruments (even rare ones). They went ahead and had their good time without us. Oh well, that is life.

When we came back to Seoul in the morning we were taken to a true Korean style hotel (named Undang) run by the most famous Korean musician and dancer now alive. This was the place I described to you. Of course, the washroom was outside and the toilets are very different, but the experience was one in a million.

When we left the next morning we were most sorry to leave this wonderful country and warm hearted people. Now we have been in Japan 5 days and I will write soon again, but my best to Mrs. Kreag and your class.

Much love,
Daddy

TUESDAY, APRIL 25, 1961

Dearest Lisa—Nicholas—Lucy:

Our Japanese visit is going by so quickly. For one thing, we are busier in making music and the big city of Tokyo is less interesting to visit than all the previous places. If you look on your map, you will see that Japan is a long stretch of many islands running mostly north to south. The land volcanic. Some volcanos are smoking even today and there are many earthquakes. In the old days, whole cities were destroyed from earthquakes and typhoons because the houses were mostly made of light wood and rice paper (like the three little pigs). Today, like the wisest pig, they are building houses of stone and brick. Japan has many people—over 90,000,000! And Tokyo is the largest city in the world! Even bigger than NYC and it is a mess. If you think New York City traffic is bad, you don't know anything. It takes half an hour to go a few blocks and in the rush hour you can't get anywhere. Outside of the downtown area, the streets are so small that there are traffic jams every minute (and there are lots of cars!) Japan is the most industrialized country in the Orient and they make everything.

Time out for a sight of magic. We just flew past the sacred mountain of Fujiyama. The highest mountain in Japan (almost 13,000 ft.) and a volcano that is always topped with snow. The day is breathtakingly perfect and the landscape is unbelievably beautiful. This country is full of paradoxes (a paradox is a situation in which two things that shouldn't be together, are together.) For instance, Japanese people are very old fashioned in their ideas about tradition and how they live. Yet they have the most modern machinery to make things. Another paradox, the Japanese people are extremely emotional in their feelings about their country and their desires (and very intense as personalities)—yet their art and tradition is calm, meditative, slow in motion.

Almost all the big cities were destroyed in the war and have been rebuilt in the last fifteen years. This may be why Tokyo is not a very pretty city. But Kyoto (which was not bombed by agreement) the ancient Capitol of Japan is one of the most interesting and beautiful cities in the world. Our first stay in Tokyo lasted two days and Isaac Stern was in the same hotel so we had a lot of fun together. We met Pablo Casals (who is

here with a Japanese cello pupil) and Isaac brought Margot
Fonteyn (the great English ballet dancer) to one of our television
broadcasts. Also we visited a large music school called Musashino
College (which has 2,000 students). We toured a tremendous
new building and played for the students in a modern
auditorium. We did not have a single concert in Kyoto. (We
did play at a former pupil's music school and for this we were
given a car to take us around for two days by the city!) Noviko
Kosai (our student) is married to a young economics professor at
Kyoto University and his father is an important Shinto Priest in
Kyoto. He is a very wise and wonderful man. Very worldly and
direct. Also the main religions in Japan are Buddhism (followers
of the great Buddha who lived many centuries ago in India) and
Shintoism. Shinto derives from love and worship of nature and
one's ancestors.

Nowhere in the world do people create gardens as they
do in Japan. In Kyoto we visited many of them (some at
imperial palaces and residences; some, just gardens). Many are
a combination of ponds (with lilies, goldfish, turtles, etc. in
them) various tress from tall pines to the dwarf trees (hundreds
of years old but not taller than you are), many kinds of flowers,
stone lanterns, arches, stone bridges over ponds of the water, or
log bridges or just plain wooden arches, swans and ducks and
beautiful temples and pogodas. We even visited a mountainside
moss garden. All kinds of green mosses underneath the trees. And
some of their most famous gardens are made only of white sand
(raked in patterns to represent waves, or sky or something) and a
few beautifully placed rocks! The palaces, residencies shrines, and
temples are all filled with the most beautiful paintings (on walls
and screens) from early Japanese history.

The earliest people here were called Aimu and they still live
on the northern island of Hokkudo. Then the true Japanese
people came over the Japan Sea from Korea and China. They
have received their cultural heritage from these places also. Even
their language uses Chinese characters. Their paintings are full

of animals, birds, nature scenes, and of course, people. There are a lot of trees and Japanese art has a tremendous sense of balance and proportion. What is that? Suppose you have a room and you fill it up with everything—furniture, clothes, lots of pictures, etc. That is not in good taste. But if you take a room and only put a few simple things in it that suit the size, color, and style of that room, and in themselves are beautifully made and are placed in just the right spot; that is proportion, good taste, and art. And all Japanese rooms are like this.

Such was the room where we took part in a "Tea ceremony." Noviko's father-in-law took us to the birthplace of the Tea ceremony (one room was 450 years old) and an ancestor of the present family was the first great master of the Tea ceremony. Today, this place is also used to teach teachers how to improve their ability to conduct a Tea ceremony. I'm sure you will wonder how all this can happen over drinking a cup of tea? Well, this is the symbol of old Japan (like flower arranging—where you study all your life how to arrange flowers). Here is what happens. First we took off our shoes and entered a room with very little light. Along the walls were six pillows (to sit on your knees). We sat down. When my eyes became accustomed to the dark, I saw that in one corner, hanging from the ceiling (ceilings are low, because most Japanese people are quite short) on a chain, was a pot of boiling water sunk in a square hole in the floor, steam coming out of a little square hole in the pot (charcoal fire). Near the pot was a simple open shelved table of beautiful lacquer. (Lacquer is the art of decorating a piece of wood with as many as 30 coats of lacquer paint all rubbed down smooth.) On this table were only a bowl with a small wooden egg beater (of thin bamboo and a ladle, serving spoon) in it, and a small tea bowl and a napkin. A young lady (usually the ceremony is conducted by a man) entered the room on her knees and bowed twice, touching the floor with her head. Then she went to the area of the table. An assistant did the same thing and brought in six tea bowls. The first lady (in a magnificent

kimono with an obi sash in back) took the ladle and beater out
of the cup and placed them on the floor. Then she took the tea
bowl and ladled out some crushed (powdered) green tea and
put it in the boiling pot. Then plates were served out and three
small pieces of strange candy were put on each plate. With each
serving the young lady faced each person and bowed low (as did
we, all) as she served. Then she ladled some tea into her tea bowl,
and then poured it back, wiping her bowl meticulously (and the
ladle). Finally, she thought the tea just right and poured some in
a tea bowl (like a soup bowl made of the most beautiful pottery
and each one different), served each person one at a time. As the
bowl is placed in front of the drinker, it is turned away from the
drinker. As you drink you hold the bowl in both hands. Were we
surprised! The tea (I forgot—the lady beat the tea hard with the
beater) was thick like a pea soup and tasted just like alfalfa. (ugh)
But you get used to it. The drinker is supposed to drink it all in
three and a half sips. Then she passed the bowl (lacquer) around
for us to admire and collected our things with more bows to
the floor. One is only supposed to talk calmly and impersonally.
"What a nice day." "It is good to see you," etc. Everything was
put back just as it was and we quietly got up and went on.

We were taken to the tourist part of the house where
foreigners can sit on real chairs and experience part of this
ceremony, and we also went to their new building across the
street where they teach these ceremonies. We were told it takes
two or three years to learn the basic part and one never stops
studying all one's life! Isn't that something!

We also visited Mr. Kosai's Shinto Shrine. Gardens with
upward curved temples. People come to special places, pull a
card that rings a bell and with head bowed, hands folded, they
meditate (think) for a few moments. You only go when you feel
like it. We also had lunch at the Losai house (consisting of rice
cakes covered with eel skins, bean cakes, and other small fish,
etc.) Japanese food is stranger and to my taste not as appetizing
as Chinese food. They eat Sukiyaki which they make right in

front of you. (There is a restaurant in New York that does this and I will take you) and they eat tempura which is frying food like shrimp or vegetables in a boiling fat for a few seconds. In one dinner we had a soup with a whole fish head in it. And we had octopus tentacles! And they love sour vegetables.

In Kyoto, besides visiting temples and palaces we also visited the Sion district which is where the young Geisha girls (like Korean Kisaeng) are trained almost from childhood. Their makeup and dress is traditional and you can see it on almost any old Japanese print. (The reason my writing is so scribbly bad is that I am always writing these letters on planes, cars, and now a train from Osaka to Nagoya.) Very special and complicated hairdo, beautiful kimono with the traditional obi (sash) in back and white socks with one toe plus getas (wooden shoes). The front of their face is painted chalk white, reddish tinges in the corner of their eyes and a funny design on the back of their necks. We went to a cute variety show put on with over 100 Geishas. On one side, a whole row, playing the traditional large drum with two sticks. The other side, another row of girls playing shamisens (a banjo type instrument with a long neck). On the center stage, dancing scenes were presented. One clever one depicted a group of girls in a night village scene catching fire flies. The fire flies were tiny light bulbs hung on wires and all you could see were the lights going on and off. Actually these girls are primarily entertainers for small parties. Our first concert in the Tokyo festival was a big occasion and two unexpected members of the audience caused quite a stir. The first was one of the Princes of the Royal family who granted us an interview at intermission. We didn't ask for it—but were conducted to a room where we had tea and pastry and carried on a conversation through an interpreter. We played a Ravel movement as an encore at his request. The second person was none other than the new Ambassador from America, Mr. Reichauer who came backstage with his beautiful Japanese wife to congratulate us. We were honored since he had just arrived and is extremely busy.

The Japanese inn outside of the city of Fukuoka is very much like the Korea style hotel. A little more solidly built and the young serving girls put their hands over their mouths and giggle. We arrived after the concert and my room was just perfect in the taste of its decorations and furnishings. The floor is covered with soft straw mats called Tatami. There were flower arrangements in a vase. (You can study flower arranging the way we study music.) There is a big squat jug called a Hibachi with ashes in it and a charcoal fire with a tea kettle steaming on an iron frame. The furniture is only a foot high because you sit and sleep on the floor, and there is a screen with a mountain painting on it as well as drawings of Chinese characters (called calligraphy) hung on the wall.

We had a Japanese dinner. When the girl served us she knelt down to set things on the low table. First we had three small dishes (with sauce). The first was raw fish rolled around the hard yolk of an egg. Then there was crab and chicken liver as well as sour celery, bamboo shoots (thick), cucumber, small birds and octopus tentacles. Then there was tempura (ebi), meaning fried shrimp —with ginger root and horseradish. And broccoli with lots of soy sauce and two kinds of soup, one with a fish's head in it (including the eye, ugh!) and one of small oyster-like-clams— which was wonderful. And of course warm sake wine and green tea. I had to wear the Japanese kimono with a sash around the waist and after the meal was finished my bed mat was ready— now here I lean over the pillow writing it all down.

Imagine, Mr. Medd's two young children, aged 3 and 4 (he is the American Information officer here) cannot speak English— only Japanese, and the southern island of Kyushu dialect at that! You know, this letter is never going to end (maybe?) so I will leave the next 50,000 words for the finale of our Japanese visit. See you in less than a month.

Love,
Daddy

MAY 5, 1961

Dearest Lisa and everyone,

   This is the most exciting day of all. Right at this moment we
are 8,000 feet above the Cambodian jungles. Once in a while
we see the great Mekong River and look into the country of
Thailand (also known as Siam). We will land in southern Laos in
a town called Pakse and there the Royal Laos Airlines will have a
plane to fly us to Vientiane which is the capitol of Laos. Perhaps
you know about the difficult struggle going on here, where the
non-communist countries are trying to keep these areas from
becoming communist. In Laos, there is fighting going on just
forty miles from where we play our two concerts and of course
we hope the fighting will stop. Ambassador Harriman just came
through Saigon and he was not too encouraged. All of Southeast
Asia is threatened, and in Viet Nam where we just played the
country is practically controlled by terrible bands of communist
guerilla fighters. They hide in the jungles and come out at night
and terrorize the villagers and farmers and kill anybody they
want to. Even in Saigon where we stayed, they come in secretly
and throw hand grenades into buildings and crowds where
Americans or important people are. We played our concert in
a movie house and before we were allowed to play, the police
checked every seat and place for the possibility of finding a
bomb that might explode during the concert. Westerners do
not dare to go to the beach nearby or out of the city very far
because they might be shot as many already have.
   So you see, this is not a happy place. Yet the Vietnamese
people are a wonderful people and I am glad to have made their
brief acquaintance. Like most Asian people they are very short.
They are light brown in color and have very black hair. The
women wear it long. They are most handsome and their eyes are
somewhat slanted thought not so much as Chinese or Japanese.
Their cheek-bones are not as high. Their appearance contains a

gentleness and softness (which in the women, combined with their exquisite costume, makes them amongst the most beautiful women in the world). The female costume is at once colorful, graceful, flowing and breathtaking. First there is an under slip or blouse which can be white or black. And a type of Chinese silk pajamas also white or black. Over this the dress of bright color (all colors of the rainbow are used, of beautiful pattern and design) is worn. There is a round collar, long sleeves, and a length close to the ankles. The pajamas slightly show. But the unusual part is the split up to the hip on both sides so there is a front and back "apron" that flows in the breeze.

The men usually wear shorts and shirts or some pants. Saigon is a French built city (the country was once part of the French Empire) and contains over 2,000,000 people. It is situated on the Saigon River. There are a lot of walled gardens and rich colonial villas (where the foreigners live along with the rich Vietnamese). I could appreciate them more if I didn't see so many poor people, beggars, filled with disease and eating very little. The country is not the worst by far (I am told India is much worse) but it tears my heart to see some of the pitiful sights I have seen.

We are now in the land of hot, hot, hot. We were very lucky because our hotel rooms (overlooking the river) were air conditioned. To go in the room from the outside was like going into an ice-box. To come out was like walking into an oven. You have to change your clothes very often and take a shower at least three times a day. It is so hot that you cannot work too hard or move too fast and almost everybody takes a siesta between 12pm and 12:30pm in the afternoon. Even the poor children lie down on a doorstep in the shade and sleep. In Asia the market places are the most interesting of all and Saigon is no exception.

Time out while we land in Pakse. I will continue in the Laotian plane. (On this plane are some American children, father is a missionary and they are going to join him in the jungle land of Laos. Six boys, named Timmy, Tommy, Teddy (7 years old), Terry, Torry and Tillman.) (On the airfield at Pakse were many

Laotian soldiers with guns and real ammunition. We had our
pictures taken with some of them.)

Back in the air going north and back to the marketplace
in Saigon. One has to get used to some strange things. People
squat on their feet and sit this way for hours. Women constantly
chew Betel nut. They dip the nut in some lime and hold it hard
between their teeth. Then they spit a lot because the lime causes
one to salivate. The spit is bloody red, and over the years their
teeth become a lovely, ugly black! Then the smells! Of food, and
mold, and human beings. If you have a delicate "smeller" don't
go to an Asian market. Babies run around naked, old men sit
and talk and sometimes smoke bamboo water pipes. Everybody
chattering, girls in beautiful costumes shopping, animals being
slaughtered, food, clothes, hard-wares piled up in each shop.
Most people barefoot and unfortunately—too dark to get
good pictures of such a miraculous scene. We also visited two
religious shrines. The people are mostly Buddhist (but a form
of it peculiar to Southeast Asia). The Chinese influence is there
but the Indian character is stronger. The first shrine we went to
is a tomb of a famous ancient general and his wife. The king of
the country was mad at this general and when the general was
buried in the tomb, the king had the tomb whipped 100 times.
There are many statues and burning coals at places where people
buy incense sticks and place them upright to burn and as they
do this they pray. Inside the temple are various rooms with many
imposing statues (some very big) of Buddha, sitting or standing.
His hands always in one of a few accepted positions.

The people take round boxes of sticks and shake them for a
long time. Finally they allow one stick to fall out. This one has
a number which then they take to a priest and he gives them
their fortune. Also, if they have a problem or hope they take
two kidney shaped stones and as they kneel praying they let the
stones fall and how they fall tells them if their wish will come
true. They hire "wise, older men" to read documents or longer
prayers to the images. But at the second temple, which was the

most fascinating (more Chinese influences) the most impressive sight was countless spiral-like springs, coils of incense hung from the ceilings. If you wish to burn this incense in honor of your ancestors you can pay for one month of burning or even 6 months (costs about $8.00).

We also went to a Vietnamese folk opera (very much like Chinese opera) with colorful costumes and comedy routines but we didn't see classic plays. These are (I am told) very beautiful and a young man at a party sang some of these chants from the country's long epic poem (wet nurses and mothers sing this to the children) and it was singularly beautiful. We also went to their national conservatory where they played on their classical folk instruments. Very much like Chinese, and one young group played a Mozart string quartet for us and think of it, two of them had never had a lesson on their instruments, and the quartet was self-learned from records. Unbelievable!

The embassy gave us a reception where many ambassadors and important political people from different countries came and the concert was considered a great success.

Then we had a great to-do about getting to Laos. The Vietnam airplane flies to Pakse in Southern Laos. There it meets the Royal Laos plane and they exchange passengers. For some reason the Vietnamese people decided Laos wasn't flying so they cancelled their flight. We had a big uproar and even agreed to pay $350 more to take the plane ourselves—but when we got to the airport, there were other passengers and at Pakse the Laos plane was there and they had their return passengers. I finish this letter after our Laos visit (en route to Bangkok) but Laos was one of the greatest experiences of my life—so I will have to write again.

Love,
Daddy

MAY 10, 1961

Dearest Lisa (and everybody),

Here I am flying over the gulf of Siam and in Bangkok at the
Royal Palace I saw where Anna taught the children of the King
of Siam many, many years ago.

I must tell you not only of my visit to Siam but also to Laos.
I already told you how Laos is having a war that the people
don't want but the Communists are pushing. Every day you
can see headlines in the newspapers about it. We flew from
Saigon to a town in South Laos called Pakse and changed planes
to go to Savanna Khet and finally Vientiane which is where
the government of Laos is. Laos is shaped like a boomerang.
Vientiane is on the river and when you look across you can see
Northern Thailand which is the true name for Siam. The Thai
and Laotian people are related and cross back and forth between
the two countries. These countries are the land of elephants.
There used to be white elephants and they were considered
sacred. There are lots of tigers, monkeys, and poisonous snakes in
these places. When we walked in a flooded temple (called Wat)
we were warned to look out for some snakes as there are kinds
that are sure death if you get bitten (and no antidote).

Well—we thought that Vientiane would be full of soldiers
and people would be scared because some of the fighting is only
a few miles away. (Last December there was fighting in the city
and then all of the American families were moved out.) But
the city is quiet and lovely. Of course, my bags were not on the
airplane and I had a bad time until word came that they were
left in Pakse. (I had to borrow clothes for our main concert.)
The bags were brought by military plane the next day. Laos
was very much like Korea in primitiveness and warmth of the
people. The market place was the most fabulous of all and I
have some marvelous pictures of such things as women buying
live beetles (big ones) for eating! Also ant eggs and many other

strange foods. One thing that the Thai and Laos people take on picnics is this: they make a paste out of the bugs and mix this raw with sticky rice. Then they take a young bamboo pole and make it hollow. They push the paste in when and when they are hungry they just peel down a bit of bamboo and there is a tasty meal. There is no wonder that there is much sickness in some of these countries. You should see the meat lying in the sun with hundreds of flies on it! The women wear a very pretty skirt with local material and I have a shawl for you of this. They sew gold and silver into the cloth.

All houses in this part of the world are built on stilts because there is much rain and the ground floods. And the lizards! They are everywhere. On the walls of our hotel rooms, and one on the outside wall was 16 inches long! They are very good because they eat flies and mosquitoes (we had to sleep with mosquito nets around the beds because there is so much danger of being bitten by malarial mosquitos).

Like Saigon, this was the first quartet concert in the country of Laos, and it was well attended. Even the Laos Premiere and his wife, as well as the American Ambassador, Mr. Winston Brown. Mr. Brown, who I am sure has much more important things to do (and his group of American staff members) turned out to be quite a wonderful person and a music lover. We had lunch at his house and he gave a special party for all the representatives of foreign governments plus Lao people, Thai Prince Hwan, a recent president of the United Nations Assembly, and Senator Dodd who is on a tour of the area; at which we played the Schubert "Death and Maiden" quartet out of doors. After a few bars, a ripe mango from the trees above fell and knocked over my music (but was put back on the stand by the French Ambassador) and there were a few more attacks and the wind blew all kinds of twigs on our heads. But we didn't stop and were admired not only for our playing but our ability to continue under "fire." That was the closest we came to real warfare.

We got very used to the Lao and Thai greeting which I once described to you. Finger tips touching and up in front of the face with head slightly bowed. And, the food is very interesting. Like Chinese but much more peppery. Some of the fruits are very exotic. Mangos! Yum. But the most interesting is a purple fruit about the size of a small apple. Inside is a white large center (the seed) but that is what you eat. Adlai Stevenson was in Bangkok and he didn't know about what to eat so he ate the outside and was very unhappy because it is most "mouth puckering" and bitter. The inside tasted like a mixture of tangerine, banana and sugared grapefruit. Yum!

Laos and Thailand are the lands of the Buddhist priests. (Burma, too.) Hundreds of them on the streets and in the temples. All in colorful orange robes (and no girls or women are allowed to touch the robe). Boys started studying for priesthood at very early ages (10 or 11) and everybody studies a little even if he will not become a priest. We visited the great Laos national monument called That Luang. It is very high and the top part is shaped like a graceful turret. Under the eaves were gigantic beehives and I wouldn't want to stir them up. Nearby was a village with a "long" house (where all through Melanesia and Polynesia the men or elders meet to decide important matters). All over there were preparations for an important festival day, called Fireworks Festival. They were making long rockets on stands and very colorful. These are carried to a special spot and at the climax of the festival they are fired off. Some men were getting drums and gongs and other instruments prepared. They would spit on the big drum head and massage it. The big gongs had wonderful "out of tune" tones. Other men were slicing off layers of green bamboo and carving wonderful designs from them and then building little houses out of them. The children were all racing around having fun (with or without clothes

on—because it is so hot). The next morning we came back and
already people were celebrating. We were really amazed because
this turned out to be one of their most important festivals (the
festival of fertility). Many groups of men and boys (women do
not take part) with some of the men dressed as women and all
of them painted and in strange costumes danced from house
to house singing chants and playing drums, cans, and Klenes!
This is a tremendous instrument and a little like the Chinese
and Japanese one. (I am bringing one home.) It is made of
many thin bamboo reeds and sounds like a little organ. These
groups danced the famous dance of Laos called Lamuong. It is
extremely graceful and hypnotic. At each house they blessed
it and the man of the house came out and offered a potent
fermented rice drink to the dancers (soon they got very drunk).
The purpose was to ensure that the people in the house would
be blessed with the arrival of a new baby in the ensuing year.
There were lots of costumes that alluded to the parts of people
that help to make babies and even the children took part in this.
In America this would never be allowed. Not because we are
more civilized, but because we are more socially restrained by
our own customs.

Anyway, the celebrating was one of the most exciting things
I have ever witnessed and I'm sure this will be the high point
of the trip. Before we left Laos, we also went to a country fair
(to raise money for the temples) and the main attraction was a
dance arena where the young Laos men paid to dance with the
young Laos girls and they danced the Lamuong. At one point
we were invited to take part and that must have been some
sight because even though it is a simple dance, we were very
awkward compared to the graceful movements of the men. The
women have to move their hands in a very difficult way. But the
men don't, except for the older men who dance much more
beautifully.

We were sorry to leave Laos. Bangkok had to be a bit
disappointing afterwards and though it had new interests, it was

a letdown. First of all, Bangkok is a very big and quite modern
city and it is very expensive. Then we were not able to see any of
the great Thai dancing or hear them play. We did visit the royal
palace and it is just like a fairy palace with strange statues and
giants and thousands of different painted rocks and the buildings
are like children's drawings. There is an emerald Buddha in
one building and that is very impressive and we saw the throne
room. We also visited two houses where there are great personal
collections of Thailand art (many Buddhas) and I went on a
Klong trip along the canals where people live and I will finish
this in the next letter.

Love,
Daddy (Bob)

MAY 14, 1961

Dearest Lisette, (& all),

I'm afraid that my last letter (May 12th) was the dullest of
a rather dullish lot and besides, much too stuffy-grownupish.
Remember the game we used to play, when we would name the
animal we thought each of us was? Mommy was a Cheetah and
I was a Buffalo. When it comes to letter writing that's just what I
am. Heavy, lumpy, brown-black and little not so bright.

Well, I'm going to shed my skin (and some weight after all
these Siamese and Chinese feasts). Shall I be a tiger? They still
roam around the jungles here and affluent (there I go again—
that means wealthy (rich) and a bit more important) people in
Siam like to receive tiger heads with silver plated mouths as gifts
of esteem (respect). No. Obviously, I can't be a tiger.

How about a monkey? When we went to visit the house
of Mr. Thompson (he is the man who started the whole silk-
making in Siam and his house is full of the most beautiful

things)—we saw a spider monkey who is the pet of the house. He is bashful, but likes his friends. He will bite if you bother him and his cousins in the jungle will throw coconuts and mangoes at you and make an awful racket. No—I can't be a monkey.

How about a goose? You know that people keep geese because they keep the snakes away (something about the smell and the dung of the geese that bothers the snakes). Or maybe a mongoose? They are marvelous. The are not geese at all and I remember a wonderful story about Riki-Tiki-Tavi, and the Indian mongoose who is a hero and saves a family from a bad cobra snake. A mongoose can jump backwards and he is so quick that when the snake strikes out from his coil he misses and then the mongoose grabs the snake's head and breaks it in his teeth. I'd like to be a mongoose, but I don't jump backwards well enough.

Should I be the snake? On no—then nobody would like me. Once a lady in Siam came home and sat down because she was very tired. She asked her servant if he would bring her some lunch. The servant said, "You come over in the dining room and I serve you." She said, "No, I'm too tired, bring the food here." He said, "No, you come, missy, dining room." (That's how some people speak English here.) She got mad and got up and said, "Oh, all right, but I don't know what's wrong with you today," and then she walked toward the door, and quickly the servant took a gun out of his pocket and shot a Krite dead that was hanging on the lamp right where the lady had been sitting. (A Krite bite is worse than a Cobra and you are dead in a few minutes.) Well, aren't you glad that the servant was so wise, because if he had said to the lady, "Missy, Krite, him 'bove you, lamp" she probably would have screamed or jumped and surely then the Krite would have bitten her!

No—No—No—I won't be a snake! Elephants are nice, but I'm not big enough. And Vultures that fly around in the sky looking for a dead animal to eat are too repulsive. I rather like the lizards on the walls. Even the bigger ones that make such

strange noises at night, but I think I'd rather not be one (like
the purple cow). And then there are frogs. We saw a frog in the
corner where a wall touched the ceiling and the lady said that
this frog has legs that stretch over a foot long when he jumps
and he can jump from the floor all the way to the ceiling. And
like our little chameleon lizard (remember) he can change his
color.

But I don't want to be him because if you touch him you get
a rash which never, never comes off. And I don't want to be a
fish because then I'll end up being eaten in a sweet and sour dish
by some Chinese business man—and in pieces with chopsticks,
too—ouch!

What shall I be? I'll just have to wait and when I see you in
Honolulu in June you will decide for me.

Do you know that the man who ran the concert in Bangkok,
when he came to Siam for the first time, with his wife twenty-
five years ago, they came from Burma and they had to cross the
Siamese peninsula (water)—water on elephants!

And also I met a lovely young man who plays the violin and
knows a great deal and is extremely intelligent. His home is
in Pakistan and he has invited you and Nicholas and Mommy
and me to visit with him in a mountain valley in the Himalayas
(highest mountains in the world) where the tribe of people called
the Hunzas live. (They are the healthiest people in the world and
live very long. Many of them live over a hundred years.)

After Siam (Thailand) we flew south to Singapore that is
an island off the Malay Peninsula (there goes that word again).
Singapore is a big city and the island is a little country. But they
would like to join the Federated United States. The states won't
let them because the Malay people there have a slight majority
(more than) of the population (over the Chinese) and Singapore
is mostly made up of Chinese people. The Malay States fought
a terrible war to stop the Communists from ruling the land and
they don't want to upset the control they now have. Malaya is a
remarkable place.

It is well governed, it is prosperous (natural rubber from rubber trees—they plant them and tap the sap and make rubber from it) tin (one third of the word gets its tin from Malaya) and many other things. It's the only place on our whole trip where we can drink tap water, eat all the uncooked vegetables and eat butter, milk, etc. without being afraid to get dysentery.

There was quite a commotion in Kuala Lumpur, capital of the Malay States where we played.

The flagship of the 7th U.S. Navy fleet was near there and Sargent Shriver (President Kennedy's brother-in-law) was also there setting up the Peace Corps (maybe you will join someday?)—where young people go to underdeveloped countries to work with the people. Admiral Griffen the Commander of the 7th fleet (which has a very important position in this dangerous area) came to the concert and we met him at the reception afterwards. What a rarity! He is a military man who loves chamber music. (Like Ambassador Brown in Laos who plays Mozart sonatas on the piano.) Say—how is your piano playing? Besides not writing me any sweet letters, I haven't heard a thing about your piano lessons. Well—you can tell me in Honolulu. It certainly was fun to walk the streets of Kuala Lumpur. People in this part of the world speak the Malay language (one of the simplest in the whole world.) And the men wear white shirts and trousers with a beautiful colored shawl around their waist. The women wear the sarong skirt. We took a ride with a terrible driver out of town to the famous Batu Caves. There is a Buddhist Shrine inside, but you have to climb thousands of stairs to get to them. They are at the top of a limestone cliff and in the heat of this part of the world, it was very hot climbing up. Inside the cave it was cooler but very wet. Quiet, except for the squeaks of millions of bats. The roof and sides of the cave form scary, fantastic shapes and it is very, very tall inside.

It certainly is fun to be in the part of the world where the main tree is the tall palm tree. After Kuala Lumpur, we flew back to the city of Singapore to give our concert there. I finally got what I have always wanted and Lucy, too. A profound lava stone head of Buddha from a very famous area of Java (near Burobudur, the great monument of this part of the world.) It cost a lot of money and weighs at least 25 lbs, but it thrills me to look at it. Even Claus (who really does know something about this) likes it.

Mr. Goh (who put on the concert and is the main violin teacher in Singapore) had his two young wonder-violinists play for us—two brothers ages 11 and 17. They lived on the streets and had a crazy father, but they are being properly cared for now. You should hear them play. Wonderful! The Consul General gave us a party at his residence, and what a 'palace' that is! Whatever the difficulties of diplomatic life, the living is certainly paradise (mansions and servants). The Consul's wife went shopping with us the next morning and all too soon our visit to Singapore and Malyasia was over. We flew back over Malaya (along the famous Malacca straits where seafarers have sailed since the beginning of human civilization) and saw hundreds of open tin mines which from the air look like small ponds of greenish water and sand pits surrounding them. Finally we stopped for 30 minutes at Penang (a little island off north Malaya) and then flew off across the straits to make our first stop in Sumatra, Indonesia at the city of Medan—and here begins a strange tale which I will relate in the next letter.

Love,
Daddy (Bob)

P.S. You see—I started out with fun and soon became sober-serious again. What a dull father you have!

May 22, 1961

(You might get this letter before my preceding one)

Dearest Lisa,

This is my last day on the Asia tour and my last travelogue
letter. Tomorrow I leave Indonesia and the visit here has lasted
9 days. This has been the most difficult part of the trip and
the most tiring. It is the hottest, the most annoying, the most
frustrating, most uncomfortable, but also most exciting.

We flew from Penang, Malaya over the Malacca straights
(water) to Medan in northern Sumatra, we entered the country
of Indonesia. This area was mostly a colony of the Duth until they
won their independence after World War II. It is enormous and
made up of thousands of volcanic islands. In Java we went by Mt.
Meraysi which had sent streams of lava and ash over some villages
and was still smoking when we saw it.) From the top of Sumatra
over to the Easternmost Island is almost 4,000 miles. Even though
it is made up of islands it has a land mass of some 900,000 square
miles. (The island of Borneo is bigger than the state of Texas.
Sumatra is one of the wildest countries in the world and in one
part the fierce Atje tribe lives. Even today, they kill strangers and
practice some cannibalism (eating human beings). The jungles ae
so thick in vegetation and full of swamps (poison snakes, bugs,
crocodiles, and everything else like tigers and pythons) that there
is very little traveling in the countryside. Medan where we landed
is the biggest city and here we met the "police-state." The police
at the airport were very severe and wanted to see everything
and make it difficult. Claus was taken into a little room to be
examined twice (sometimes they strip off your clothes). (Also,
they can take away your money or cameras or anything if they
feel like doing so.) It took us over an hour for this and we went
through the same procedure every time we entered or left the
airport. (Leaving Medan they refused to let our luggage go on

the same plane until the local contact finally persuaded them. In Sananeng we had to hide our cameras or they would take them away. Anytime an important politician or any soldier wants to get on a plane, the airline just takes anybody they want off the plane to make room. Even diplomatic officials.)

This is the first country where there is no air conditioning at all and what heat! And our poor violins! When we played concerts in Medan 2 in Djakarta, Bandung, and Samareng, the sweat poured down the head to foot and flowed over the instruments like small rivers.

The men in all of Indonesia (there are many different races)— mostly wear a little round black hat (Americans call them "peachies") colored or white shirt, and very elegant long sarongs made of a stiffer material than the women's sarongs. The women wear light shawls and long graceful sarongs made of many different styles of cloths. One of the most interesting is Batik and that is a cloth that is very artful. The old ones are stamped and dyed by hand and are extremely beautiful. Marriage dresses and dancers' costumes have much gold and silver thread and are very heavy (as are the headdresses). I should add that the people are as poor as I've ever seen and many people's clothing consists of a pair of tattered pants, on a moth eaten, torn shirt or skirt. (Children are very often naked.)

We were lucky, because the American consul was delayed in Malaya and we stayed at his home. The market in Medan was, as all markets are, lively, smelly, fascinating. I've told you enough about such markets and I have enough movies to show you. One slight difference here was that the people were friendly and jokey at the same time that many did not like to have their pictures taken. Also, everywhere, mothers are nursing their babies while they work.

The Sumatran people are different than the Javanese, more direct and honest, and they feel that the Javanese (who are the most populous) run the country for themselves. (There are still rebel soldiers in Sumatra. After seeing mile after mile of Sumatran jungle (from the airplane, 900 miles Medan to Djakarta—capitol of Indonesia) I'm glad we didn't have to land in the country of the Atjes because I wouldn't make very good stew.

It was very different in Djakarta, Java. Java is the most densely populated area in the world and after driving over a good bit of Central Java and seeing houses lining the road for most of the way, I'm sure it's true. Djakarta is an ugly conglomeration of low lying buildings, shacks, Betjos (bicycle cabs) and 3 ½ million people.

One thing—this country is about the dirtiest in the whole world, the food is so dirty that almost anything gives one dysentery (we ate very little, the whole week) and you can't drink any water unless you see it boiled in front of you. The people are mostly barefoot and 90 percent suffer from hookworm which saps your vitality. Most of the babies struggle very hard to live but many die from sickness before they are two years old. The people eat mostly rice and fish and in the country we saw thousands of people in the rice fields. Their feet in mud and water up over their knees, planting, gathering up, making bundles, and drying, shaking, pounding, and carrying rice. With their balancing stick they carry loads that you or I couldn't possibly carry. After the two concerts in Djakarta we drove up into the mountains to Bandung. On the way we had to pass a very wild and dangerous area where at night, bandits and Moslem fanatics rob and kill travelers. (We went in the daytime but we still wondered.)

After the Bandung concert we started early the next morning and drove from 6am to 8pm from Bandung and Semareng. This was a remarkable trip. The first part was in the mountains (and quite cool). The jungle was thick and green; palm trees everywhere, also giant ferns and millions of flowers. The valleys were deep and muddy waters rushed down the hills. As the land flattened out, the rice fields in lovely terraced designs came into view. It is never cold here so there are four growing seasons and four crops of rice, so someone is always getting his field ready. They have water buffalo here who pull the plows and the

farmers sing a plaintive chant or song to keep these big strong
animals calm and happy while they work. On the road it was
nice to see drivers of carts splashing water on their oxen to keep
them cool. The girls all wear the peaked straw hats and they
are sometimes very, very beautiful. We passed by fishing villages
where men were mending nets or fixing graceful boats.

The exciting moment of this trip was stopping where a
village puppet story (Wayang) was in progress. In front the men
sat watching the play. Then there was a banana log and hundreds
of puppets with all the characters from the Ramayana Hindu
stories. The story teller sits crossed-legged behind the log and
moves the puppets and tells the story to the accompaniment
of the music from the Gamelan orchestra. There are drums,
wooden xylophones, gongs, bells, flutes, even an Arabian violin
called a rebab. The story teller's wife played a xylophone while
her baby nursed at her breast and with her free hand she fanned
the baby and herself. Her little girl lay on the floor and hit
a metal instrument every few seconds in time with the rest
of the music. Crowding around the musicians were all ages
of children and women, talking, screaming, eating, playing,
watching and listening. We ran around taking millions of
pictures and marveling at the experience. Finally we took out
our instruments, music and stands and right on the dirt floor
we played Haydn and Bartók for the village people. When we
would play fast or high or snap pizzicato they would laugh and
clap their hands, just like little children. It is something to see
these people laugh. I would call it liquid laughter because the
smile ripples across the whole face like a flowing brook. And as
they laugh their eyes are bright stars in a sunny sky.

The two hours of our ride were on such a bumpy road, full of
holes, that my stomach was up where my throat is and nothing
stayed in its right place. Even so—we put our things in the hotel
room in Semareng and went to a Wayang Orang performance.
This is the same kind of story as with puppets, but played by
live actors with masks and wonderful costumes. The actors

and actresses move in a manner that suggests the movement of
puppets. The story we saw was about a bad, bold monkey king
and how he was defeated and of course the gamelan orchestra
played all the time. When we went to sleep the room was very,
very hot. I have crossed the equator for the first time in my
life. Also, we had to use mosquito netting to keep the malaria
mosquitoes from biting us. The very next day we again got up
early and drove another 13 hours before we came back and
played our last concert of the tour. But we did this because
we wanted to see two very great monuments. The Hindu one
called Pranganan and the Buddhist one called Burubudor. They
are as big as the biggest New York buildings and are wonders
of the world. On the walls are what we call bas-reliefs which
are half sculptures made out of rock telling many stories. There
are thousands of them along with the most beautiful statues on
these two monuments. At Prangbanan, many school children
your age were visiting and we had our pictures taken with them.
One little girl fell down many steps, but besides bruising herself,
I don't think she was badly hurt. On this trip, we also stopped
at Djakarta, a city that Claus Adam lived in from his third year
to his sixth. This city is the cultural center of Java where the
little girls learn to dance so beautifully. Here I bought you some
lovely dance costumes and one wonderful hat which is hard to
carry so I wear it myself.

When we played our concert that night we were so tired that
I am afraid we did not play very well. When you walk around
the streets at night and it is still very hot you see whole families
sleeping on the dirty sidewalks, on little steps in front of shops
and anyplace they can rest. The music of street gamelan players
fills the air softly and the candles at the night marketplace flicker
with a dreamy unreality. The smells are just as strong as ever but
the darkness of night envelops everybody and everything in a
merciful blanket of semi-secrecy and then, as I trespass through the
alleys, avoiding the refuse under my footsteps and the scurrying
rats with their bubonic, beady eyes; averting my gaze from too

direct a look at the pitiful, tattered and huddled half forms wearily escaping from the pitiless, sunny reality of day, then I feel the pulse that is Asia, and all the fabulous, wondrous, magical events I have witnessed on our triumphal tour fade to triviality and away from my loved ones, I walk alone slowly and cry.

Dear little Lisa, the above is for a Lisa grown up, and for a Lucy and for myself, but the trip is over and its mark will always be with me. I hope someday you, too, can make such a trip.

The flight back to Djakarta, the ambassadors reception and our last flight (each his own way) is anti-climactic. The next few days I will find us the house in Hawaii that we will live in together again and where I will also collect my feelings and thoughts. Tell Mommy and Nicholas that I will telephone you all sometime before you fly, most likely on May 28 on Sunday (before bedtime).

All my love,
Daddy (Bobby)

Robert and Lisa, after a Juilliard String Quartet concert, mid-1960s

PART VII

Coda

[CREATIVE EXPRESSIONS]

Robert frequently wrote poems and letters to his wife, Lucy.

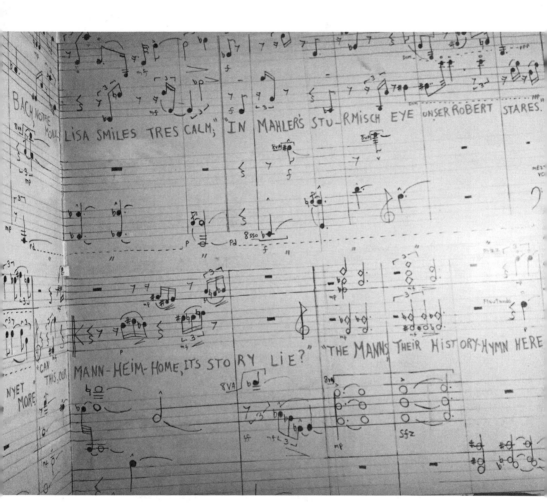

Robert's composition, which he drew on their apartment's kitchen wall, incorporates all the family names with corresponding musical notes.

[PHOTO GALLERY]

Robert as a baby, with his parents, Anna and Charles Mann, circa 1923

Robert rehearsing, 1964

*Robert and Nicholas
playing, 1960s*

*Robert and Nicholas Mann
duo flyer*

OPPOSITE: *Robert and
Nicholas, fashion shoot
for* Esquire

*Robert and Lisa,
Aspen, late 1960s*

Lisa and Lucy, at the Pierre Hotel, early 1960s

Robert and Lucy's close friend Leo Kok, Lisa's godfather. Leo was a Dutch resistance fighter in World War II, and owned an antiquarian book store in Ascona, Switzerland.

Robert and Lucy, Place de la Contrescarpe, June 1977

Robert and Lucy, 1970

The Lyric Trio performing at Seiji Ozawa's Matsumoto Festival

Robert and Lucy in front of her paintings of them

Robert and the Juilliard String Quartet with Martin Cornelissen in the Anechoic Chamber of the National Bureau of Standards, testing old and new instruments, March 1976

Juilliard String Quartet playing for Arthur Rubinstein in his apartment, Paris 1976

Robert with Robert Sirota and Elliott Carter, 2009

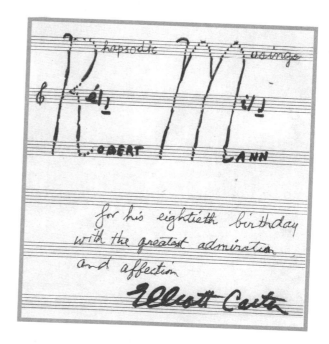

Elliott Carter's birthday card to Robert on his 80th birthday

The Babbitt Clarinet Quintet was a commission by Juilliard School of Music for the Juilliard String Quartet's 50th anniversary. Pictured are Charles Neidich, clarinetist, and the Juilliard String Quartet standing, Milton Babbitt, sitting.

Robert with violinist Anahid Ajemian, friend, colleague, and fellow Naumburg Competition winner

Robert with close friend Mark Sokol (1946-2014), of the Concord String Quartet

Robert made a number of duo recordings. He is pictured here with friend and colleague Stephen Hough, 1983 Naumburg Competition winner.

William Steig drawing of Juilliard String Quartet for their 50th anniversary

Juilliard String Quartet celebrating its 50th anniversary, 1996, cake made by Hansi Adam

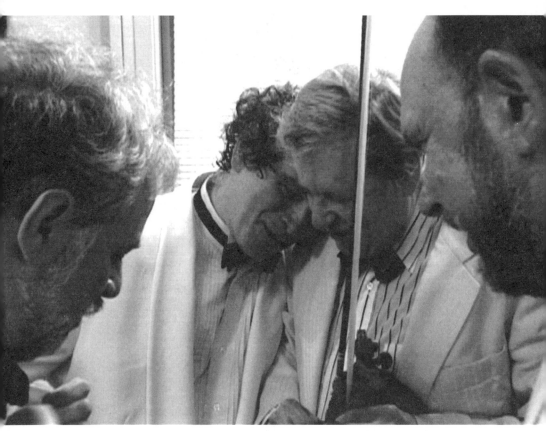
Robert backstage after his last Juilliard String Quartet concert, 1997

Robert coaching with Nicholas looking on, Robert Mann Chamber Music Institute, 2014

Juilliard String Quartet was named Musicians of the Year,
Musical America *magazine, 1996.*

*Robert, surrounded by quartets he has coached and with whom he has played, at the
Manhattan School of Music, 2009, Robert Mann tribute event. Pictured are members
of the Brentano, Tokyo, Pacifica, American, Shanghai, and Mann Quartets.*

PHOTO CREDIT: CHARLES ABBOTT

The Cold War between Apollonia and Dionysia

Dear Papa,

I cannot write poetry; I am not a poet. I cannot communi-

cate with light and shadow; I am not a painter. I cannot even

through movements and pantomimes reveal my feelings, my

thoughts; I am not a dancer. I am a musician. Tomorrow at

★*Cannabich's, I shall play all my congratulations for your

name and birthday on the Clavier.

And one tone after another, boasting amongst other things of illustrious genealogies and prowess in war (with words); supplicating deities, intoning the mysteries of love, as well as inducing buffalos to turn water wheels (with tones); and every stumbling step of the way till tomorrow their divine, fallible, inventive, intermittently rational voice of human beings has been contending with reason, with emotion,

---

★   Christian Cannabich (1731-1798), German violinist, composer and Kapellmeister

with both noble and nasty disposition, which words and which tones are the true and which are the false.

One certainty, words and tones together shared the same time-continuum with powerful effect. But the word-speakers held the word to be supreme and commanded the ordering of tones, while the tone-singers defiantly innovated and reordered their own tones as they dared.

From this endless struggle, the makers of tones, the shapers of words, the political moves of both as well as the under- and over-privileged audiences, have been, with unrestrained zeal, chipping and chopping away at the function and meaning of a growing body of tones and words defined as the art of music.

Igor Stravinsky stated in his Harvard lectures: "The poetics of the classical philosopher did not consist of lyrical dissertations about natural talent and about the essence of beauty." He continued, "Aristotle's poetics constantly suggests ideas regarding personal work arrangements of materials and structure." The poetics of music is exactly what Stravinsky was going to talk about; that is to say that he would not use music as a pretext for pleasant fancies.

Since Stravinsky imposingly took care of the poetics of music, but generously avoided the seductive path of pleasant fancies, I, with proper regard for you, Stravinsky, and myself, shall steer clear of the techné of my craft. I do not promise to avoid the pleasant fancies if they help me in any way to clarify and expose some of the confusion generated in the heat of that endless conflict I might title, "The Cold War between Apollonia and Dionysia." What you may ask, is that? Perhaps words on the objective and subjective elements in music will turn on a small light in the direction I hope to explore with you.

While the words "objective" and "subjective" possess semantic validity in the realm of philosophy, their application to the art of music has been most impressive. Reason and poetry both share the use of words. Tone shaping and emotional affect can share the same functioning in sound. The *Encyclopedia Britannica* holds Friedrich Nietzsche (1844-1900) responsible for the modern belief that the followers of Apollo and Dionysius were inimical to each other. I think it valuable to list some associative terms that are generally linked with each deity:

Apollo: God of the Sun—motion—harmony—the golden mean—objective—scientific—dispassionate—pure—formal—stricter than free—traditional—proportional—consonant—law abiding—entertaining—classic—noninvolved—cool—impersonal—relaxed—mind oriented—music for its own sake—non dramatic—non programmatic—loyal to the text—artificial—reasonable—rational.

Dionysius: God of wine—of ecstasy—night—catharsis—subjective—orgiastic—passionate—uninhibited—improvisatory—informal—more free than strict—innovative—revolutionary—involved—personal—intense—hot—dramatic—dissonant—propagandistic—programmatic—expressionistic—romantic—baroque—sensual—decadent—chaotic—natural—irrational.

In *Cratylus* Socrates pointed to the fact that Apollo was the God of harmony; musicians and astronomers both affirmed that Apollo made all things move together. Flowers of Orpheus, the musician, during the sixth century, acknowledging allegiance to the god, Dionysius, in reality worshipped within the cults of Apollo as well, thus creating some of the early philosophical confusion over Apollonia and Dionysian distinctions. I tend to believe the Orphic movement was more Apollonian than Dionysian (its favored instrument, the Apolline lyre). Delphic prophecy was reasonable, not rapturous. Asceticism, not exhilaration were embodied in the rhythmic stresses of words and plucked strings. How very different from the character of the instrument of the true followers of Dionysius, the double-fluted Aulos regarded in sound and symbol as ecstatic, orgiastic and phallic. These two instruments, Lyre and Aulos have come to represent the conflict between sobriety and ecstasy, reason and unreason, objectivity and subjectivity.

The number of cultural and social influences that shape musical taste are far more mysterious than a simple intuition of what is good or bad, right or wrong, or a simple development of a plucked string or a windblown tube. Bronislaw Malinowski (1884-1942) reported that

Trobriand Island singers were no less successful with the ladies than their music. "For" say the Trobrianders, "the throat is a long passage like the vulva and the two will attract."

"Greenlanders," and I hesitate to add most rock singers of this world, while singing, bend their knees at regular intervals, at times step forwards or backwards, turn half around, twist and contort the body; Greenlanders, the upper half, Elvis Presleys, the groin. Apropos of Dionysian body movement, the Juilliard String Quartet once received the following letter:

Dear Sirs,

When Camilla d'Urso began the study of the violin, her father made her practice with her right heel on a fragile china saucer so she could learn to play without excess motion. I have seen Heifetz playing as beautifully as it is possible to play on the violin—with no squirming.

Gentlemen of the Juilliard Quartet, (excluding the cellist who plays with dignity), I doubt that your parents made you practice with your right heels on a basket of snakes. Some of us attend concerts to hear the music, objet to having our attention distracted from your accuracy in playing by all this swaying, wiggling, foot patting, head jerking and doing the Twist to Beethoven's Quartets. PLEASE STOP IT! It is unmusical and unprofessional.

On the other hand, if you are so embarrassed by your musicianship, try baying like hounds in the rests. Then we will stay at home and you can draw perhaps some of the public that is flocking after the Beatles.

Yours in deep sorrow,
A Library of Congress Listener

While Chinese civilization had established a science of music millennia earlier than the Greeks, the physical system of musical tones and their properties are known to us today as having been established by Pythagoras. The followers of Pythagoras (including Euclid) sixth century B.C. were the Western World's pioneers in establishing the mathematical relationships of the harmonic overtone series.

The Chinese had endowed musical tones with non-musical connotations. The tone called KUNG (C flat) was equated with "lovely winds murmur—wood—mercury—north—black; the tone SHANG (D flat)—spring—water—Jupiter—east—violet; CHIAO (E flat)—autumn—Earth—Saturn—center—yellow; CHIH (G flat)—winter—metal—Venus –west—white; and the tone, Yü– summer—Mars—fire—south—red.

The Pythagoreans paradoxically established the foundations of not only a science of tones, but a mystical, transcendental art form based on the emotional response to numerical relationships. From such thought and theory developed two rather playful characteristics of the art of music: a pure love of tone-ordering according to the rules of a game evolving out of the physical properties of sound: and the pure delight in the mastery of the physical properties and challenges of musical instruments (resulting in a class of professionals called virtuosi.)

Both Aristotle and Plato came to regard music and musicians with a most conservative and skeptical eye and ear. With their heightened sense of ethos and duty they could not view music as anything but a way to something higher in value: Aristotle always the observing analyst and scientist, Plato, distraught by the power of music to accomplish good or evil. Neither of them ever tired of reminding us that the professional musician or virtuoso was vulgar, while describing their performances as vain, glib, boorish and unmusical; maintaining that technical polish was of ascending importance. Here, now in the twentieth century, as a practicing composer-performer, I find myself completely beguiled by Aristotle's disapproval of stress on style of delivery, or virtuosity for its own sake, on impressing the audience in a bid for applause instead of concentrating on the substance of the music, its truth and virtue. His three requirements for a good performance (right use of tone, understanding of harmony, right use of rhythm) are still valid today. Aristotle did shock Plato by writing: "Music for public performance should be no better than the type of audience which enjoys it."

Timotheus of Athens, one of the avant-gardists upsetting the peaceful state of Plato and Aristotle has been quoted as saying, "I do not sing of the past;" "in novelty is power," and "to hell with the old muse." (Shades of Boulez shouting, "Schoenberg is dead.") However, whether the defender of the faith or destroyer of rules, no one could fail to be touched by Socrates in the last Platonic essay that, "He (Socrates) could not understand the injunction he often received in his dreams to compose music, for he had always practiced philosophy and this was certainly the highest and best music." There were a few early Greek philosophers who could live without music; among them Philodemus of Gadara, the Epicurean, ca. first century B.C. who added insult to injury when he said: "Music is irrational and cannot affect the soul or the emotions and is no more an expressive art than cookery.

The Romans, more preoccupied with government and things military considered music more of an addendum to the already developed Greek art. Greek musicians were so swelling the ranks of gigantic, Roman orchestras and choruses that Seneca the Younger (4BC-65AD) lamented there were often more performers on stage than spectators in the audience. Wealthy ladies competed with each other in patronizing special stables of virtuosi prodigies whose efforts to outplay each other in technical displays and sensational interpretations fed petty jealousies, enlarged the ranks of professional cliques and bribed contest judges: (activities as familiar to us as to Plato and Aristotle.)

The ferment and evolution in music, growing out of Hellenic artistic dynamics, by this moment in history had completed a full circle. While there may have occurred interesting and unique diversions at specific moments in musical history, the main stage of human involvement with the musical art seems to repeat itself over and over, the only new element being the names of places and the cast of participants in battle. Oh yes, I do admit to music-technological evolution but I believe that not unlike a mystical or sexual experience, the inner character, quality and depth of artistic experience has not changed significantly.

The early Christian attitude towards musical function, both objective and subjective, followed the predestined path of previous purgations, borrowing from the pornographic pagans as well as the heretical Hebrews; censoring the use and enjoyment of music for its own sake, considered by now, a Dionysian sin; (confessed St. Augustine, "When I am moved not by the singing but with the thing sung, I float between peril of pleasure and an approval custom") altering and simplifying as did the inflexible, but inexhaustible Pope Gregory while collecting and codifying the Christian world's liturgical music. However, pleasure and preoccupation with music presented the same difficulties as pleasure and preoccupation as sex. Authority may try very hard to direct, suppress or reshape such pleasure, but after the roar of battle subsides, the observation can be made that though many casualties resulted the original impulse that has run its course is still present and the power structure must either ignore it or join it. The powerful Christian hierarchy chose wisely to join it. After all, the options were not that inimitable to Church faith. The Christian God easily could embrace the extravagant praise of both a well-directed, Dionysian devotion or an ingenious Apollonian, polyphonic invention as well as any Greek deity could. And that which could not be embraced was wisely tolerated with eventual victory in mind. Thus, the young St. Francis and the many aberrant Abelards spent their early days very much in the tradition of the medieval jongleurs, minstrels, troubadours and minnesingers, making street music, conning the peasants of the countryside with musical theater, ghost composing the love songs of less creative knights in armor, all before accepting the vows of strict abstinence and pure thought.

The Council of Lyon in 1274 and the Papal Bull of Avignon in 1324, both said no! to the use of many-voiced polyphony in church. "Singers deprave the melodies with incessant running to and fro." However, this did not prevent Guilliaume de Machaut (1300-1377) from describing music as a science that would have us laugh, sing and dance. Meanwhile, lesser fanatics attacked from both sides of the musical battlefield with ax and ink: the medieval church banning the major diatonic scale as modus lascivious and Calvin's musical henchman. Ulrich Zwingli (1484-1531) allowing the great Zurich organ to be hacked to pieces while the organist stood by helpless and weeping.

Then, how ecumenical that Martin Luther (1483-1546), religious performer, played both the modern lyre and aulos (the lute and the flute). And, found joy in the simple folk song as well as more complex polyphony. "How strange and wonderful that one voice sings a simple melody, while three, four or five other voices are also sung. These voices play and sway in joyful exuberance around the tune and with varying art and tuneful sound, wondrously adorn and beautify it."

Three music-craft evolutions became entangled in the greater Apollonia—Dionysian battle: the attitude towards rhythm and its notation which became a crucial rallying point of both forces for freedom and the forces for strict time; the fixing and tuning of tones which became a pawn of the forces for ever increasing chromaticism on one hand, and the forces for harmonic law and order as well as melodic simplicity; and finally, the mechanical measuring of rate of tempo or speed which became the battle cry of both attacking forces, slow, medium or fast, depending not only on one's heartbeat but on whether one's heartbeat remained loyal to Dionysian extremes of fast and slow or to Apollonian moderation of a golden mean.

At this point a brief overview of battle forces might be useful. Authorities controlling an ordered compliant music; a music that served and pleased but did not overexcite or challenge, indulge in excessive technique or emotion, remaining self-effacing and object oriented. All this comprised Apollonian territory. The theatrical, the self-indulgent virtuoso, the emotionally abandoned, perpetrator of extremes and intense involvement along with the subjectively committed musician and uncontrollable innovator; all inhabited Dionysian land. The masters of tonal (ordering) both in composition and the playing of instruments could join either side, depending on the moment and the personal inclination and indeed, in some cases like counter-intelligence, play both sides of the field. Andreas Vogelmaier (sixteenth century) recognized one of the hottest areas of philosophic unrest: "It seems as if theory and practice were ever to be at strife, for the man of science, who never hears music, and the musician who never reads books, must be equally averse to each other." Kepler (1571 -1630), in the spirit of Pythagoras had composed musical tones to the related movement of planets.

Descartes (1596—1650), in the spirit of both Plato and Pythagoras and a confirmed Apollonian, attributed moral values to rhythm. He suggested the desirability of using rhythms which neither enervate nor overexcite the passions.

Blaise Pascal (1623-1662) in 1647 responded for the Dionysians with a new idealized view of musical history comparing childhood to the unadorned, simple melody of the Chinese, Hindus and Greeks; youth to the many voiced, anonymous, medieval, Christian praises of God; and manhood as the triumphant and final age of musical reason, individual genius and the drama of the whole life of mankind. For the skeptic who preferred to remain above the scene of battle, there was Baruch Spinoza (1632-1677) whose only illusion to music was, "that it is good to the melancholy, bad to those who mourn and neither good nor bad to the deaf." After 1700 the war raged on in two arenas. The conflict over the philosophy and function of music, and the conflict over the interpretation and response to that music.

While Baroque music may sound serene and familiar to us now, the complaint of Giovanni Artusi (1540-1613), then held, that it was bombastic, strident, cacophonous and much too bold in dissonance and chromaticisms. Shakespeare (1564-1616) in *Much Ado About Nothing* had prophetically sounded the Dionysian challenge a full century earlier: "Now divine air! Now is his soul ravished! Is it not strange that sheep's guts should hale souls out of men's bodies?" In 1607, the forlorn heroine's musical lament in Monteverdi's opera, "Arianne" caused listeners to melt in tears. Thirty thousand people crowded St. Peter's Square in Venice to hear the great organ virtuoso, Frescobaldi (1583-1643) perform in a style "now languished, now lively, in accordance with the affections of music." My daughter once wrote a paper titled "Social Economic Status of Musicians of the 18th Century," which stated that: "musical distinctions and divisions did separate geographical areas, South Germany down through Italy where ecstatic church music, brilliant operas and violin virtuoso musicians dominated the scene; whereas to the North in Germany through England where instrumental and vocal music was less brilliant, more intimate and more serious." In this irreverent age of reason, Swift, Sterne, Addison and others were quick to parody the serious Baroque and the unnatural opera. Gottfried Wilhelm Leibniz (1646-1716) was equating musical beauty with an unconscious counting of Pythagorean-based numbers. The two great English musical historians, Hawkins and Burney, both confirmed Apollonians; accounted music at best, an amusement. Jean-Jacques Rousseau (1712-1778) in France, Johann Adolf Scheibe (1708-1776) in Germany belittled the contrapuntal giants of the time, maintaining that it was much more difficult to write a simple, affecting melody than accomplish the most complex contrapuntal feat.

After Johann Sebastian Bach's death in 1750, Baroque was dead and the Brandenburg concerti were sold as waste paper. The Apollonians were gathering force behind Rousseau stimulated inflected, Rococo, Gallant witty and amusing defense works of non-complicated, natural entertainment; the Dionysians were biding their time quietly building their strength in the constant commitment musicians made to the doctrine of affections which implied that the composer use as much as possible, musical materials that evoked a recognizable emotional response in the performer who in turn would translate this state of feeling to the listener. Words strategically placed in the score became a powerful tool for communicating to the performer, the composer's intention. Italian instrumental prowess (not unlike today's ubiquitous Coca Cola) spread the use of Italian words in preference to other languages throughout Europe. Friedrich Wilhelm Marpurg (1718-1795) compiled a list of words other than slow (adagio) and fast (presto) to program the performer's mind; such as doloroso, languido, pomposo, maestoso, affetuoso, amoroso and mesto. All composers have since indulged.

Of course one can declare, "I am passionate while feeling no passion whatsoever or feeling passionate inside but in no way communicating the passion outside." The same is valid for music. On a different level, the composer's or performer's choice of tempi and dynamics were directly related to the corresponding effect. Johann Joachim Quantz and Matteson, seventeenth century, attributed non-musical connotations to individual tones very similar to the Chinese and Greeks. Major keys were described as gay, fresh, and serious. Minor keys were sad, gentle, flattering. Both agreed that the key of E minor was especially sad, desperate and suffering. Chromatic and unusually related intervals, melodic or harmonic used at the right moment were a direct method in obtaining emotional affect. Irregularity of melodic line, rhythmic pulse and structural shape was another means of creating affect. Finally, the expanding use of an enlarged spectrum of tonal color and dynamic intensities which became very pronounced in the second half of the eighteenth century was at the very core of this most important doctrine of affections. [Haydn, Opus 20, Affetuoso]

While composers were committed to some phase of the Apollonian—Dionysian conflict, it was the performer of music who like the helpless but increasingly important chess pawn, not only was involved in battle but placed in the forefront of attack or defense, quick to be sacrificed or become the scapegoat for hero-composers of either side or the critics, both partisan and scavenger.

From the copious advice out of the mouths of Carl Philipp Emanuel Bach (1714-1788), Daniel Gottlob Türk (1756-1813), Georg Muffat (1653-1704), Leopold Mozart (1719-1787), and all the scriptural, ensuing performer-composers, Robert Schumann (1810-1856), Carl Czerny (1791-1857) etc, on how music should be played, we at least know the geography of the conflict and cannot cry that we weren't forewarned when entering the battle arena. Rubato or strict time beating; intensity or relaxation; overall unity or unforgettable moment; extreme contrasts versus middle of the road homogeneity; all touched by how fast or loud or clear; this plethora of advice intending to lead the innocent through dangerous territories, hopefully avoiding a fatal ambush.

A contemporary story could illustrate the tradition. A young pianist was accepted for an audition by the great but puritanical conductor, George Szell in his hotel room. On his arrival the young man noted with alarm that there was no piano in the room. Szell reassured him that it would be sufficient for the young man to use the top of the table and to address it as if it were a keyboard, that he, George Szell could recognize the intentions of the young musician by the movement of his hands and fingers. With grave apprehensions, the young man placed himself at the table and began to 'play' the opening phrase of Beethoven's Fourth Piano Concerto. After a few bars he stopped but Maestro Szell motioned for him to continue. The young musician reached an irrevocable decision, he arose and said, "This is ridiculous" and proceeded to leave. Mr. Szell said, "Why are you so upset? I can tell quite well how you are interpreting the piece." The young man replied, "That's not the problem; if you must know, I don't like the tone of your table!"

The earlier hero-composer musicians advised more soberly. Johann Joachim Quantz (1697-1773) spoke of repeating a section slightly quicker in order not to put the listener asleep. P.E. Bach also warned against, "indolent hands that put us to sleep." Obviously, one of the sins of a too slow tempo was allowing the audience to take forty winks.

Werner Herzog (b. 1942) aptly writes about African music making: "The real art of master drumming does not consist merely in playing beautiful contrasting themes. A true master must time his utterances to replenish the listener's physical and aesthetic energy at the right psychological moment." Philipp E. Bach, Wolfgang Amadeus Mozart, Hector Berlioz, Felix Mendelssohn, Frederic Chopin, Johannes Brahms, Claude Debussy, Arturo Toscanini, Béla Bartók, and the Budapest String Quartet all described, loved and adhered to that elusive rubato which does not break up or arrest an underlying pulse. On the other hand, Thomas Mace (1613-1670) wrote of taking "liberty with time, sometimes faster, sometimes slower as we perceive the nature of the thing requires, "Thus the gauntlet is thrown down; are you a strict time or a free time musician? Certainly Beethoven, Wagner, Liszt, Dvořák, Mahler, Schoenberg, Nikisch, Furtwangler and the Juilliard Quartet favored more declamatory freedom from the tyranny of pulse.

Jean-Jacques Rousseau (1712-1778) in his Dictionaire de Musique, 1775 had written: "The musician who renders only notes, keys, scales and intervals without comprehending the meaning, even if he is precise, is but a 'note-gobbler.'

Türk illustrated the pitfalls of incorrect musical phrasing in 1789 by the shifting of a comma in the following sentence: "He lost his life (,) not (,) his property." Anton Reichardt describes Niccolò Jommelli (1714-1774), the Italian violinist conducting the notorious crescendo of the Mannheim Orchestra thus: "The audience gradually rose from their seats. It was not until the following diminuendo that they realized they had almost ceased breathing."

By the nineteenth century, the growth of commercial publishing houses and concert halls added a new dimension to the struggle. The defender of fidelity to the composer's manuscript could stand between the two armed camps along with those Pythagoreans (science-sound-mystical connotation) whose allegiance shifted (sides) depending on the particular issue of the conflict, John Keats (1795-1821) aptly described this central ground when he wrote that genius possessed the capacity to "walk the empyrean and not be intoxicated." Beethoven (1770-1827) reaffirmed that "music, verily is the mediator between the intellectual and sensuous life." Haydn (1732-1809) was the first composer to notate as much as possible in the score to aid the performer to realize the proper effect in the music. To the publisher and performer he proclaims a new battle cry: "loyalty not only to notes, but tempi and even articulations in his compositions." (Mozart quote)

The conquering hero of apotheosis, disrespector of traditional authorities and values, the great Dionysian breaking down the door of fate; this is the ever persisting picture of Beethoven. But like Haydn, he demanded absolute loyalty to the composer's notated concept. It is well known that Beethoven expected the performers of his music to practice long and hard to achieve this 'true' interpretation of the score. The Englishman, Mr. Smart wrote that at an informal first performance of Beethoven's Opus 132 string quartet the deaf composer grabbed the second violinist's instrument to demonstrate when he observed that person not articulating certain notes as short as were notated. An excellent description of the composer—performer battle arena was written after the first performance of Opus 127. "Not enough room to sit down—the four quartet players had hardly room for their stands and chairs. They were some of the best virtuosi of Vienna. They had dedicated themselves to their difficult task with the whole enthusiasm of youth and had held seventeen rehearsals before they dared play the new enigmatic work." (The Juilliard Quartet has spent over 500 hours preparing the Elliot Carter 3rd String Quartet.) "The difficulties and secrets of Beethoven's last quartets seemed as insurmountable and inscrutable that only younger, enthusiastic men dared, play the new music while the older and more famous players thought it impossible to perform. The listeners were not permitted to take their task easily. It was decided to play the work twice."

Hector Berlioz (1803-1869) another unique hero in musical histories battlefield. Painfully honest and articulate, he joined Beethoven and the growing legion of musicians who accepted no less than absolute loyalty to the composer's original intentions, but also demanded of the performer (and listener) a total involvement in the realization of the work. Verdi (1813-1901), who suffered the unceasing impulse of prima donnas and long-breathed tenors to rearrange the score to suit their own talents and egos, was despotic in his demand for unconditional surrender to the text of his music. Baritone Felice Varesi (1813-1889), refusing to repeat a scene as he had rehearsed it 150 times already, was told by Verdi: "You will put on your coat and rehearse it for the 151st time!"

There is a present day tendency to think of the nineteenth century as belonging to the spoils of Dionysia but the results of conflict were far from decisive and there were strong enclaves under the Apollonian flag. Certainly Goethe (1749-1832) who felt uncomfortable in Beethoven's presence diplomatically represented the Apollonian forces when he observed that: "Music is something innate and internal, which needs little nourishment from without, and no experience drawn from life." Perhaps the most renowned Apollonian of the 19th century was Felix Mendelssohn. His brilliant mind and urbane temperament became a rallying ground for objective music making at its best. He held high the banner of fluent tempos and strict time keeping. He once admonished a pupil: "Never sing a song as that one falls asleep, Madame, not even a lullaby." (There is that musical fear of putting the listener to sleep reappearing.) Mendelssohnian style was such a rage in Paris that Berlioz wryly remarked that, "during exams at the conservatory, the pianoforte started playing Mendelssohn's *G Minor Concerto* of its own accord at the approach of the pupil."

Mendelssohn's classic principles were destined to clash with Wagner's highly emotional and declamatory concept of musical performance. They both attended a concert where the conductor took the 'Tempi di Menuetto' movement of Beethoven's Eighth Symphony almost as fast as the composer had indicated on Maelzel's metronome. Wagner overheard Mendelssohn bravoing the tempo choice and wrote in his diary: "I thought I was looking into an abyss of superficiality, into complete emptiness." For Wagner, a true, German adagio could never be played too slowly and all the fast, 'superficial' allegros were being perpetrated on his dear organ-German folk by guess who? Obviously, the descendants of those ancient, decadent, sneaky Dionysian Orientals masquerading as respectable German and French Jewish musicians.

It is a curious fact of history that Fredrich Nietzsche (1844-1900), a long time defender of Wagner's aesthetic beliefs and the religion of Dionysia, later on, turned against and crucified Wagner as a false prophet, untrue to life.

Another warrior-hero fought valiantly against hypocritical elements in musical activity. "How I dislike quarreling about tempos," wrote Robert Schumann; "an allegro played by one who is cold by nature always sounds lazier than a slower tempo by one of sanguine temperament." And then there is the mysterious case of Frederic Chopin. Every contemporary account from the field of battle will resound with the mighty feats of improvising, dynamically thundering, orgiastic forays perpetrated by countless pianists battling in Chopin's revered name. But back to the words of that master-warrior himself: "I could not have learned to play the piano in Germany. There, people complain that I perform too softly, too delicately. They are accustomed to the piano pounding of their own musicians." Commenting on a Liszt performance, Chopin asked, "Must one always speak so declamatorily?"

On the other hand, the triumphs of a new breed of virtuoso-warrior was indeed heartening to the Dionysian that had never forgotten the humiliating defeats of earlier virtuosi at the hands of Greek philosophers and medieval popes.

There is a wonderful satire of Franz Liszt, "The conquered pianos lie scattered around him, broken strings float like trophies, wounded instruments flee in all directions, the audience look at one another in dumb surprise as after a sudden storm in a serene sky. And he, Prometheus, who with each note has forged a being, his head bent, smiles strangely before the crowd that applauds him wildly."

While the portrait of Liszt is clear, there is one virtuoso-warrior whom I believe to be quite misunderstood. Unlike the "decadent virtuosi" of Hellenic times, Niccolò Paganini (1782-1810), for all his unique mastery of the instrument, brought a very special spirit to music best described by Clara Schumann: "In the adagio the artist seemed as if transformed by magic. No trace remained of the preceding tour-de-force. A soulful singer in legato style and of a tender simplicity, he drew forth celestial tones that came forth from the heart and penetrated the heart."

As the fires of commercialism grew rampant, Hugo Wolf inhabiting a purer atmosphere of Dionysia attacked the Philistines in their acoustical coliseums: "Why in the name of heaven, must the scorching fire of enthusiasm always come out thru the hands and feet? Why must there be clapping and stomping? Do the public's hands and feet constitute the moral lightening rod for the electrified soul? I say, that if when the last notes of a profound piece has barely ceased to resound, and you are again jolly and pleased and your babble and your criticizing and clap, that you have seen nothing, felt nothing, heard nothing, understood nothing, nothing, nothing—not a thing!"

On the sidelines of the main areas of conflict, the ethnic and nationalistic musician-soldiers held steadfast to humanistic and programmatic values. Smetana, approaching deafness said, "I do not wish to write a quartet in formal style, but wish to paint my life in music."

What have the philosopher-warriors been up to during the 19th Century attainments of Dionysian ecstasy?

The great Apollonian White Knight Immanuel Kant (1724-1804) had thundered from the right: "Music was just enjoyment!" Hegal (1770-1831) the Dionysian Red Knight answered from the left: "In musical tones a whole scale of passions can echo and reverberate."

Schopenhauer (1775-1860) in the center maintaining that music didn't express any particular feeling but an abstraction of it. Kierkegaard could only send a love letter to Mozart in 1843: "I have you to thank that I did not die without having loved."

But it was Eduard Hanslick, critic-philosopher-attacker of Wagner, defender of Brahms and Apollonia who issued the manifesto of objective interpretation drawing from Kant's critique of pure reason: "Music," Hanslick stated, "must consider only the art 'object' and not the perceived 'subject.' "The interpreter must think only in terms of sound. Music is to be played but not to be played with."

To counteract the effect of so mighty a philosophical ally - the Dionysians brought forth their 19th century champion, Nietzsche who decreed that all ambiguity shall cease and there would be no further traffic between the two great powers. For Nietzsche, music was preeminently the art of emotion; but "it must be true to life!" It is no accident that he crucified Wagner as a false prophet—untrue to life.

By the end of the 19th Century—the armies of Dionysia were encircling the musical globe. Light-headed dancing to the tunes of Johann Strauss brought back deeply rooted memories of Corybantic mysteries and therapeutic curves.

Is it possible that Bach's sober saraband was the same lascivious dance that inspired Spanish authorities in 1583 to punish all who danced it with 200 lashes?

Is it true that Queen Elizabeth I, age 56, danced every morning for physical fitness to the sprightly rhythms of the galliard?

Certainly the Dionysis-oriented Wagnerian-Mahlerites, commanding musical forces of thousands taking off into the heavenly space of eternal time, were justifiably arousing desperate defenders of the intimate, the supersensitive, the fragile microsound in musical art. Whether such defenders were makers of sound such as Debussy, musical nonsense such as Satie, or makers of critical words such as Shaw, fought side by side (creator and deflator) wresting the artistic prizes away from the apocalyptic expander of unbridled tonal ecstasy.

One composer-warrior seems to have fought this battle entirely within the confines of his own internal life.

Like the strange case of Chopin, Arnold Schoenberg in the 20th century is greatly misunderstood. His descent out of Wagner and Mahler in the light of early works such as Verklaete Nacht. and Gurre Lieder is indisputable. But as he progressed into the farther realms of Pythagorean tone order—he was and is still accused of treason to Dionysian, itself. Nothing could be more untrue.

If Schoenberg and his twelve tone technique was a Pythagorean father—Alban Berg was his Pythagorean son—who remained a steadfast mystic involved in the magical properties of numbers related to musical tones and structures. Schoenberg's other great pupil, Anton Webern, embodied the tone spirit of the holy ghost.

He was the ideal, fragile world of microcosm. I think this quote of Confucius almost 2500 years earlier explains Webern's ethos to me: "From the depth of sentiment comes the clarity of form and from the strength of the mood comes the spirituality of its atmosphere; the harmony of the spirit springs forth from the soul and finds expression or blossoms forth in the form of music"

The war of Apollonian and Dionysian will rage on, I'm afraid, as long as humans breathe.

Power centers will always react to what they perceive as threats to their control.

Decadent jazz performers were fined and imprisoned in the Soviet Union in 1928—banned from Ireland in 1934. Is the innovator in music castigated any less for his so called "decadent—formalism in the Soviet Union's Central Committee resolution of 48 than the innovator who threatened anarchy in the ideal Greek state. And, now I would return to our master of the "poetics of music," Stravinsky.

I will grant that of all the makers of sounds he is the greatest shaper of words that I know. Lucid, specific and insightful, he plays upon words when he sternly warns his interpreters that the subjective element in music be eliminated. He goes even further: "Most people like music because it gives them emotions such as joy, grief, sadness, an image of nature, a subject for daydreams or still better—oblivion from everyday life." "People" he intones, "must learn to love music for its own sake." [playing a Stravinsky work]

At this moment I expect some outraged policeman of historical propriety to pull out his badge and arrest me for taking you on this wild and speedy descent down the white water agitatos of musical history. I wouldn't blame him.

But my secret goal has been to set the stage wherein as you leave here, your mind might carry on an internal dialogue both Dionysian and Apollonian as to what in reality do the elements of objectivity and subjectivity in music represent?

I hope your dialogue will keep asking, "Can there be a state of objectivity in music at all? My present belief is that music which requires sound to exist, ears to absorb and mind to react, objectivity cannot remain. It boils down to a matter of the degree of subjectivity.

Another part of your furtive dialogue would, hopefully deal with the term romantic as applied to musical expression. Sir Donald Tovey considered the word a nuisance, but I think that all great music must contain some degree of this kind of expression. When music or its performance is criticized for being too sentimental, too romantic or vulgar, I think it is the result of gross distortion by over emphasis on the materials of the composition.

Now, who is to be the arbiter of what is distortion? [Bernstein, Gould?]

Hero worship comes naturally to most children. As one grows older the band of heroes diminishes and the intensity of worship dissipates. Today my heroes are few, but one of them, Berlioz wrote down what is certainly my credo of performance: "The prevailing characteristics of my music are passionate expression, intense ardour, rhythmical animation, and unexpected turns. When I say passionate expression, I mean an expression determined on enforcing the inner meaning of its subject, even when the subject is the contrary of passion and when the feeling to be expressed is gentle and tender, or even profoundly calm."

Mencius and The Late Beethoven String Quartets

*T*HE INSPIRATION FOR THIS EXPLORATORY EXPEDITION UP THE FRONT
face of the late Beethoven String Quartet massif arose like the phoenix
out of the ashes of two separate reactions. The first has been annoying
me for years, ever since the moment my non-musical brother challenged me to prove that the 'Lento assai' movement of Beethoven's
Opus 135 was of more import to the human race than the popular
melody, "White Christmas." If only my brother had restricted his
challenge to the arena of interpretive talent, we could have debated
happily whether the Juilliard Quartet's rendition of the 'Lento assai'
was more moving or not, than Bing Crosby's rendition of "White
Christmas." Unfortunately, while everyone recognizes that popularity
alone does not carry its own guarantee of permanence, no one yet has
set up a fool proof standard of measure for a musical composition that
avoids value judgements involving subjective or cultural attitudes.

The second reaction was the result of a more recent, "green tea"
discussion in Wei Ming Tu's Berkeley, California garden. Wei Ming
is a remarkable Chinese scholar, so when he spoke about Mencius and
the application of this great Confucian's analysis of human nature to
the aesthetic realm, the very idea inspired a continuing internal dialogue of my own on how Mencius might have regarded a late Beethoven string quartet.

The philosopher, known today as Mencius, was Meng-Tzu or Master Meng, born a little over one hundred years after the death of Confucius in the region of Shantung Province in China. He became, after the Master, the greatest influence on the School of Confucianism in China. He believed that human nature was essentially good; evil evolving only as one strayed from his original ability to love and commiserate, to distinguish right from wrong.

What does the music composed by Ludwig van Beethoven born in Bonn, Germany in Europe, 2100 years later have to do with ancient Mencius? I would begin by stating that Beethoven shared Mencius' belief in man's inherent good nature. Before I am finished I will dare to suggest that they shared much more than that. Up to the year 1823, Beethoven commanded the serious respect, love and admiration of his fellow musicians and the entire European musical community. However, as his deafness increased, he retreated into the silent places where his incredible imagination roamed. The musical world found it more and more difficult to follow him. Thus, that extraordinary musical mountain range known to us as the Late Quartets came into being, lifted into dizzying stratospheres during the four last years of Beethoven's silent existence. Noise, spoken words and other musician's music could not reach him, and his inner, creative furnace, like that of the uninhibited, Hawaiian Goddess Pele, forged into musical reality, terrifying peaks teeming with un-scalable cliffs, well protected by strange foothills of mystifying, musical materials that even the experienced musical explorer and climber could not easily traverse.

It took only three years for Beethoven to create five separate, unique musical mountain massifs with at least one unclimbable Everest, the Great Fugue.

The year 1824 saw the composition of Opus 127, Opus 132 and Opus 130 with the great fugue as last movement were completed in 1825. Opus 131 and Opus 135 and the alternate last movement Rondo for Opus 130 were finished in 1826, a few months before Beethoven's death in early 1827.

Everyone was awestruck or mystified as to how to approach these works. A small band of true believers eagerly prepared to assail these cliffs and precipices, no matter what the dangers. Beethoven himself was well aware of their inherent difficulties; both to perform and understand. His note to the members of the Schuppanzigh Quartet read as follows:

"Best Ones"—Each one is herewith given his part and is bound by oath and indeed pledged on his honor to do his best, to distinguish himself and to vie with each other in excellence. Each one who takes part in the affair in question is to sign the sheet.

(Signed) Beethoven

A contemporary ear-witness, a Mr. Smart from England described the first attempt on Opus 127 thus:

"Not enough room to sit down. The four quartet players had hardly room for their stands and their chairs. They were some of the best virtuosi of Vienna. They had dedicated themselves to their difficult task with the whole enthusiasm of youth and had held seventeen rehearsals before they dared play the new enigmatic work. The difficulties and secrets of Beethoven's last quartets seemed so insurmountable and inscrutable that only younger, enthusiastic men dared play the new music while the older and more famous players thought it impossible to perform. The listeners were not permitted to take their task easily. It was decided to play the work twice."

I regret to report that this valiant, first attempt on Opus 127 by Beethoven's Schuppanzigh Quartet failed. Beethoven somewhat ungratefully, (and I think, being a first violinist in a quartet, myself, unfairly), blamed the failure on Schuppanzigh. Unfortunately the whole quartet was roped together and if one failed, all failed. Schuppanzigh himself, confessed that he could easily master the technical difficulties but it was almost impossible to arrive at the spirit of the work. By the time Beethoven died, he had watched (he could not hear) attempts on Opus 127, 132 and 130. The year 1828, after his death, marks the first expedition up the massif of Opus 131. It has been a modern illusion that these intimidating, musical challenges were not only misunderstood but also ignored. Research has proven this to be untrue. It is known that even such virtuosi as Paganini, Wieniawski, Servais and Vieuxtemps loved to play these works. By the year 1875, (when Wagner wrote his essay on Opus 131) there is evidence of at least 1,039 public expeditions up the various late Beethoven peaks; 260 on Opus 131 alone. Even New York City witnessed three attempts on Opus 131, Boston, two.

But while the musical world has become more and more involved and obsessed with the meaning of the late quartets and their challenge to the human body and spirit, the success of reaching the rarified atmospheres of each work whatever route one chooses remains almost as elusive and unique as when they first appeared on the human horizon.

I personally was terrified by the late quartets in my early years. Gently, but firmly, loving teachers have guided me through their foothills. Slowly but surely I learned to survive for long periods of time in the region where these works exist. Out of my over forty years of group-playing with these five musical giants has come my deep conviction that they represent the most important influence of my musical life.

Yet I would be the first to disclaim that I comprehend what Beethoven intended. It is even possible to suspect that even Beethoven didn't fully comprehend what he had wrought: that is why I now turn to the ancient sage, Mencius, for help.

Mencius postulated six exceptional steps up the ladder of "self-cultivation." He who commands our liking is called (SHAN)—good. He who is sincere with himself is called (HSIN)—true. He who is sufficient and real, is called (MEI)—beautiful. He whose sufficiency and reality shine forth, is called (TA)—great. He whose greatness transforms itself, is called (SHENG)—profound. He whose profundity is beyond our comprehension is called (SHEN)—spiritual.

According to Wei Ming Tu, Mencius maintained that this spirituality, this greatness that transforms itself, that is beyond comprehension, represents a symbol of a higher station of being on the very same path as good, truth and beauty. He believed that while few might attain spirituality it was a potential for all. I might paraphrase this to say that while few might create as Beethoven did, the path for the interpreter, performer and listener is essentially the same path that Beethoven traveled.

Mencius reveals a clue relevant in the approach to late Beethoven when he emphatically states that the way of learning consists of none other than the quest for the lost heart, when he holds that the body can hardly express the feelings of the heart even though it is the proper place for the heart to reside. The Mencian heart is both a cognitive and an affective faculty. It not only reflects on realities, but in comprehending them, shapes and creates their meaningfulness for the human community as a whole.

The Confucian view accepts a human being as part of the whole rather than the end all (unlike Protagoras, the Greek philosopher who said, "Man is the measure of all things.") This Confucian attitude is vital to the understanding of Beethoven and his last works. To put it another way, completion of self necessitates the completion, not domination of things.

For Mencius, aesthetic language (such as embodied in Opus 131) was not merely descriptive, but it suggested, directed and enlightened. To respond to such a work, both the performer and the listener must bring to it what Mencius viewed as the vital spirit endowed with what might be termed, "matter-energy," a power connected to breathing and blood flow. Authentic music therefore does not create a fleeting impression on the senses, but possesses enduring virtues. There is a quaint account in Confucian analects that after hearing the music of SHAO, Confucius was in such a state of beautiful enchantment, that he could not distinguish the taste of meat for three months afterward.

By looking again at Mencius' six stages of human self-cultivation we may find in them just that elusive standard of measurement of enduring artistic value.

Stage 1: That music, which commands our liking, is called good. That music is good which is entertaining, which is understandable, that pleases. That music is good which you wish to experience again, that intrigues, that doesn't offend. That music is good which one may not like but which is liked by others.

Stage 2: That music, which is sincere with itself, is called true. That music is true which delivers what it promises, which is consistent, logical, unassuming, which does not pretend to be other than what it is, and speaks in its own voice, adhering to its own way whether it be pleasing or not; which, after repeated hearings or passage of time, still evokes a positive response in the listener.

Stage 3: That music, which is sufficient and real, is called beautiful. That music is beautiful which is both substantial and conclusive which stands for something no matter how big or small. That music is beautiful in which the cliché or predictable musical sequence does not dominate the course of musical events; in which the emotional affects aroused by the music may strain or challenge the boundaries of the music's structure but never distort or destroy it.

Stage 4: That music whose sufficiency and reality shine forth, is called great. That music is great which arouses tingling of the spine, open breathing and the formation of tears. That music is great which not only stands apart from other music of its kind, but contains special, magical moments or lucky accidents (as Stravinsky called them). That music is great which one is drawn towards and held a willing captive no matter how much one has experienced it previously. That music is great which, when experienced, remains enduring and memorable.

Stage 5: That music whose greatness transforms itself; is called profound. That music is profound in which the whole is greater than each part; which in effect transforms the person experiencing it. That music is profound which when it is simple appears complicated and when it is complicated, appears simple. That music is profound which as it evolves appears to become something new or other than it has ever been previously.

Stage 6: That music, whose profundity is beyond our comprehension, is called spiritual. That music is spiritual in which its vital force does not drain but on the contrary, recharges the emotional state of the listener. That music is spiritual which mixes the logical with the illogical, the rational with the irrational, whose physical manifestation is always ingenious. That music is spiritual in which one can know every sound and silence, may even have an understanding of its physical properties, yet whose effect while spell-binding and powerful, nonetheless, in the last analysis, remains unfathomable, mysterious, elusive and tantalizing.

I have discovered that my lifelong involvement with the five last quartets of Beethoven is definitely Mencian. I would describe the continuous sounds and silences of Beethoven's last quartets as pathways or vessels through which the music conceived in Beethoven's mind, moves. I would argue that the music of the mind is only as good and true as it is touched on by the heart; and further, this "mind-heart" power that Mencius refers to as CH'I, remains the motivation and means to achieve the oneness of heart and body, spirit and mind.

We observe that animals expend life energy out of functional need. Humans can strive (if they are possessed of CH'I) to harness that energy for emotional and artistic functions. Obviously Beethoven was in agreement with Mencius, not only about the human spirit, but about the power of an aesthetic language that draws creative sustenance from oneness with nature and the inner heart.

What about the modern day Schuppanzighs and Mr. Smarts, (performer and listeners) as we prepare for the experience of these awesome works? For the performer, the Confucian master, Mencius penetrated to the heart of the matter. He made a clear distinction between unwillingness and inability. He was keenly aware of the difference between rote performer and active participant. How did a rote performance reveal itself? By a lack of intensity, a concentration on the external form as a basis for truth and beauty; and by focusing not on the result but only on the means by which the result was attained. The master was not content that the student achieves the correct form. He tried to enable the student to create his own style, his own interpretation. In our present time, when most foods reach us in packaged form; where hotel rooms in New York, Cairo or Tokyo look essentially the same; piped in music in buildings sounding essentially the same; while we expect our machines to function at all times precisely and efficiently; it is not surprising that most career musicians, most audiences and critics are satisfied with technically superior, rote performances. Perhaps the best advice for the performer in the twentieth century about to play a late Beethoven quartet is Mencius' sixth century assertion that, the capture of the heart or profound meaning should be understood as 'the art of steering, involving a process of adjusting and balancing on unpredictable currents.'

For the listener about to hear a performance of a late Beethoven quartet I would advise that the opening of the heart and the emptying of the mind is of more importance than a conscious and perhaps artificial effort to count and catalogue the external materials and events along the way. Leave that activity to the critics and musicologists. I would caution that knowledge of the score and repeated encounters with the composition are illuminating only if, after thorough digestion and absorption into the less conscious self, they support and abet the spontaneous and vulnerable experience. Certainly they are not helpful if they become the focus and preempt the central preoccupation of the relationship between the music and the participants.

Joseph Kerman in his book on the Beethoven quartets writes that: "Each of the late quartets provides us with a separate paradigm for wholeness. Total integrity arising out of individuality of form, feeling and procedure." Maynard Solomon refers to the sense of 'pain and its transcendence' in Opus 131. Being the true musicologist, he also counted six main keys, thirty-one tempo changes and 'a variety of forms that move from fugue, suite, recitative, variation, scherzo, aria to a final sonata form. Erich Schenk makes the most interesting observation about the late quartets by showing how Beethoven's last creative urges were deeply influenced by the baroque period; preoccupation with chromatic melancholy conceptions that might be described as portraying pain, sorrow, trespass and preparedness for death: Beethoven, the 19th century revolutionary composer emulating Bach in his upward striving, constantly defeated melodic shapes and his obsession with the intensity of a single note building towards resolution one half step down or up. It is a curious fact that Beethoven entertained during the last years of his life, the idea of composing an overture based on the musical signature of J.S. Bach:

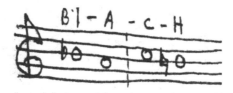

Simply analyzed, this remarkable group of notes consists of a single note (B-flat) resolving one half step down to (A-natural) and this two note pattern repeated at a higher level (C-flat to B-flat). These two groups are connected by a less intense interval (the A-flat to the C-flat) a minor third.

Now examine the first theme in the first movement of Beethoven's Opus 130:

Three two-note groups containing the half step resolution with a less intense interval of a minor sixth connecting the second and third groups.

The main theme of the big fugue last movement is even more re-velatory. The interval groups are:

Four groups of two notes, three of them resolving up and only one down. The first group connected to the second by a major sixth, the second to the third by a minor sixth and the third to the fourth again by the interval of a major sixth. A larger pattern of four notes repeated at a higher level can be likened to the Bach signature stated twice.

It is surely no accident that Beethoven, who loved Bach's Well Tempered Clavichord fugues, created his opening fugal theme in Opus 131 with Bach's C-sharp minor fugue in his mind:

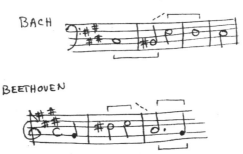

In both Bach's and Beethoven's themes there exists two half step groups connected by an interval of a major third (Bach's actually is spelled as a diminished fourth but sounds as a major third). Richard Wagner in his 1875 essay on Opus 131 refers to Beethoven's opening theme in Opus 131 as 'surely the saddest thing ever expressed in notes.'

This close Bach-Beethoven link continues in Opus 131. If we compare Bach's theme (Frederich's?) in the 'Musical Offering' with the opening motive in the last movement of Opus 131:

Again the two note pattern of a half step influenced or disturbed by the sound of an interval of the sixth. The opening motive of Opus 132 continues this mystery.

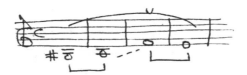

And finally, in Opus 135, the 'difficult question' motive of the last movement:

And later at the coda:

Beethoven pronounced his last five string quartet creations great; "each in its own way." I would submit to my non-musician brother that while "White Christmas" may aspire as high as Stage 3 on Mencius' score card, the Lento assai of Opus 135 and indeed all of the towering creations of Beethoven's last quartets pass every (Mencian) test of greatness and spirituality without contest. I am well aware of the conceit of my argument. No one can "prove" greatness in music any more than one can put a "price tag" on the value of human life. While these musical compositions may be beyond our musical comprehension, we can certainly think on Beethoven as we contemplate Mencius' dictum: "The great man does not lose his childlike heart."

[EXCERPT FROM ALLAN KOZINN INTERVIEW]
Robert Mann, 1st Violinist, Juilliard String
Quartet On Bartók 02/03/81

ALAN KOZINN: *How is it that you never met Bartók?*

ROBERT MANN: Well, it's very simple. He had even come to my town where I lived, Portland, Oregon, as a pianist, I think when I was there. But I didn't know about Bartók when I was thirteen, fourteen. Later before I left Portland, I had become aware of the easier piano pieces. And I liked Bartók. I went to Juilliard to study and I became enamored of Bartók. But I was not a very bright person. I could have researched him down because he was at work at times during my student days at Juilliard, across the street at Columbia University doing some work on his round discs that he had collected in the ethnomusicological trips he made with Kodály throughout Hungary, the Balkans, and even North Africa. He was working on them for Columbia at a time when I was struggling with his quartets at Juilliard, and the teachers didn't know how to teach them. So basically I missed that opportunity, and I regretted it for the rest of my life. But then you see, I was in the army in 1943–1946, and then I had no opportunity to meet him. When I got back and the quartet got started in 1946, he was dead.

So most of my connection to Bartók has been second hand through some of the people who had been very close to him. And some people who played his music and who might NOT have been close to him. My experience of Bartók is through his music, but not personally.

He was a very unusual man anyway. From what I gather from all the people that knew him, he was NOT a person who embraced you and made you feel a close part of his entourage, even if you were friends. He was a person who had enormous inner integrity, an almost steely integrity, and was absolutely the most proper person in the world. I don't think he'd have ever uttered a lie or say anything incorrect; but he also would not have—if he listened to your performance. I remember one person who told me that he listened to 3 movements of something, and after it was over the person said, "Please tell us what you would like." He said, "Well, the first movement is too slow. The second movement is too fast; and the last one needs a bit more work." That was it. Quite different from when we played all the quartets of Schoenberg for Schoenberg. We finished the first one and said, "Well, what was it like?" He started laughing, and told us, "The way you played it was a way I'd never conceived of it." We thought all my God, what have we done wrong, and he laughed some more and said, "No, but it's wonderful. I'm not going to tell you anything because I want you to continue playing it that way." A completely different personality you see . . .

Everybody's different. First of all, I ask my friend Eugene Lehner, of the Kolish Quartet, which gave the first performance of the 5th Bartók, and had played the 4th and 3rd and maybe the 2nd . . . I heard the first performance of the 6th quartet, by the Kolish Quartet. I had come in on a pass from the army and heard it at Town Hall. Lehner had already left. But he indicated very similar things—that Bartók didn't say a lot. He just told him a few things here and there. The thing is that we would play a Bartók quartet for Eugene Lehner, and he's an absolutely inspiring musician—imaginative, offbeat and everything, and yet when we would say, "But what did Bartók ask you to do there?" it would be pretty much what I'd heard—you only got certain information and that was it . . . The Kolish Quartet, which was the exciting, intellectual quartet of contemporary language in Central

Europe—Pro Arte was pretty terrific that way too . . . the Kolish knew Schoenberg and they knew Bartók, and they lived in Vienna. They were involved with Alban Berg, like Felix Galimir too. There's a certain set of musicians who were really interested in the language of their day. So, if you want my one complaint, it's that most younger musicians are NOT interested in the language of their day today.

AK: *Neither are most older ones*

RM: Well, you tend to forgive them, because they're like dinosaurs, they're on their way to extinction anyway . . . How many times can you hear the 5th Symphony of Beethoven? You can hear it, but at a certain point it's got to be given a rest and you've got to hear other things. What's going to happen is like the dustbowl. They'll get the good crop too often to take its place. I'm not talking about 10 years from now. I'm talking about 100 years from now. If you have the long view. So far the old chestnuts have held up pretty good. Concertizing is only about 150 years old anyway . . . in terms of the idea of commercial concerts.

AK: *Would you say that nowadays Bartók is part of the standard repertoire.*

RM: Oh sure, certainly.

AK: *Can you remember a time when it wasn't?*

RM: Certainly. I can remember the first time we ever played Bartók at the Buffalo Chamber Music Society—they asked us if we would program the Bartók at the beginning or the end, so that their clientele that didn't like that music could either come late or leave early. And, that's not an isolated incident. That happened a lot.

AK: *Can you remember your own reaction to the quartets the first time you looked at them?*

RM: I never had trouble with the Bartók Quartets. You see, you have two different kinds of musicians—those who are open to new language, and those who are not. You can have absolutely outstanding artists, like Pinchas Zukerman or Murray Perahia, who don't want to play contemporary music too much—or at all—and then you can have another type of musician, like an Isaac Stern, who's willing to play Penderecki and not Rochberg just because he's more conservative, but who will play some of the more far out concertos too. It's a question of almost temperament, and in our day, I was interested. I was a composer. I started composing when I was 13, and I remember by the time I got to be a student at Juilliard I once came to a lesson taught by a pupil of Joseph Joachim, Hans Letz, and into the lesson came Felix Salmond, who was the other great chamber music teacher at Juilliard. They were both ultra conservative people, whose musical experience—well, Salmonds ended with Debussy and Ravel, and, Letz went a little farther, he was a little more open, but not a lot. And, there was a refugee Dutch composer Julius Hijman, who'd just come over and needed desperately to establish himself. He scraped together enough money to give a Carnegie Recital Hall concert, and on our stands was placed a string quartet. I was in the student quartet, and Letz, our teacher, said, "Would you read some of this for us?" It wasn't too difficult and it was very non-tonal. We were playing it and Felix Salmond was getting madder and madder by the second, and finally he just took the music and threw it up in the air and said, "How can you play this blank, blank?" Letz said, "Well I guess it isn't worth it, and that was that."

So I said, "Do you mind if I take the music?" and, he said, "No, if you return it to this gentleman." The music had his telephone number, and I called him and said, "Mr. Hijman, I'm sorry but I don't think Juilliard's going to provide you with a quartet for your concert. But, I have some friends, and if you would like it performed, I think we can give a reasonably good performance of it." He was very grateful and we played it. A matter of fact, when he got a job as a teacher at the University of Texas, he gave me his upright . . . piano. He's dead now, he wasn't a great composer, but the thing is I was interested.

But you see interestingly enough, you have, my point of view about ALL composers . . . it's very hard to know what is not just surface or cliché because the clichés are being wrought at the time. There might be some substance in a cliché if it's set a certain way. And, there might be shallowness in an avant-garde approach—that's a new language altogether. So, it takes time to sift it down. Now, in Bartók's case, you've got a language that was forged out of a number of elements, and had their moment. I mean for instance, obviously the first element was the classic, traditional background. I've seen a quartet . . . in the Bartók archives in Budapest that looks like it could have been a fourth Brahms' piano quartet. Honestly, and good, by the way, a very good piece of music. Maybe it's been published since then, I don't know. Then there was the element of the kind of Hungarian tradition that was phony—which he first absorbed. I mean the Liszt, Brahms Hungarian dance type thing and all that . . . Which Bartók with his cool intellect began to take apart almost early in his life and see that this was the surface stuff and really false, so he began getting interested in ethnomusicology. That was the third element in him, which was going into the fields and listening to the peasants sing, and play (their) flute(s), and finding out what (music) was in different areas of Hungary, and what was (its) relationship to language, and then going further into the Balkans, so that by the time he composes multiple rhythmic pieces, . . . like in Mikrokosmos and the 5th Quartet, and stuff like that . . . (h)e's already synthesized, not so much taken the music and the materials, but synthesized those elements that are in this music. Even his glissandi, which sort of horrified people who were listening. (E)veryone makes a slide in Wieniawski and salon music. And, everybody loves it. But Bartók heard these peasants gliss (with a very different aesthetic) . . . he started using it in his music, and people didn't understand it. It was ancient. It wasn't new, it was old. What was new was that Bartók took all these elements, plus his own developing creativity in terms of structure, color, nature, and harmony, and all these things and created a language which basically turns out . . . not to have been such an obscure, difficult language to understand, but which is so uniquely Bartók that of all the great composers he's

one of the few that can't be imitated or followed . . . (W)hereas
Schoenberg opened up a category that hundreds and hundreds of
composers could draw from and develop from . . . (Bartók's) language
is unique. Oh, there were a lot of people who tried (to imitate him),
on certain levels . . . Many of the Socialist Republic composers, once
they got over the fact that this was not decadent formalism . . . (In the
beginning they) had to declare his music bourgeois decadence. But
finally . . . the Czechs, Poles, Romanians, and finally the Russians
came around and said, "Okay, Bartók is alright." (In) Hungary he was
their hero, he was their greatest composer.

But (even in 1949) when Shostakovich came (to the USA) . . . to a
conference of composers, he was the Soviet representative, he came to
our concert in Times Hall (in New York City) where we were playing
the Bartók's Fourth Quartet and he wrote a scathing commentary
about the quartet as an unfeeling, non-human work. And, that's the
great composer Shostakovich.

AK: *Do you think he really believed that or was he bullied into it?*

RM: In light of the recent Shostakovich diaries, or so called diaries, I
don't know. I honestly don't know. I think that Shostakovich is definitely a great composer and probably would have been greater if he
had not had these political shackles around his neck and in his mind
all of the time. But the point is, that even NOW we can play the Third
and Fourth Quartets of Bartók in the Soviet Union and have a big
reaction. I don't think that Brezhnev would love it, but then, neither
would certain of our leading politicians.

AK: *You said that it takes time for things to be filtered out.*

RM: Right . . . there's a fun book—(i)t gets tiresome, but if you read
it a little at a time it's fun, it's Slominsky's *The Lexicon of Musical Invec-
tive*—(i)n the opening he says it takes 40 years for any language or
idiosyncratic thing that is created, to be accepted by the public. Now,

there are some pieces that aren't accepted in 40 years, in fact, late Beethoven language is confusing to some of our practicing musicians today . . . I can tell you, in our early days, in the 1940s, we would get many reviews that would say the Beethoven late works are magnificent failures, or, that as theoretical works, they're the greatest, but as performing works, they don't succeed. Even as great a musician as Stravinsky, of whom there can be no greater, had his doubts, in his Norton Lectures, about the validities of the late Beethoven quartets. Th(en) h(e) subsequent(ly) began talking about how 131 was the greatest piece ever written. But he went through a period where he didn't accept that. So language is a funny thing.

With Bartók, we used to have a little flip saying that in the early days, 25% of our audiences responded medium to great, and 75% rejected it outright. And today, it's the other way around, 75% accept and 25% reject.

AK: *Looking at them yourself, did you feel immediately that they were masterpieces? It seems today that they're almost up there with the Beethoven Quartets.*

RM: Of course, see, the thing is, at no point did any member of the Juilliard Quartet ever not have the awareness that Bartók was one of our great composers. How great is a silly or unnecessary question? I mean, we don't know that he'll be considered the greatest quartet composer in the world, or greater than Beethoven, or less great, or as great—we just know he was a great composer of quartets. It's up to those people who make lists to do that. I mean, do you think that the 10 best or worst dressed lists in America is an accurate statement? I mean, come on, that's journalism at its worst.

AK: *Okay, well—how many composers' complete quartet outputs have you recorded three times?*

RM: Well that, I mean, you've got a twinkle in your eye, but the reason for that is not what you might think. Number one, the Juilliard

Quartet formed in 1946. We were studying lots of music, Beethoven, Haydn and so on. We were committed in our minds and the guy who hired us—William Schuman—was committed to our playing contemporary music. It wasn't a duty for us, we *wanted* to do it.

All serious performers have to find something to get onto the boards with. It can be a gimmick, a preoccupation with something, or a fluke of the moment. I mean, nobody would deny, whatever the worth of Van Cliburn, who's a great pianist, that he got catapulted by winning the Tchaikovsky competition in Moscow at a juncture when the cold war was hitting the fan. So there are many things. In our case, our first connection of meaning was that Schuman had been a kind of protégé to Koussevitzky and the Boston Symphony Orchestra, (and) Koussevitzky believed in contemporary music. He played the first recording of the 3rd Symphony of Roy Harris, he played Lennie Bernstein, he played William Schuman, he played this composer and that. William Schuman was a friend of his, so he got us a concert the first summer at Tanglewood. Not Bartók—we played Roger Sessions, William Schuman, Walter Piston, and Aaron Copland. That was our first concert. We made a good impression playing them. So Koussevitzky invited us back for the second summer, and by then, we were searching around desperately: What can we do that will really be significant? There had been single recordings of Bartók quartets, but nobody had, at that time (in America), played all six quartets at two concerts at that time . . . there was another quartet in Europe that did play them, the Vegh Quartet, with Sandor Vegh . . . So, we suggested it, and people who were running Tanglewood, including Koussevitzky said, "Yes, we'd like to have that." So we did it. And you know how those things happen. At that moment they'd never been done, and our performance was viable because of what we had to give, which was enormous energy. I remember at our first concert ever, at the Juilliard School, we played Bartók's Third Quartet and Kodály in the auditorium with Menuhin, and they were responsive, and we *knew* people *liked* the way we played Bartók. It made an enormous hit. There were all kinds of magazines there—the thing that really started us on our career was a marvelous article in *TIME* magazine after those

Tanglewood concerts. And, immediately Columbia was interested in our recordings, so the first thing they recorded (with us) was the Bartók Quartets. That's what got us into the records in 1948. I think they came out in 1949.

So then of course, everybody who read these articles and heard about us said, "Hey, let's get them to play those Bartók Quartets." We didn't choose to do it that way . . . Did they know what they were asking for (when they asked for Bartók or the Bartók cycle)? Well, they got it, and I'm not saying that every chamber music society hated it. Many of the people in these various societies wanted it. It's not like *everybody* hated it. 25% of the people fanatically wanted it. So there it went, and so (we) became, in those early days, the "great interpreters of the Bartók Quartets."

Now begins the interesting part of that story. As we played, dozens of cycles—dozens, in two concerts—but at a certain point, all the younger quartets started coming in (and playing them too). Like the Guarneri Quartet, the Cleveland, the Tokyo, Concord—all one after another, establishing themselves as great quartet players, and the European ones too, the Hungarian Quartet, which had older people who played them before I was born, and Amadeus, and others. And so everybody was playing Bartók.

So over the years, the Juilliard Quartet began playing a little less Bartók every year . . . (F)inally it boiled down, in the last ten years that I don't think we played a cycle in eight or nine years. And we haven't played more than two or three quartets in any one year for more than ten years. (We would say), let's keep the third and sixth this year . . . or the first and the fourth . . . or some particular place wanted a Bartók, so we'd work it up but not keep it on the repertoire. Finally (1981) became the Bartók year. And, the Juilliard Quartet still has a reputation about playing Bartók.

There was one other thing that gave it a catapult too. Which is that in 1958, we were the first Americans along with Lorin Maazel to go back to Hungary after the counter-revolution. And, we played Bartók Quartets—the Fourth and the Third—at concerts at the Liszt Conservatory, and the students and everybody made an enormous uproar.

That got into *Time* magazine too. That was perhaps the thing that catapulted us into doing a second recording set.

Now, while we're known for Bartók, so many other people have played and recorded whole cycles of Bartók that there are, believe it or not, numbers of people out in the chamber music audience who know we play Bartók but don't think about it as anything more or special than anybody else.

But in the meantime, I've got now three members of the Juilliard Quartet that have never recorded a Bartók quartet. And, THEY want to record them because we still play them well. So this year, because it's the Bartók year, we put a cycle on the books, which we're playing in the Library of Congress in two concerts, and in three concerts with Brahms in between, at Alice Tully Hall this Spring, March and April.

(W)hen we were talking about repertoire with CBS, they said, "Well, the set from the 1960s is still selling, but its 20 years old, and the new group wants to do it, with digital and all that, so let's do it again." So that's why we're doing the third set. None of what I'm telling you takes away from the fact that we DO think that Bartók was one of the great quartet composers of all time. But, that's not the only reason we are (recording) it (for a) third time.

AK: *How has the interpretation changed? Other than new members? What were the changes between first two recordings of the cycle?*

RM: I think that I could best point (that) out by saying that (in) the early years, Juilliard Quartet was characterized by enormous incisive rhythmic thrust, forward motion. Another quartet, (a) very great quartet that played them all during the same years—the Hungarian Quartet—it's style was different. It was more European; the incisiveness was—it was smoother attack, they were maybe more interested in the lyric sonority—which was another way of looking at it. I think if you want to ask what changes have come over the years with the Juilliard, it's that we've tried, without compromising either virtue, to include within conception and the performance of conception, more elements of both, rather than overload heavily with one side or another.

That's been the change. Those elements that are lyric, or not so incisive or thrusting have been toned down in their articulation. Whereas other areas we have tried to keep the power and the thrust . . . You might say it's become more chromatically orchestrated in terms of all the possible potentials of the music, rather than emphasizing certain priorities at the expense of others. The third set of recording, well, I'd like to leave it to you as a listener to decide. We're going to do them in May.

AK: *I've seen a purported quote from Claus Adam: "We discovered that it was music." That doesn't sound likely, but do you know if he actually said that?*

RM: That literally, I can't conceive of his having ever said... It's not only not .. true, it's not even good apocrypha; I don't think he'd ever say a thing like that . . .

By the way, I could make that statement in all fairness about certain music. Music that I have always loved, but which has been harder to get at the meaning of. There was always enough elements in the music to challenge the Quartet or myself to understanding it or wanting to play it, but because I didn't really understand all those elements so well, I think I missed the board on many levels. But as I began to understand its musicality on many levels I began to interpret it in a much more meaningful way. I think that's happened, many times (with certain music). But not with the Bartóks . . .

AK: *You mentioned the early piano quartet that was almost like Brahms. But can you see a direct line to and from Bartók . . . in the quartet literature itself?*

RM: Well, certainly, his very earliest works—he wrote a piano quintet you know, earlier than the 1st quartet. He wrote an earlier violin sonata. You see in all the compositions of a significant composer, the mainstream, it would be very hard to find one whose earliest efforts at composition didn't show some connection to . . . his predecessors. And in Bartók you find Liszt, you find Brahms; as a matter of fact there's a section in the first movement of the 1st quartet that in terms of its whole tone preoccupation and color it would be hard for me to think that he HADN'T in some way discovered Debussy and some of the things that were going on the West Coast or Europe, near the Atlantic. I think he must have been affected by many things.

AK: *Is there a point where he ceases to be affected by them?*

RM: I don't think anybody ever reaches that point, even if you take people who seem to have broken off completely. Take Edgard Varèse. Varèse started out writing music that was very impressionistic, then expressionistic, like Alban Berg, and so on, and influences of French color. And all of a sudden he starts getting into Ionizations and things like that. Milan Kundera, the Czech-French writer, misinterprets him as not dealing in notes anymore, well, that's not true. He's not talking about non-validity, just that it's not music as we know it anymore. I find in all of Varèse's work a relationship to the music of before him.

Bartók . . . hit his high point of pushing in his own language farther than he'd ever push anything again in 1927, 1928, 1929. From that moment on there began to be not a receding from that high point, but an encompassing of less uncompromising elements. By the time you get to the 5th quartet, in 1935, and works from then on, till his death, they are more classically and harmonically oriented. They are more encompassing of things that wouldn't disturb the Felix Salmonds of my life. He could listen, almost, to the 6th quartet. He could never listen to the 3rd quartet. That just killed him; but he could listen to the 6th quartet because already Bartók was including certain elements by then. The solo violin sonata, written in the latest years, is a complete classical reorientation; as is the 3rd Piano Concerto compared to the first and second. So there's always . . . a strain in history that's always there . . . —even improvisational methods used by some of the Avant garde composers w(ere) used in earlier days . . . And combination rhythms—just take Elizabethan madrigals, moving from 3s to 4s—I mean, my God, that's no different than Bartók moving from 2s to 3s to 4s.

AK: *Where are the lines of descent from Bartók?*

RM: In my earlier life, I was very much influenced by Bartók, but I think that I would stick to my statement that it . . . was harder to be a disciple of Bartók and still continue a creative urge, than it was say other composers, like Webern. For instance, it's wrong maybe to mention names, but a fairly good composer like Tibor Serly, who was Bartók's disciple and tried to follow the language of Bartók and continue composing like that, didn't do so well. No, a composer like Leon Kirchner developed his own language and avoided the trap of being a Bartók disciple.

AK: *Having performed other music by Bartók, the solo violin sonata, etc . . . do you feel closest to the quartets?*

RM: Obviously, in terms of just sheer weight of experience. There's no Bartók quartet that I haven't played at least 300 to 400 times, maybe more. The solo sonata I recorded once. I've played it maybe two dozen times. The 1st and 2nd sonatas I've played two, three dozen times in my life, and the *Contrasts*, two to three dozen times. I've played the piano quintet only once—that wasn't available for years, and when it was finally available, one had a problem. Bartók himself didn't want it performed. But there's a way, if you don't destroy your piece, then the rest of the world always earths out everything of every notable person . . . some of it's viable, or else some of it is momentary and goes by the wayside. I mean, certainly the quintet is in that category... The same thing for the early violin concerto, not the big one, but the one that's called the 2nd Concerto. The Hungarian composer Szidor Bátor actually asked me to study the material, and he showed me a card in Hungarian that stipulated that Bartók didn't want it performed. But, Bátor arranged certain events where it came out and got published and performed.

Composers are very touchy about what they think is good and bad. Now, the world may say, well, you don't know, in posterity, that . . . maybe your worst work will turn out to be your most famous or considered your best, or vice versa. The creator of a work of art somehow feels that unlike human life, which is holy . . . (if you birth a child you can't destroy it)...if you birth a composition and you don't like it, you can tear it up. For instance, Stefan Wolpe, my composition teacher for a while, wanted to write a quartet for the Juilliard Quartet in the worst way. And, over the years I would say, "Come on Stefan, where's our quartet?" And, he would say, and without exaggeration, "You know I've literally written 16 quartets and torn them up."

Bartók handed the score of his violin concerto, which he wrote for Stephie Geiringer, who I think he was enamored of—I'm not sure, but I think so—and he gave her the score with the understanding that she would not perform it. He incorporated the slow movements into one of the *Portraits* for string orchestra, so it's a beautiful work, and didn't give that up. But he didn't want the other movements performed.

The same thing with the quintet. He did that and submitted it to a French composition contest. And I don't think he even got honorable mention. And, he was a very depressive type. When he realized he hadn't even gotten honorable mention, he went through agony and even debated whether he should continue being a composer, because if the world rejected him he couldn't be any good.

So then, at one point, Josef Waldbauer, the violinist who had a quartet and was a friend of Bartók in Budapest, wanted to cheer him up and give him encouragement. So they gave a concert of his chamber music, including the piano quintet, and the 1st and 2nd quartets, I think. After the performance, Bartók gave Waldbauer the manuscript . . .

I didn't know Waldbauer, but at a certain point he came over to America and taught at the University of Iowa for many years, and I know his son, Ivan Waldbauer, who needed to get a job and parleyed this manuscript that had been in his possession to the Bartók estate, archives. He . . . was a musicologist and a musician, and there was some mutual interest there. So they got a hold of that manuscript and made a Xerox of it, and that's what I first saw. And, the Bartók estate then asked the Juilliard Quartet if we'd be interested in giving the first performance in America. However, the estate here was at arms point with the communist/socialist government in control of the publishing house in Budapest . . . In poor Bartók's time, there was no money coming in (from his compositions), but by now thousands come in every year from music and performances and all that. And, the publishing house in Budapest, naturally, wants all music sold in America, England, Japan and anywhere else, so that royalty should come to Budapest . . . (A)nyway, the Budapest publishing house didn't have any international copying laws to deal with . . . so they put out a printed version of the quintet.

Now, Bartók, during that first performance, according to Waldbauer, had played different piano parts in many places, out of his head—he'd recomposed. He told Waldbauer that the work should not be performed again until he worked out the piano part. The Bartók archives or musicologists in Hungary claim to have found in Bartók's effects a written down amount of changes from the score. And, they've published that version, and that's the one that's played now. That's the one the Juilliard Quartet played. But no one knows whether (Bartók) really composed them or somebody else did, just to get around his desire not to have it performed.

We performed the so-called new version. I don't have the Xerox of the old version, but I've seen it. We haven't recorded it—not that we wouldn't. I happen to think it's a very nice work. I think it shows Bartók in his early formative period, it's worth playing. I wouldn't agree with Bartók that it's not. Maybe this (published) version is his and he *would* agree with it being played. After all, look at Paul Hindemith who changed his mind about many of his early compositions and recomposed them to fit his later conservative bent in harmonic construction. I could even imagine someone disliking what they did in early times and recomposing it later. Many composers have done that. So it's possible Bartók would have changed his mind.

I can quote you Elliott Carter. We played a program recently in which Sammy (Rhodes) played an early Carter work for viola and piano. At first, Elliott was sort of holding his ears in anticipation saying, "I can't believe it's any good; that's when I was a young composer and I really might be embarrassed." But then he heard it and said, "You know, I shouldn't be ashamed of that piece. It's a very nice piece!" And, he changed his mind. So, it's possible that if Bartók was anything like these other people that he might have written it and said, "Ooof, " and torn it up or made sure that nobody ever saw it. So, there's some leeway in what you might think is a composer's own knowledge or his own children.

AK: *Why not revisit the Barók Sonata and other works you recorded in the 1950's?*

RM: No one's asked me. I've got so many irons in the fire that if I had priorities, it would be . . . the Beethoven sonatas with Emanuel Ax. There are so many things one is involved in . . . I would love to do it but wouldn't search it out. I almost did another version with William Masselos in the 1960s—we tried making the record, with a Meyer Kupferman work . . . had one day to record; didn't work out. One other Bartók work I have played, and I love it, I've played it twice in my life—Springfield, Ohio and Chicago Symphony at Ravinia; that's the concerto.

AK: *Do you think he tended to be more lyrical and conservative in his orchestral works than in his quartets?*

RM: A good question. The *Concerto for Orchestra* was an attempt to write something, without compromising himself, which (people might) want to . . . play . . . more—like the 3rd piano concerto. (I)f you think of the 2nd piano concerto, that's very uncompromising in terms of his language..(but) it's hard for me to think of it as difficult. And, even the 1st concerto . . . is somewhat neo-classical. He ran (a) parallel existence to Stravinsky on certain levels. I mean, the opening of the last movement of the 4th quartet, with that syncopation; he wasn't necessarily imitating Stravinsky's *Rite of Spring*, but they were both going down the same path at certain times. That kind of orchestral writing is as densely uncompromising as any of his music. On the other hand, he did allow his contrapuntal elements more free reign in chamber music than in the broader based symphonic (works) . . .

Sometimes people ask do you ever get tired of Bartók quartets, and I've pointed out that one can, under certain conditions, get tired even of one's own mother. There are certain works that, because of the nature of what they give and what they obscure, and the way they're constructed in which they're so complete, that one never gets tired of them. For instance, I never get tired of Beethoven Opus 95 and Opus 135, and the third Bartók. Those works I can play morning, noon and night, and never get tired of them. I can't say that for any other Bartók quartet. It isn't even a question of how great the quartet is. I'm not sure the third is his greatest quartet; in fact I wouldn't say that. It's a fascinating thing. You learn this not by thinking about it, but by experience. When we've repeated on a tour over and over again a particular work and you think, does the saliva still work before the concert. I can be sick and tired, or have a 102 fever, or be absolutely mad at my colleagues and not want to play the concert. And yet, when it gets to the moment I'm going to go out and start the third Bartók, there's kind of an inner smile and a feeling that I'm glad to be alive to be able to play that piece again. Nothing can get in the way.

AK: *What is it about the 3rd?*

RM: I don't even pretend to understand. I've tried to put into words about how it's constructed, how it reveals certain things, and how it keeps certain things to itself. There is an enigmatic aspect about art, and that's why words are ultimately insufficient. You cannot capture the greatness in words—you can only monkey around the periphery of it. And hope that somehow you can catch somebody else so that they might get a little key and get into that mysterious center too, you see. Now, interestingly enough, I'm always deeply moved by the 6th quartet, but I couldn't repeat it as much.

There are certain emotions that are unlocked in performance as well as in other things. For instance, at one point I was going through Wilhelm Reich therapy, which is a very strong, overwhelming thing. I was telling my therapist that I was afraid that if I really let myself go in performance, that I might just break up on stage and wouldn't be able to continue the performance. I guess maybe he understood, or else had more confidence in what held me together. He said, "Why don't you try. Let yourself go and see what happens." A couple of days later, we were playing a Bartók cycle in Boston. At the beginning of the program we played the Bartók 2nd Quartet. Now, the 2nd Quartet is where Bartók crosses the bridge from the past into his own language, returning only peripherally at the end. And, at the point where he crosses is the last movement. As my friend Eugene Lehner says, that movement is the great beginning of abstract Hungarian aesthetics in music, where the ethos is absolutely undeniable and unmistakable—where the language is completely unique, with nothing of the past. But it's also one of the most bleak, sad pieces of music ever written. Wagner said that the (Beethoven's) Fugue Opus 131 is the saddest piece of music he knew. I don't think it is—but *this* is. As I start playing it (in this concert) and allowing myself to respond—you know, a performer has to respond but still keep some control over activity; (y)ou've got to keep your finger in the right place and still in a sense direct the traffic of the interpretation, even though you're responding as well— . . . the tears started streaming down my face as I was playing. I thought, oh my God, I'm going to break up and start sobbing and everything; but I didn't. Somehow, the emotion that went through me was like breathing. First you breathe a shallow amount and then you learn you can breathe deeper. At first you just tickle yourself and think Oh God, will I get hyperventilated or something—but eventually your system begins to take in more oxygen and you begin to develop something. Well, that sadness I felt began to plumb deep into my being. I don't want to sound mystical—but I was able to tolerate greater sadness and greater feeling. And by the time I was finished, I wasn't feeling triumphant. But I was definitely feeling I had experienced something on a profound level that I had never experienced before in my life. Now whether I fooled myself or not, I don't know. But that happened in the 2nd Bartók quartet.

Look, I love them all. It's like if you have six children . . . you love them all to varying degrees. Each one has its own place. It comes down to that list again—are you going to say this is best, this is next—

no, you're going to be able to tolerate many kinds of things. When somebody says who is your favorite composer—it's only games. I think maybe if I had to pick a group of compositions of one composer because I was in prison and that was all I was allowed, it would have to be the late Beethoven quartets . . . but what about the Mozart or the Haydn quartets? I might end up taking the Haydn. First of all there are more of them; and as I get older I see more in them.

It changes. It's hard to say I don't like the Bartók as much as the Beethoven. On its own level I'd be bereft if I had to give up the Bartók quartets. Absolutely bereft.

JUILLIARD STRING QUARTET FAMILY TREE

⌒ FIRST VIOLIN ⌒

1946-1997 Robert Mann

1997-2009 Joel Smirnoff

2009-2011 Nick Eanet

2011-present Joseph Lin

⌒ SECOND VIOLIN ⌒

1946-1958 Robert Koff

1958-1966 Isidore Cohen

1966-1986 Earl Carlyss

1986-1997 Joel Smirnoff

1997-present Ronald Copes

⌒ VIOLA ⌒

1946-1969 Raphael Hillyer

1969-2013 Samuel Rhodes

2013-present Roger Tapping

⌒ CELLO ⌒

1946-1955 Arthur Winograd

1955-1974 Claus Adam

1974-2016 Joel Krosnick

2016-present Astrid Schween

After starting their career under the management of the Juilliard School of Music, the Quartet signed with Colbert Artists Management (then Colbert-LaBerge Concert Management) in 1954. They have enjoyed a long and fulfilling relationship.

ACKNOWLEDGMENTS

This book is the result of the unwavering vision of Lucy Rowan Mann. It would not have become a reality without the invaluable help of Lisa Mann Marotta, Debra Kinzler, and Nicholas Mann. Our deep gratitude also goes to Stephen Viksjo for his creative cover designs, Kyle Werner for his research help, Joel Krosnick, Earl Carlyss, Ann Schein, Samuel Rhodes, and Bonnie Hampton for their collaboration on musical facts and photographs, Manhattan School of Music and the Juilliard School of Music libraries for allowing us access to some of their archival photographs, Allan Kozinn, for allowing us to reproduce his interview with Robert Mann, and Alan Miller, who generously shared with us the interviews he did of Robert Mann, for his documentary film, *Speak the Music*. Finally, we would like to acknowledge the help of Miranda K. Pennington and Pauline Neuwirth, of Neuwirth & Associates, for their roles in bringing this book to the printed page.

Robert's 97th birthday celebration. Pictured are close friends Debra Kinzler, Connie Emmerich, and Bonnie Hampton, with Robert, Lucy, and Lisa.

INDEX